Divrei Mishkan T'filah

Delving into the Siddur

Delving into the Siddur

Rabbi Richard S. Sarason, PhD

CENTRAL CONFERENCE OF AMERICAN RABBIS | 2018/5778

CCAR Press, 355 Lexington Avenue, New York, NY 10017
(212) 972-3636
www.ccarpress.org

Library of Congress Cataloging-in-Publication Data
Names: Sarason, Richard S., author.
Title: Delving into Mishkan t'filah = [Mishkan divre tefilah] / Rabbi Richard S. Sarason, PhD.
Other titles: Mishkan divrei t'filah
Description: New York, NY : Central Conference of American Rabbis, 2018/5778. | Includes bibliographical references. | Includes excerpts of the text of Mishkan divrei t'filah in Hebrew.
Identifiers: LCCN 2017037850 (print) | LCCN 2017039103 (ebook) | ISBN 9780881233124 | ISBN 9780881233117 (pbk. : alk. paper)
Subjects: LCSH: Siddurim--Commentaries.
Classification: LCC BM674.34 (ebook) | LCC BM674.34 .S37 2018 (print) | DDC 296.4/5--dc23
LC record available at https://lccn.loc.gov/2017037850

Designed and composed by Scott-Martin Kosofsky
at The Philidor Company, Rhinebeck, New York

Printed in U.S.A.
10 9 8 7 6 5 4 3 2 1

Contents

Preface

WORSHIP IS, and must be, much more than simply reciting the words on the pages of a prayer book. That insight has been repeatedly stressed by the liturgists and liturgical scholars of our generation, following the lead of anthropologists and other students of ritual.[1] But Rabbinic Judaism historically has been a liturgical tradition, with prescribed forms and words—and so, for Jews, the words *do* matter. The Rabbis who composed our liturgy over the generations viewed words as powerful, creative, even cosmic, forces: according to the theology of the Torah, the world itself was created through the agency of divine words. In a similar vein, according to the biblical narrative, God was revealed to the people Israel at Sinai through the medium of words. The Torah, in Jewish tradition, is the tangible embodiment, in written form, of those divine words. The psalms and other biblical prayers provide both the models and the lexicon for rabbinic prayer; these are viewed as powerful and efficacious words. And the rabbinic ideal of *talmud Torah*—the ongoing and perpetual study of Torah—is the study of words and the creation, through commentary, of yet more words. Judaism is a highly verbal tradition, since words (as well as deeds) are viewed as the intermediaries between humans and the Divine.

While contemporary Jews might not view the words of the prayer book in the same freighted fashion as did their ancestors, it certainly remains the case in our own day that a well-turned phrase or a word in its proper time and place (*davar b'ito*) remains powerful and can unlock inner doors of feeling and conviction—particularly when those words are sung or chanted.[2] Our prayers should be understood as poetic: the words are allusive and point to something more than themselves, something that words cannot fully grasp or encompass. To pray (mostly) the same Hebrew prayers as did our ancestors—while interpreting them in our own fashion, in our own context—links us across time and space as one eternal family.

So while it is certainly the case that a new prayer book is not a magic bullet that by itself can generate moving and convincing worship—that is much more a function of how the book is used—the prayer book nonetheless can upend our habitual thinking with new and challenging words; can provide solace, enlightenment, and inspiration with well-chosen and beautiful words; and, if used wisely and well, can facilitate, rather than hinder, a powerful—even transformative—worship experience. Such is the goal of *Mishkan T'filah,* the North American Reform Movement's most recent prayer book, published in 2007.[3] The book's novelty is that it provides multiple simultaneous interpretive and performative options for every prayer, and prayer section, in every worship service. This innovation must be credited to the book's editor, Rabbi Elyse D. Frishman, and Rabbi Judith Z. Abrams, originally her co-editor and then later consulting editor. The prayer book also provides both religious/spiritual and explanatory commentaries at the bottom of each page.

A 1994 survey of what Reform congregants wanted in their worship and in a new prayer book indicated, among other things, that they wanted to understand what they were saying in Hebrew—particularly now that so much of the traditional Hebrew text had been restored in Reform worship.[4] They also wanted to understand the logic of the liturgy itself: the structure, background, and meanings of the various services and the individual prayers. How can the prayers on the page become the prayers of the heart? How can the historical prayers of the community become also the personal prayers of the individual? The first step in that process must be one of *iyun t'filah,* of contemplation, study, and learning about those prayers of the community—and how they might be personally internalized, even if that requires some interpretation. Hence the title of this book, *Divrei Mishkan T'filah,* literally "Words about *Mishkan T'filah,*" but actually commentary on and study about our newest prayer book.

This volume began its journey in 2007–8 as a project of the Reform Movement's Joint Commission on Worship, Music, and Religious Living, on which I have had the privilege of serving since 2003 and which I now serve as vice-chair representing Hebrew Union College–Jewish Institute of Religion. As *Mishkan T'filah* was being published in the fall of 2007, several of the Worship Commission's working groups considered how they could help introduce the new prayer book to the Reform Movement's members by generating useful and informative learning content. It was decided that writing a series of essays about each two-page spread of the prayer book for weekly dissemination on the Union for Reform Judaism's daily-study e-mail blast, "Ten Minutes of Torah," would be the most effective and timely way to help teach about the prayer book and its contents. The idea was to generate three essays, distributed over three weeks, for each two-page spread, all written by members of the Worship Commission—rabbis, cantors, and congregants. The first week's essay would deal with the spread's "right-hand page," the Hebrew text and its faithful English translation. It would discuss the logic and meaning of the prayer or prayer section, its history, and its treatment historically in Reform prayer books, including *Mishkan T'filah*. The second week's essay would be, in the spirit of the "left-hand page," a personal meditation on the spread's prayer. The third week's essay, by a cantor, would deal with a variety of musical settings for the spread's prayer texts and provide some brief audio-file examples. The materials in the present volume are mostly revised and updated versions of the "right-hand page" Ten Minutes of Torah essays, all of which were written by me. The series ran on Thursdays as "Delving into *T'filah*" between May 2008 and January 2013. That same month, after completing our multiple commentaries on *Mishkan T'filah*, we began a commentary series about the prayers for the High Holy Days, in anticipation of the new Reform *machzor*, *Mishkan HaNefesh*, then in the process of formation. That series continued through February 2014. The new *machzor* was published in the summer of 2015 and was subsequently joined in 2016 by its own commentary volume, *Divrei Mishkan HaNefesh: A Guide to the CCAR Machzor*, by its editor, Rabbi Edwin C. Goldberg—who had also been a member of the Worship Commission in 2007 and helped to formulate our Ten Minutes of Torah project at that time.

I owe a debt of gratitude to all of my fellow members of the Worship Commission during those years who worked diligently with me on the completion of this project. Our intention was that the materials would continue to remain available for use and study by anyone who was interested in them. Initially they were archived on the URJ website, but unfortunately they are no longer available electronically. Hence the urgency of this volume to keep at least some of these materials accessible.

Rabbi Sue Ann Wasserman and Cantor Alane S. Katzew, at that time the heads of the Department of Worship, Music, and Religious Living at the

URJ, who staffed the Joint Commission, and Rabbi Joan Farber Glazer, who managed and edited Ten Minutes of Torah at the URJ, and Rabbi Victor S. Appell, who succeeded her in that position, all supported this project from the outset. It was Cantor Katzew who subsequently prodded me to assemble my Ten Minutes of Torah essays and publish them in book form. Rabbi Hara E. Person, publisher and director of the CCAR Press, who also currently provides staff support for the Worship Commission, has enthusiastically endorsed bringing this project to the CCAR Press and has provided sound editorial guidance throughout the process. To all of these exemplary colleagues I offer my most profound gratitude. I also thank the staff at the CCAR who all have a role in the life of this book, including Ortal Bensky, Debbie Smilow, Sasha Smith, Carly Linden, and Rabbi Dan Medwin, as well as CCAR Chief Executive Rabbi Steven A. Fox.

Finally, to my wife, Anne Arenstein, and our sons Yoni and Michael: your love sustains and affirms everything that I do.

Richard S. Sarason
Cincinnati, Ohio

Introduction

JEWISH WORSHIP is a living organism. The service as we know it today is a product of many eras, places, and sensibilities. In addition to being a ritual manual and guide to daily piety, our prayer book is truly a textbook of living Judaism, embodying our history and our evolving ideas about God, the world, and our relationship to both. It contains the words of prophets and priests, sages and poets, philosophers and mystics, all juxtaposed with each other. The language of Jewish prayer is poetic. It is modeled on and includes large portions of the psalms and other prayers in the Hebrew Bible, the *Tanach* (the traditional abbreviation for the three parts of Scripture: *Torah*, "Instruction"; *N'vi-im*, "Prophets"; and *K'tuvim*, "Writings").

While much of the language is biblical or based on biblical models, the liturgy itself was first shaped by the Rabbis (masters, teachers) of the late first through seventh centuries of the Common Era (CE) in the Land of Israel and Babylonia. Jews had always prayed, but prayer as the primary expression of Jewish public worship became common only after the destruction of the Second Temple in 70 CE, when daily sacrifices no longer could be offered. (Some groups of Jews outside the Land of Israel who did not have access to the Temple and others, like the community of the Dead Sea Scrolls in the Land of Israel who withdrew from the Temple in protest against the perceived illegitimacy of the Maccabean priesthood in the second century before the Common Era [BCE], engaged in regular communal prayer even before the Temple was destroyed.)

In place of the twice-daily sacrifices, the Rabbis instituted a thrice-daily Prayer of Eighteen Benedictions, the *T'filah* (the "Prayer"), later called the *Amidah* (the "Standing [Prayer]"), or the *Sh'moneh Esreih* (the "Eighteen [Benedictions]"). The *T'filah* was to be prayed by and on behalf of the entire community; down to our own day, it remains the core of each Jewish worship service. The three daily prayers correspond roughly to the three main demarcations of the day—sunrise, (after-)noon, sunset.

The *T'filah* serves a twofold purpose: it expresses the community's praise of God and gives voice to their needs; simultaneously it expresses the hopes and needs of each individual Jew and encourages each person to insert his or her own private prayers. Here is an attempt to address the ongoing tension between the needs of the community and the needs of the individual. This is also the reason why, in traditional worship, the *T'filah* is recited twice, once by each person privately and then by the congregation together, led by the *sh'liach tzibur* (prayer leader, "agent of the congregation"). As *Mishkan T'filah* attests, contemporary worship still struggles to balance the needs of the individual worshiper with those of the congregation.

The other early liturgical unit, dating from at least the first century CE, is what the Rabbis call *K'riat Sh'ma*, "Recitation of the *Sh'ma*." Traditionally, this comprises the twice-daily recitation—"when you lie down and when you get up"—of three biblical paragraphs, Deuteronomy 6:4–9, 11:13–21, and Numbers 15:37–41, framed by rabbinic benedictions appropriate to evening and morning recitation. The combination of these two originally separate liturgies—the *T'filah* and *K'riat Sh'ma*—is the origin of the multifaceted Jewish prayer service as we know it.

Other elements of the service were to follow. The Rabbis endorsed the pious custom of preparing oneself to pray by coming early to the synagogue in the morning and reciting psalms (*Mishnah B'rachot* 5:1). In time, this became a regular part of the morning service, the *P'sukei D'zimrah* ("Verses of Song"), psalms and praises recited before *Bar'chu*. Similarly, the Babylonian Talmud (*B'rachot* 60a) prescribes a series of blessings to be recited, as an act of personal piety, upon waking up and beginning each new day. Later, these were incorporated into the public synagogue service and became the *Birchot HaShachar* ("Morning Blessings") unit with which the morning service now begins. The custom of public reading from the Torah in the synagogue on Sabbaths and Monday and Thursday mornings and of reading also from the Prophets (haftarah, "conclusion" of the scriptural reading) on Sabbaths is very old; it goes back to the late Second Temple period. After the Temple's destruction, this was combined in the synagogue with the rabbinic liturgies. The conclusion of the daily services with the *Aleinu* prayer ("Let us now praise"), on the other hand, is a relatively late custom, originating in the Rhineland around 1300, in the wake of the Crusades. (The prayer itself is much earlier; it is part of the Rosh HaShanah liturgy.) And later still is the service of *Kabbalat Shabbat* ("Welcoming the Sabbath"), which began as an esoteric ritual practice of sixteenth-century kabbalists (mystics) in the Land of Israel and was not at all associated with the synagogue setting.

Jewish liturgical and ritual creativity has never flagged. Even as elements of the service became fixed, there was always a countervailing impulse toward spontaneity and improvisation. Our earliest rabbinic sources, the Mishnah, *Tosefta*, and Talmuds (on which, see below), suggest that although the Rabbis early on fixed the content and structure of the liturgy (themes, number of benedictions and their relative lengths), the actual wording of the prayers was not (or at least not completely) fixed. Only the concluding benedictory phrases (such as "Praise to You, Adonai, who brings on evening") are explicitly prescribed in the early literature. Opening phrases occasionally are mentioned as well.

Both the Mishnah and the Talmuds bear witness to an ongoing debate over the desirability of fixing the precise wording of the prayers. On the one hand, fixed prayers are easier to teach and easier to memorize; they allow worshipers to "flow with the words." But spontaneous, creative, and fluid wordings force worshipers to think about what they are saying and to respond with *kavanah*, intentionality: "When you pray, do not make your prayer a matter of fixed routine, but an entreaty for mercy and grace before the Omnipresent One" (*Mishnah Avot* 2:13).

Even when fixed wordings seemed to have won out, new poetic versions of the basic prayers were often created. Elegant and elaborate hymns (*piyutim*) were written and performed in synagogues on Shabbat and festival mornings (some of these are included in the festival services in *Mishkan T'filah*). These poems incorporated rabbinic midrashim (interpretations) on the day's Torah reading and interwove them with the themes of the benedictions and of the day. They are, perhaps, the earliest "creative liturgies." The creation of liturgical hymns (like *Adon Olam*, *Yigdal*, and *Y'did Nefesh*) in different styles, reflecting changing aesthetics and theologies, has continued down to the modern period.

The first "prayer book," *Seder Rav Amram* ("The Order of Rav Amram"), a manual of the liturgy of the entire year (including rules and practices) with fully written-out prayers, dates only from the last half of the ninth century, during the Islamic period; before that time we have no full written texts of any of the standard prayers. *Seder Rav Amram* was composed by the head of the Talmudic academy in Sura, Babylonia, in response to a request from a Jewish community in Spain (possibly Barcelona), for guidance about the "correct" order of prayers as practiced in the Babylonian rabbinical academies. It became the basis particularly for the Sephardic rite of Jews who lived in Islamic countries. Many other manuals detailing liturgical laws and customs of various local and regional Jewish communities were to follow.

The various medieval prayer manuals contributed to the fixing of Jewish prayer texts and customs. But at the same time, a variety of pious and mystical movements created new rituals, customs, and texts; they also infused new meanings into old ones. Pietists in the Rhineland in the twelfth century (*Chasidei Ashkenaz*) and kabbalists (mystics; literally "receivers" of mystical traditions) in fourteenth-century Spain, Provence, and later in the Land of Israel (particularly the circle around Isaac Luria in Safed in the sixteenth century) made major contributions to the liturgy, including numerous hymns (like *Anim Z'mirot, Y'did Nefesh,* and *L'cha Dodi*) and customs (like *Kabbalat Shabbat* on Friday evenings and *Tikkun Leil Shavuot*, the all-night ritual of Torah study on the eve of Shavuot). Ultimately, it was the invention of the printing press, and the expense of publishing every local variation, that led more than anything else to the standardization of prayer texts.

The modern reform of Jewish liturgy began in early nineteenth-century Germany. Initially, the concerns were aesthetic and cultural: how could the style of Jewish worship, for a community entering into mainstream Western culture, be brought into conformity with contemporary middle-class Lutheran and Reformed Protestant expressions of religious edification and piety? Early reforms included shortening the service and eliminating repetitions; introducing a German-language sermon, hymn singing, and art music with a choir and organ; and emphasizing decorum in the conduct of services. Subsequently, theological concerns became important as well: there was a strong desire to "say what you mean and mean what you say." Rituals based in superstition ("folk religion") were eliminated, as was the mention of angels. The hope for some kind of spiritual immortality after death replaced that for physical resurrection. The expectation of a future messianic age in which the evils of social life would be ameliorated was substituted for the belief in a personal Messiah. In general, Jewish particularism was toned down in favor of a prophetic universalism. Prayers for the ingathering of the exiles to the Land of Israel and for the reinstitution of the ancient Temple sacrificial rituals were eliminated; these no longer expressed the political and religious aspirations of Western European Jews.[5]

By the beginning of the twentieth century, most Reform liturgies in Europe were fairly "moderate" in their style and content, still retaining a good deal of Hebrew language and tradition. In the United States, however, what became "classical" Reform was fairly radical, eliminating much Hebrew and many traditional practices. The first edition of the *Union Prayer Book*, published in 1894–95, embodied the spirit of the 1885 Pittsburgh Platform, the first manifesto of Reform Judaism in North America.[6] It was the work primarily of more radical German Reformers. Subsequent revisions (1918–22, 1940–45) reflected the growing influence on the movement of Jews from Eastern Europe, who had greater attachment to Hebrew and to traditional customs.

Gates of Prayer (1975) and *Gates of Repentance* (1978), the next North American Reform liturgies, displayed the sensibilities of the post–Six-Day War period, combining acute awareness of the Holocaust and the State of Israel with a growing interest in the Hebrew language and traditional ritual forms. The first impact of the feminist movement that began in the late 1960s and the entry of a significant number of women into the Reform rabbinate over a decade later can be seen in the gender-neutral editions of *Gates of Prayer* (1994) and *Gates of Repentance* (1996). Their fuller impact is felt only now in *Mishkan T'filah*, which also reflects the spiritual sensibilities of the maturing postwar "baby boom" generation and the search for personal meaning both within and outside of the communal context. A deeper exploration of Jewish tradition (including the mystical tradition) and Hebrew liturgy has been part of this search. *Dor dor v'dorshav*: each generation refracts Jewish tradition and Jewish worship through its own lenses. *Mishkan T'filah* explicitly acknowledges that fact but also strives for continuity among the generations.

Having noted the importance of an egalitarian, gender-inclusive or gender-neutral liturgy in *Mishkan T'filah*, I must point out that in the pages below, I sometimes will depart from gender neutrality and use gendered (which, in context, means masculine) pronouns in translations of traditional texts. The sole reason is to provide an accurate representation of these texts when discussing their historical, premodern meanings. All discussions of the renderings in *Mishkan T'filah* itself will retain the gender-neutral usage. Translations of most liturgical passages are from *Mishkan T'filah,* except where a more literal rendering is deemed necessary. Translations of most biblical passages that do not follow those of *Mishkan T'filah* are from *TaNaKH: A New Translation of THE HOLY SCRIPTURES According to the Traditional Hebrew Text* (Philadelphia: The Jewish Publication Society, 1985).

Let me now identify briefly the literary sources of rabbinic liturgy, as these are cited in this volume:

1. The Mishnah ("Memorized Teaching"), the earliest rabbinic text, edited in the Land of Israel around 200 CE, is a succinct anthology and study book of early rabbinic law and custom. Its contents are compiled in sixty-three tractates, arranged into six orders. The first tractate, *B'rachot* ("Blessings") deals entirely with liturgies, prayers, and blessings. The public Torah reading is discussed in Tractate *M'gilah,* which deals primarily with the reading of the Scroll of Esther on Purim. Other prayers and liturgies are discussed in tractates that deal with the festivals, fast days, and the rituals of the Temple. References in this book to the Mishnah prefix the italicized letter "*M.*" to the name of the tractate, followed by the chapter and paragraph number (*M. B'rachot* 1:4, for example).
2. The *Tosefta* ("Supplement") is the earliest commentary on the Mishnah, edited in the Land of Israel sometime in the third century CE. It contains additional traditions and alternative versions of traditions that are as old as those in the Mishnah, as well as commentary on the Mishnah. Some of the traditions included here are the earliest building blocks of the two Talmuds. The *Tosefta* broadly follows the arrangement of the Mishnah. References in the commentary to the *Tosefta* prefix the italicized letter "*T.*" to the name of the tractate, followed by the chapter and paragraph number (*T. B'rachot* 2:1, for example).

3. There are two Talmuds ("that which is learned"), one from the Land of Israel and one from Babylonia. The former is briefer and generally thought to have been completed first, sometime in the fifth century CE; the latter was likely completed about a century later. Both are framed as commentaries on the Mishnah and follow its order, but they include voluminous other materials. The Babylonian Talmud became the primary source of later Jewish law (halachah) when Babylonian Jewry later found itself at the center of the Islamic empire, in the eighth century CE. References in this book to the Talmud of the Land of Israel (also called the Palestinian Talmud, Jerusalem Talmud, and *Talmud Y'rushalmi*) prefix the italicized letter "*Y.*" to the name of the tractate, followed by the chapter, paragraph number, and folio and column number in the standard one-volume edition printed in Krotoshin, Poland, in 1866 (for example, *Y. B'rachot* 2:1, 4c). References to the Babylonian Talmud prefix the italicized letter "*B.*" to the name of the tractate, followed by the folio number and side in the standard edition printed in Vilna, Lithuania, in 1880–86 (for example, *B. B'rachot* 11b).
4. Tractate *Sof'rim* ("Scribes"), composed probably in the eighth century CE in the Land of Israel, is a manual for Torah scribes that includes a list of Torah readings for special occasions, an account of the Torah service, with a full liturgical text, as well as the earliest full references to the *Kaddish* and an account of its liturgical use. (Scholars deem it likely that this liturgical material is a later addition to the original text, possibly from as late as the eleventh century.) *Sof'rim* is sometimes called one of the "minor tractates of the Talmud," because it is often printed in sets of the Babylonian Talmud, although it is not part of the Talmud. Reference is made in this book to the standard printed edition found in the back of the *Avodah Zarah* volume in the Vilna edition of the Babylonian Talmud. An English translation may be found in the Soncino *Minor Tractates* volume. Reference is also made to the critical edition of Michael Higger (New York, 1937), which numbers the paragraphs differently.

The following midrashic and homiletical texts are referred to in the text:

1. *M'chilta D'Rabbi Yishmael* is an early (third century?), mostly legal midrash on the Book of Exodus, compiled in the Land of Israel.
2. *Sifrei B'midbar* is an early (third century?), mostly legal midrash on the Book of Numbers, compiled in the Land of Israel.
3. *Sifrei D'varim* is an early (third century?), mostly legal midrash on the Book of Deuteronomy, compiled in the Land of Israel.
4. *Vayikra Rabbah* is a homiletical midrash on the Book of Leviticus, compiled in the Land of Israel in the fourth to fifth centuries CE.
5. *Midrash Tanchuma* is a homiletical midrash on the Torah, compiled in the Land of Israel sometime between the sixth and eighth centuries CE. The edition published by Solomon Buber (Martin's grandfather) in 1885 transcribes a manuscript that differs from the standard printed edition. Both editions are cited according to the *parashah* (weekly Torah reading) and paragraph number (thus, *B'reishit*, 10).
6. *Seder Eliyahu Zuta* is a homiletical text compiled in the Land of Israel in the eighth century CE that stresses the value of Torah study and ethical behavior. It is cited according to chapter number (*Seder Eliyahu Zuta* 17).
7. *Sefer HaZohar* ("The Book of [Divine] Radiance"), the major work of Spanish Kabbalah from the end of the thirteenth century CE, takes the literary form of a homiletical midrash in Aramaic on the Torah. The interpretations are all symbolic of processes that take place within God, who has ten primary aspects or dimensions (*s'firot*). The *Zohar* is cited according to the *parashah* (weekly Torah reading) and the folio number and side in the standard edition (Vilna, Lithuania, 1882); thus, *Vayak'heil*, 206a.

The following medieval halachic liturgical compendia are referred to in this volume:

1. *Seder Rav Amram,* the first "order of prayer," was composed by the *gaon* ("eminence," head of the rabbinical academy) Amram ben Sheshna sometime before 875 CE in Sura, Babylonia. It heavily influenced all subsequent rabbinic prayer rites, but especially that of the Sephardim (Jews in Spain and other Arab lands).
2. *Siddur Rav Saadyah,* a treatise on prayer and liturgy, was composed by the *gaon* Saadyah sometime before 942 CE in Sura, Babylonia. The work was composed in Judeo-Arabic, with the liturgical texts given in Hebrew. It was known to Mediterranean Jewish communities in Arab lands but, because of the language of its composition, was less known and not copied in Central Europe. It was quoted in Sephardic legal-liturgical works and only rediscovered among the writings in the genizah of the Ben Ezra Synagogue in Cairo (the Cairo Genizah).
3. *Machzor Vitry,* the first major liturgical work of Rhineland Jewry (Ashkenazim), was compiled by Simchah ben Samuel of Vitry (now in France) in the twelfth century.
4. *Siddur Rashi* is a legal-liturgical manual from the Rashi school (not written by Rashi himself), from the area between France and Germany in the late eleventh century.
5. *Sefer HaManhig,* by Nathan ben Avraham of Lunel (Provence), is a legal-liturgical manual written in Toledo in 1205.
6. *Kol Bo* ("Miscellany," literally "everything's in it"), compiled by Shemaryah ben Simchah, details the liturgical customs of German Jews in the thirteenth and fourteenth centuries.
7. *Seder HaYom* ("The Order of the Day"), by Moses ibn Machir, who lived near Safed in the late sixteenth century, is a liturgical work heavily influenced by the Safed kabbalists, but not significantly by the teachings of Isaac Luria.

Finally, a word is in order about the term *b'rachah,* "blessing" or "benediction," as it applies to rabbinic prayers. The term refers to any expression of praise to God that begins or ends with the words *Baruch atah Adonai* ("Blessed/Praised are You, Adonai"). This verbal formula is both the germ and the formal hallmark of all rabbinic prayer. The opening blessing of the *T'filah,* for example, begins with this formula, and every one of its eighteen/nineteen blessings ends with it.[7] Similarly, the first blessing that precedes the *Sh'ma* begins with it, and all of the blessings surrounding the *Sh'ma* end with it. This formula at the end of a prayer of multiple sentences is called a *chatimah* (literally "seal"; rhetorically, "peroration" or "conclusion"), and serves to "round off" the blessing by recapitulating or summarizing its theme. In *Mishkan T'filah,* these Hebrew *chatimot* appear at the end of each alternative English version of the prayer (including the translation on the right-hand side of the page) and serve as markers to indicate that it is time to turn the page.

Abbreviations and Page Number References

Mishkan T'filah was printed in two different versions, resulting in three different possible paginations. There is the complete version of *Mishkan T'filah*, made up of Shabbat, weekday, and festival prayers. There is also the two-book set, made up of a Shabbat-only volume and a separate weekday and festival volume. For this reason, page number references within this book are coded as follows:

C	Complete version
Sh	Shabbat volume
W/F	Weekday and festival volume

OTHER ABBREVIATIONS

B.	Babylonian Talmud (*Bavli*)
GOP	*Gates of Prayer*
M.	Mishnah
MT	*Mishkan T'filah*
T.	*Tosefta*
UPB	*Union Prayer Book*
Y.	Jerusalem Talmud (*Y'rushalmi*)

Weekdays

Introduction to Weekday Services

Most Reform Jews are more familiar with the services for Shabbat than with weekday services, since, with the exception of those who have attended Reform summer camps or NFTY events, have been to shivah minyanim in the homes of mourners, or have participated in services at URJ Biennials and other public functions, they have not attended many or any such services. Most North American Reform congregations do not hold weekday services—although some do, and that number is slowly growing. But the more familiar Shabbat services are best understood as variations and elaborations of the weekday services, which form the core of traditional Jewish worship.

Traditionally, daily worship takes place three times a day: in the morning (*Shacharit*), afternoon (*Minchah*), and evening (*Arvit*). Shabbat, the festivals, and the High Holy Days include an additional (*Musaf*) service, corresponding to and commemorating the biblically mandated additional Shabbat and festival sacrifices that took place in the Jerusalem Temple on these occasions. (Most North American Reform prayer books eliminated the *Musaf* service, for reasons of redundancy and the association with Temple sacrifices, but most European Reform prayer books retained—and retain—them, and they are retained in Israeli Progressive prayer books, as well as some of those in Australia, New Zealand, South Africa, and South America.)[8] Yom Kippur also has a fifth service, *N'ilah* ("closing" or "locking" of the Temple gates) at the end of the day.

The morning service is the longest of the daily services, likely because people are most fresh for worship and study as soon as they have awakened. The core of the morning service is the recitation of *Sh'ma*, with its accompanying blessings, and the *T'filah/Amidah* ("Standing Prayer"). The text of the *Sh'ma* and Its Blessings is identical every day of the year (although different musical modes are used to chant the blessings depending on whether the day is a weekday, Shabbat, festival, or High Holy Day). The text of the *T'filah* contains an invariant core of three benedictions at the beginning (*Avot V'Imahot, G'vurot, K'dushat HaShem*) and three at the end (*Avodah, Hodaah,* and *Shalom*). On weekdays, there are thirteen[9] petitionary benedictions in the center. Since petitions are deemed inappropriate for Shabbat, these are replaced on Shabbat with a single benediction, *K'dushat HaYom,* which deals with the theme of Shabbat rest. On the festivals and High Holy Days, this benediction is expanded to encompass the relevant themes of the day.

On weekdays only, the morning *T'filah* traditionally is followed by penitential supplications, *Tachanunim,* which are related thematically and rhetorically to the *S'lichot* prayers for forgiveness recited on Yom Kippur and the days that precede it. Most North American Reform prayer books have omitted these, because their rhetoric of self-abasement is deemed too strong; many European and Israeli Reform prayer books have retained this section but abbreviated it significantly. Traditionally, they are not recited on Shabbat for the same reason that the intermediate petitions of the *T'filah* are not recited then: Shabbat is a time for rest and joy, not for petition and supplication.

The Torah is also read at Monday and Thursday morning services—just the first section of the reading for the following Shabbat; the same text has been read at the previous Shabbat afternoon service.[10] Since the main Torah reading is on Shabbat mornings, the rest of the week provides just enough to whet the appetite. The liturgy for removing the Torah scroll from and returning it to the ark is also less elaborate on weekdays and on Shabbat afternoons. (For more on this, see p. 83.)

The *Sh'ma* and Its Blessings are preceded on weekdays, as on Shabbat, by the Preliminary Morning Service (*Birchot HaShachar,* "the Morning Blessings" and accompanying prayers, and text study of biblical and rabbinic passages), all of which were originally recited at home. The texts are identical on weekdays and Shabbat. Following this, and immediately preceding *Bar'chu,* are the *P'sukei D'zimrah* or *Z'mirot,* psalm texts that constitute preparation for prayer. More of these are recited on Shabbat than on weekdays, including Psalm 92, the psalm for the Sabbath day.

The concluding portions of the weekday service, following the *T'filah* and (on Mondays and Thursdays) the Torah reading, are basically identical with those on Shabbat—*Ashrei* (Psalm 145 with additional verses), *Aleinu,* and Mourner's *Kaddish,* followed by more psalms. (In a traditional Shabbat service, *Ashrei* is recited before returning the Torah scroll to the ark, before *Musaf*, while *Aleinu* and Mourner's *Kaddish* follow *Musaf*.) The traditional service also includes what is called *K'dushah D'sidra* between *Ashrei* and *Aleinu*. This is another recital of the *K'dushah* and its Aramaic interpretive translation, together with other biblical verses that look forward to Israel's redemption. (On Shabbat, this is postponed until the afternoon service.)

The structure of the afternoon and evening services is basically identical on weekdays to what Reform Jews know from Shabbat. There is no Torah reading, however, on weekday afternoons. The service consists solely of *Ashrei*, the *T'filah*, and concluding prayers. The evening service consists of the evening recitation of the *Sh'ma*, the *T'filah*, and concluding prayers. On Erev Shabbat, the service begins with (or, to be more precise, is preceded by) the *Kabbalat Shabbat* ritual—the singing of seven (actually eight; see p. 120) psalms and the hymn *L'cha Dodi* to welcome Shabbat.

The key to understanding the Jewish worship service is its structure. It may be helpful to visualize this structure as follows:

WEEKDAY MORNING	**SHABBAT MORNING**
1. Preliminary Morning Blessings	1. Identical
2. Preparatory psalms	2. More psalms (incl. Psalm 92)
3. *Sh'ma* and Its Blessings	3. Mostly identical
4. *T'filah*: 18 (19) blessings	4. *T'filah*: 7 blessings
5. [*Tachanun* (penitential prayers)]	5. Omitted
6. Torah reading (Mon., Thurs.—abbreviated)	6. Torah reading (full)
7. *Ashrei* (Psalm 145 plus add'l verses)	7. Identical
8. [*K'dushah D'sidra*]	8. Postponed to afternoon service
9. *Aleinu*	9. Identical
10. Mourner's *Kaddish*	10. Identical

WEEKDAY AFTERNOON	**SHABBAT AFTERNOON**
1. *Ashrei*	1. Identical
—	2. [*K'dushah D'sidra*]
—	3. Torah reading (abbreviated)
4. *T'filah*: 18 (19) blessings	4. *T'filah*: 7 blessings
5. *Aleinu*	5. Identical
6. Mourner's *Kaddish*	6. Identical

WEEKDAY EVENING	**SHABBAT EVENING**
—	*Kabbalat Shabbat*
1) *Sh'ma* and Its Blessings	1) Identical
2) *T'filah*: 18 (19) blessings	2) *T'filah*: 7 blessings
3) *Aleinu*	3) Identical
4) Mourner's *Kaddish*	4) Identical

Traditional prayer books begin with the weekday morning prayers, since the earliest prayer codes (such as the Babylonian *Seder Rav Amram* and the early Ashkenazic *Machzor Vitry*) first list the blessings to be recited upon awakening in the morning and beginning the day—a logical place to start. The Shabbat, festival, and High Holy Day prayers, however, begin with the evening services, since that is when these special days begin, and the evening liturgy already includes special prayers for these days. *Mishkan T'filah*, on the other hand, following the example of its predecessor *Gates of Prayer* (1975), begins with the weekday evening service—likely because Reform Jews, being more familiar with the model of the Shabbat services, expect to see the evening service first. Our commentary, however, will begin with the weekday morning service, since that is the basic service of the day.

Modeh Ani
Giving Thanks upon Awakening

The weekday morning service in *Mishkan T'filah* begins with texts and actions, such as donning tallit and *t'fillin* for those who wish to do so, that help us prepare for worship. Many Reform Jews know the brief prayer *Modeh Ani* (C, pp. 24, 186, 288, 414; Sh, pp. 68, 170; W/F, pp. 24, 150) as a song or as a prayer that children learn to recite upon waking up in the morning, just as they often learn to recite the *Sh'ma* before going to bed at night. The prayer indeed was composed to be recited immediately upon awakening in the morning—at home, not in the synagogue—as an expression of gratitude for the gift of renewed life. It thanks God for having "restored my soul to me in mercy." Behind this powerful image is the Talmudic understanding that "sleep is one-sixtieth of death" (*B. B'rachot* 57b) and the kabbalistic idea that when a person is asleep, their soul leaves their body, returning to it only when they wake up. Hence, waking up in the morning is a compassionate divine gift ("great is Your faithfulness"). The prayer itself was composed under the influence of Kabbalah and appears for the first time in the sixteenth-century prayer manual *Seder HaYom* (1599) by Moses ibn Machir, who had lived for a time in Safed and was a contemporary—though not a disciple—of Isaac Luria.

There is yet another aspect of this prayer that is noteworthy: it does not mention the divine name. Rather, God is referred to as "ever-living Sovereign [*Melech chai v'kayam*]." This is a response to a halachic quandary that goes back to the early post-Talmudic era. The Babylonian Talmud (*B. B'rachot* 60b) prescribes a series of blessings upon waking in the morning that accompany each of our actions as we regain our consciousness and prepare for the new day (for example, opening our eyes, stretching our limbs, sitting up, putting our feet on the ground, getting dressed). As we shall see below, these blessings (known collectively as the *Birchot HaShachar*, the morning or dawn blessings, and labeled by Rabbi Chaim Stern in *Gates of Prayer* as *Nisim B'chol Yom*, meaning "miracles of every day") are now recited all together in the synagogue instead of one by one accompanying the appropriate actions at home. The *geonim*, legal authorities of the early Islamic period in Babylonia, forbade people to recite any blessings that included the divine name before they washed their hands in the morning—since who knows what those hands might have been touching during the night that could have rendered them unclean? *Seder Rav Amram*, the first prayer manual, thus requires people first to wash their hands (with the proper blessing), face, and feet and only then to recite the rest of the morning blessings in a series all together, rather than each before its appropriate action. In Spain, the blessings were all moved into the synagogue, to ensure that everyone, no matter how unlearned, could fulfill them (and see below, p. 19). But this wound up nullifying the original intent—to express one's gratitude to God immediately upon waking up in the morning. *Modeh Ani* was composed to address that felt need of both Jewish piety and halachic precision: it expresses gratitude for the soul's return to the body *without* invoking the divine name, and thus passes muster on both accounts.

Next follow the blessings that accompany the donning of tallit (C, pp. 26, 190, 289, 416; Sh, pp. 72, 171; W/F, pp. 26, 152) and *t'fillin* (C, p. 28; W/F, p. 28). These had been omitted from most Reform prayer books in the nineteenth and early twentieth centuries, particularly in North America, once distinctive Jewish prayer garb had been discarded as too foreign for Western societies. The blessings were restored in *Gates of Prayer*, as many Reform Jews in the second half of the twentieth century began to explore and reclaim more traditional practices. The blessings themselves derive from the Babylonian Talmud (*B. B'rachot* 60a). The biblical verses that precede the donning of the tallit and follow the wrapping of the *t'fillin* were added to the ritual by Lurianic kabbalists in the sixteenth century. *Bar'chi nafshi* is Psalm 104:1–2. Its image of God "wrapping Yourself in light as in a garment" recalls our activity of wrapping ourselves in the fringes (*tzitzit*) of the tallit and suggests that this human activity has a divine model and analogue. Hosea 2:21–22, "I will betroth you to Me forever," is often recited or sung at weddings (and can even appear on wedding rings). Its recitation when winding the strap of the hand-*t'fillin* three times around the middle finger suggests that this action is a sign and acknowledgment of God's betrothal of the Jewish people and is another human imitation of the divine model.

Mah Tovu
Entering a Place of Prayer

The Tzanzer Rebbe was asked by a Hasid: "What does the Rebbe do before praying?"
"I pray," was the reply, "that I may be able to pray properly."
—Louis Newman, *The Hasidic Anthology*, 1934, p. 332

ALL PRAYER requires preparation. We cannot simply drop everything and pray. We need to move ourselves (or let ourselves be moved) to a different place: physically, mentally, emotionally, spiritually.

And so our liturgy at the very outset helps us to transition, to prepare to pray. The first portion of every service is preparatory. The first text that we encounter in the morning service every day is *Mah Tovu* (C, pp. 30, 192, 290, 418; Sh, pp. 74, 172; W/F, pp. 30, 154). This a not a prayer, but a series of five biblical verses that relate to the theme of prayer and of preparing to worship.

The first of these verses, *Mah tovu ohalecha Yaakov / mishk'notecha, Yisrael* ("How fair are your tents, O Jacob, / your dwellings, O Israel"; Numbers 24:5) is taken from the story of the gentile prophet Balaam, hired by the Moabite king Balak to curse the invading Israelites. God, however, saw things differently; whenever Balaam opened his mouth to curse Israel, only blessings came out—including this one! The verse appears here, however, because of its rabbinic interpretation in the Babylonian Talmud (*B. Sanhedrin* 105b). The Rabbis identified Israel's "tents" and "dwellings" in the verse with their synagogues (*batei k'neisiyot*) and study houses (*batei midrashot*): for the Rabbis of the Talmud, *these* are the places in which Israel truly dwells, in prayer and study. And for this reason, the early post-Talmudic authorities ruled that this verse should be recited whenever we enter a synagogue (*Seder Rav Amram*, Babylonia, ninth century; *Machzor Vitry*, France, twelfth century). It helps us to focus on where we are—and who we are. (By the way, the Hebrew word for "dwellings" in this verse, *mishk'not*, is the plural form [with second-person singular possessive suffix—"*your* dwellings"] of the noun *mishkan* in the title of our siddur, *Mishkan T'filah*, literally "a dwelling-place of prayer." The word also appears in a verse below, from Psalm 26:8, *mishkan k'vodecha*, "the dwelling-place of Your glory.")

The four remaining verses are all from psalms. They evoke feelings of awe and reverence upon entering God's house. In their biblical contexts, these verses refer to entering the Jerusalem Temple; but the Rabbis refer them, once again, to entering the synagogue, our place of prayer and divine encounter:

וַאֲנִי בְּרֹב חַסְדְּךָ, אָבוֹא בֵיתֶךָ;
אֶשְׁתַּחֲוֶה אֶל־הֵיכַל קָדְשְׁךָ, בְּיִרְאָתֶךָ.

Vaani b'rov chasd'cha avo veitecha,
eshtachaveh el heichal kodsh'cha b'yiratecha.

I, through Your abundant love, enter Your house;
I bow down in awe at Your holy temple. (Psalm 5:8)

יְיָ אָהַבְתִּי, מְעוֹן בֵּיתֶךָ;
וּמְקוֹם, מִשְׁכַּן כְּבוֹדֶךָ.

Adonai, ahavti m'on beitecha
um'kom mishkan k'vodecha.

Adonai, I love Your temple abode,
the dwelling-place of Your glory. (Psalm 26:8)

וַאֲנִי אֶשְׁתַּחֲוֶה וְאֶכְרָעָה
אֶבְרְכָה לִפְנֵי יְיָ עֹשִׂי.

Va'ani eshtachaveh v'echraah,
Evr'chah lifnei Adonai osi.

I will humbly bow down low before Adonai, my Maker.

This is not a direct quote, but a rephrasing of Psalm 95:6, changing the verbs from first-person plural exhortations ("Let us bow down") to first-person singular descriptions ("I bow down"), since this is now being recited by individuals entering the sanctuary.

וַאֲנִי תְפִלָּתִי־לְךָ, יְיָ, עֵת רָצוֹן.
אֱלֹהִים בְּרָב־חַסְדֶּךָ, עֲנֵנִי בֶּאֱמֶת יִשְׁעֶךָ.

Va'ani t'filati l'cha, Adonai, eit ratzon.
Elohim, b'rov chasdecha, aneini be-emet yishecha.

As for me, may my prayer come to You, Adonai, at a favorable time.
O God, in Your abundant faithfulness, answer me with
Your sure deliverance. (Psalm 69:14)

This verse, too, is (partly) here on account of its rabbinic interpretation: the Rabbis indicate that the "favorable time" to offer up a private prayer to God is that time when the congregation is praying (*B. B'rachot* 8a).

Contemplate these verses the next time you enter a synagogue. Hopefully they will enhance your experience of prayer and worship, as they were meant to!

Asher Yatzar
Our Bodily Needs

While the *Mah Tovu* verses were intended to be recited upon entering the synagogue, the texts that follow in the morning services of our prayer book (C, pp. 32–48, 194–211, 291–300, 420–437; Sh, pp. 76–93, 173–182; W/F, pp. 32–48, 156–173), collectively referred to as *Birchot Ha-Shachar* ("the Morning Blessings"), were not originally intended for synagogue use at all. All of this material originates in the Babylonian Talmud, mostly in *B'rachot* 60b, where these are all separate blessings to be recited privately by individuals in specific circumstances—mostly upon awakening in the morning, arising, getting dressed, studying Torah, and so on.

The first of these blessings in our prayer book is *Asher Yatzar*, which praises God for the intricate workings of our bodies, and particularly for our plumbing (gastroenterologists and urologists, take note!). In the Talmud, this blessing is not specifically intended for morning recitation; it is to be recited upon leaving an outhouse (today, a bathroom; so, yes, there is a blessing in Jewish tradition for going to the toilet!).

The final chapter of *M. B'rachot* deals with blessings occasioned by special events or experiences: beholding natural wonders; building a new house; escaping from a dangerous situation; accepting God's providence, whether for good or for ill. The Mishnaic ruling to which our Talmudic discussion is attached (9:4) deals with escaping from a dangerous situation. The Talmud lists the blessings to be recited and provides further examples. One of these is safely navigating an outhouse and the human activities that take place there (remember what that's like in early childhood and old age!). The Talmud lists blessings to be recited both upon entering and upon leaving. The blessing before entering requests permission from the ministering angels who accompany a person on his way to wait for him and to protect him while he attends to his human needs. (I retain the masculine language of the original to honestly reflect the sources in their historical context.) The blessing recited upon emerging from the outhouse is the one we have in our prayer book here:

> Praise to You, Adonai, our God, Sovereign of the universe, who formed the human body [literally "man"] with skill, creating the body's many pathways and openings. It is well known before Your throne of glory that if one of them be wrongly opened or closed, it would be impossible to endure and stand before You.

There follows a dispute over how this blessing should be concluded. Rav suggests: [*Baruch atah Adonai*] *rofei cholim*, "Blessed are You, Adonai, who heals the sick." To this Samuel objects: But do we then consider the whole world—everyone who needs to go the bathroom—sick?! Instead, we should say, *rofei chol basar*, "who heals all flesh." That is to say, our bodies' natural processes are considered to be a form of divinely induced healing. Rav Sheshet suggests a different conclusion: *mafli laasot*, "who works wondrously." If we are properly attentive, it is indeed miraculous when our bodies work the way they are supposed to. (Anyone who has had to deal with illness knows that; the trick is always to be grateful for what we have while we have it.) Finally, Rav Papa suggests that we combine the two formulae of Samuel and Rav Sheshet: *rofei chol basar umafli laasot*, "who heals all flesh, working wondrously." This indeed is the *chatimah* ("seal"), or peroration, of the blessing that has appeared in all prayer books since the ninth century.

In the traditional siddur, this blessing appears immediately after that for washing one's hands—the first in the series of the Morning Blessings. Early post-Talmudic authorities did not allow any blessings invoking God's name to be recited in the morning until after a person had washed their hands and cleansed their body (and see above, pp. 7–8). Only then could God's holy name be invoked in purity.

We, too, must attend to our physical needs before we can pray. This blessing asks us to consider and be grateful for the daily miracles of our bodies and the intricacies of our vital organs when they are working properly (*mafli laasot*), and to pray for divine assistance in healing when they are not (*rofei chol basar*).

Elohai N'shamah
For Our Souls

After praising God for the intricate workings of our bodies, we give thanks for the return of our souls—of our consciousness—each morning upon awakening (C, pp. 34, 196, 292, 422; Sh, pp. 78, 174; W/F, pp. 34, 158). This blessing also derives from the Babylonian Talmud, *B'rachot* 60b, where it is prescribed as the very first thing to say every day upon waking up, while still in bed. The text there reads as follows:

> *Upon awakening, one should say:*
> O God, the soul which You have put in me is pure.
> You fashioned it within me; You breathed it into me, and You preserve it within me.
> You will remove it from me at some future time, and You will restore it to me in the future age.
> As long as the soul remains within me, I will give You thanks, Adonai my God and God of my fathers, Sovereign of all worlds, Master of all souls.
> Praised be You, Adonai, who restores souls to dead bodies.

Immediately before this text in the Talmud is a prayer to be recited before going to bed at night, that is, before letting go of consciousness. This prayer includes the requests that "bad dreams not trouble me . . . and lighten my eyes [in the morning], lest I sleep the sleep of death." The blessing upon awakening thus responds directly to this last concern with gratitude that our consciousness, our soul, has returned to us.

Our rabbinic ancestors viewed sleep as an analogue to, and anticipation of, death ("Sleep is one-sixtieth of death" [*B. B'rachot* 57b]; and see above, p. 7), because it involves a loss of consciousness and mobility. In sleep, the soul was thought to detach itself from the body and have its own independent experiences (dreams). Awakening was experienced as the return of the soul to the body. The language of our blessing reflects these ideas: sleep anticipates death, and awakening anticipates (and provides a basis for belief in) the resurrection of the dead. Thus, the *chatimah*, or peroration, of this blessing—"who restores souls to dead bodies"—refers to *both* waking up in the morning and resurrection of the dead, the ultimate "waking up."

Problems with the traditional understanding of death and resurrection led Reformers in the nineteenth and twentieth centuries to alter this blessing. German-language paraphrases of the (unaltered) Hebrew in many nineteenth-century prayer books omit all references to resurrection and deal only with the present experience of awakening each morning. The first (1895) *Union Prayer Book* and subsequent revisions provide this blessing only in English. The first reference to resurrection is rephrased to refer instead to the soul's immortality: "Thou hast preserved it in this body and, at the appointed time, Thou wilt take it from this earth that it may enter upon life everlasting." The *chatimah* is changed to "Praised be Thou, O God, in whose hands are all the living and the spirits of all flesh"; the language is drawn from Job 12:10, "In His hand is every living soul and the breath of all humankind." *Gates of Prayer* (1975) restores the Hebrew text but eliminates (in both Hebrew and English) the phrases referring to death and resurrection. The *chatimah* of the *UPB* is retained, now provided in Hebrew as well. The wording of this blessing in *Mishkan T'filah* is identical with that in *GOP*.

In recent years, this blessing has become a favorite for musical settings (such as those of Debbie Friedman and Shefa Gold), perhaps because of the renewed interest in spirituality, with its emphasis on the nonmaterial aspects of our lives. In any case, this blessing—like the ones before and after it in the prayer book—requires us to focus on those things that we too often take for granted until we lose them: the miracle of waking up each morning and our return to consciousness, as well as the intricate workings of our bodies. Proper attention to these daily miracles should elicit from us constant feelings of gratitude.

Birchot HaShachar
The Morning Blessings

The series of short blessings that follow *Elohai N'shamah* (C, pp. 36–40, 198–202, 293–296, 424–428; Sh, pp. 80–84, 175–178; W/F, pp. 36–40, 160–164) together are called *Birchot HaShachar*, "the Morning Blessings," because they originally were to be uttered each morning upon waking up, getting dressed, getting out of bed, and so on. Later they were moved into the synagogue and recited as a unit independently of the actions that first prompted their recitation. Later still, the entirety of the morning liturgy before *P'sukei D'zimrah* ("Verses of Song," the psalm texts) came to be called *Birchot HaShachar*, "the Preliminary Morning Service." To distinguish these specific blessings from this larger section of the service, Rabbi Chaim Stern, in *Gates of Prayer*, decided to label them *Nisim B'chol Yom*, "For Our Blessings"—since that is their theme. *Mishkan T'filah* keeps this Hebrew label, translating it more accurately as "For Daily Miracles." (The expression comes from the next to last blessing in the *T'filah—Modim anachnu lach . . . v'al nisecha sheb'chol yom imanu*, "We give You thanks . . . and for Your miracles that we experience every day.")

All (except one!) of these blessings derive from the Babylonian Talmud, most from *B. B'rachot* 60b and three (the so-called identity blessings; see pp. 20–21) from *B. M'nachot* 43b–44a (and *T. B'rachot* 6:18). *B. B'rachot* 60b describes how a person should express gratitude for every activity upon awakening anew to conscious and purposeful life each morning:

1. Upon hearing the rooster crow, one should say:
   Blessed are You, Adonai our God, Ruler of the universe,
   who has given the rooster understanding to discern between
   day and night.
2. Upon opening one's eyes, one should say:
   Blessed . . . who opens the eyes of the blind.
3. Upon straightening and sitting up, one should say:
   Blessed . . . who releases those who are bound.

4. Upon getting dressed, one should say:
   Blessed . . . who clothes the naked.
5. Upon rising, one should say:
   Blessed . . . who raises up those who are stooped over.
6. Upon touching the ground, one should say:
   Blessed . . . who stretches out the earth upon the waters.
7. Upon walking, one should say:
   Blessed . . . who prepares the steps of man.
8. Upon putting on shoes, one should say:
   Blessed . . . who has provided for my every need.
9. Upon fastening one's belt, one should say:
   Blessed . . . who girds Israel with might.
10. Upon putting on one's head covering, one should say:
    Blessed . . . who crowns Israel with glory.
11. Upon wrapping oneself in a fringed garment [*tzitzit*], one should say:
    Blessed . . . who has sanctified us with His commandments and commanded us to wrap ourselves up in fringes.
12. When one puts *t'fillin* on one's arm, one should say:
    Blessed . . . who has sanctified us with His commandments and commanded us to lay t'fillin.
13. [When one puts *t'fillin*] on one's head, one should say:
    Blessed . . . who has sanctified us with His commandments and commanded us concerning the mitzvah of t'fillin.
14. Upon washing hands, one should say:
    Blessed . . . who has sanctified us with His commandments and commanded us concerning the washing of hands.
15. Upon washing the face, one should say:
    Blessed . . . who removes the bands of sleep from my eyes and slumber from my eyelids.

And may it be Your will, Adonai my God, to accustom me to Your Torah and that I adhere to Your commandments. Lead me not into sin, transgression, temptation, or shame. Bend my impulses to serve You. Keep me from bad men and bad companions. Incline me to my good impulses and good companions in this world. Grant me, this day and every day, grace, favor, and mercy in Your sight and in the sight of all who behold me. Bestow lovingkindness upon me. Blessed are You, Adonai, who bestows lovingkindness upon His people Israel.

The artistry and piety of these blessings lies in their metaphorical application of powerful biblical imagery of divine creation and salvation to mundane human activities:

a. The first blessing cites Job 38:36, "Who put wisdom in the hidden parts? Who gave understanding to the *sechvi* [*mi natan lasechvi vinah*]?" The word *sechvi* occurs only this once in the *Tanach*. Its likely meaning, on the basis of the parallelism between the two halves of the verse, is "mind," but the Rabbis, in several Talmudic passages, clearly understand it as "rooster," hence the use of this verse in this blessing.
b. Psalm 146:7–8 describes God as *matir asurim*, "who frees the captive / those who are bound"; *pokei-ach ivrim*, "who opens the eyes of the blind"; and *zokeif k'fufim*, "who lifts the fallen / makes those who are bent stand straight." Blessings 3, 2, and 5 artfully apply these descriptions of God's mighty acts to the daily human experience of waking up, when we bestir ourselves from the "bonds" of sleep (parallel to the "bonds" of death). How better to express the miraculous in our everyday lives?
c. Blessing 4 alludes to the imagery of Genesis 3:21, where God makes garments of skin for Adam and Eve, "and clothes them [*vayalbisheim*]." This is another application of primal Creation imagery to the "new creation" that takes place for us every morning upon awakening.
d. Psalm 136:6, referring to God's creation of the world, uses the phrase [*l'*]*roka haaretz al hamayim*, "[Praise God], who stretches the earth over the waters," an allusion to Genesis 1:9–10. Blessing 6 invokes this image of Creation every time our feet newly touch the ground upon descending from bed.
e. Blessing 7 derives its imagery and language from Psalm 37:23, "The steps of a man are made firm by Adonai [*mei-Adonai mitzadei gever konanu*]," and Proverbs 20:24, "A man's steps are decided by Adonai [*mei-Adonai mitzadei gaver*]."
f. Blessings 9 and 10 derive their language from Psalm 65:7, "[O God, our deliverer . . . who is girded with strength [*ne'zar bigvurah*]"; Proverbs 4:9, "She [Wisdom = Torah, for the Rabbis] will

> adorn your head with a graceful wreath; crown you with a glorious diadem [*ateret tiferet*]"; and Psalm 103:4, "[God] surrounds/crowns you with steadfast love and mercy [*hamatreichi chesed v'rachamim*]."

Thus, the Morning Blessings literally wrap us in biblical imagery of divine goodness, to which the appropriate human response is gratitude.

How, then did these Talmudic occasional blessings for waking, getting up, getting dressed, getting washed, and so forth, end up being recited "in a heap" in the synagogue? The process was in two steps, both of them documented in the earliest post-Talmudic prayer manual, *Seder Rav Amram* (Babylonia, before 875 CE). The rabbinic authorities in early Islamic Babylonia ruled that God's name must not be pronounced in the morning after waking up before one has washed his hands, face, and feet (think of Muslims washing before entering a mosque for prayer). So, first one washes and recites the blessings for hand-washing (*al n'tilat yadayim*) and for going to the bathroom (*asher yatzar*), and *then* one recites all the rest of the blessings as a group. A later gloss in several manuscripts of *Seder Rav Amram* notes that the custom of Spanish congregations was for the prayer leader (*sh'liach tzibur*) to recite all of these blessings out loud in the synagogue at the beginning of the service, in order to make sure that all of the Jews in the congregation thereby fulfilled their religious obligations (since, in the days before printed prayer books, not everyone knew how to recite these blessings at home on their own—and the Rabbis weren't sure that they even did this!). Although no less an authority than Moses Maimonides objected to this custom—since it violated the original intent and purpose of these benedictions—the custom held and spread to other parts of the Jewish world.

The one short blessing in our prayer books that is not Talmudic in origin is "Praise . . . who gives strength to the weary [*hanotein laya-eif ko-ach*]." The language derives from Isaiah 40:29, "[God] gives strength to the weary, fresh vigor to the spent."

The blessing is first found in early Ashkenazic liturgical texts (*Machzor Vitry*, France, late eleventh century), together with several other blessings (like *magbiah sh'falim*, "who raises the lowly," and *someich nof'lim*, "who supports the fallen") that are no longer recited because they are essentially redundant. (The Babylonian-style texts in the Cairo Genizah also add some of these other blessings, while the texts that follow the rite of the Land of Israel have *none* of the short blessings at all, since they all derive from the Babylonian Talmud!)

Finally, there are the three "identity" blessings that derive from the *Tosefta, B'rachot* 6:18 and are discussed in both Talmuds (*B. M'nachot* 43b–44a and *Y. B'rachot* 9:2, 13b).[11] Since these blessings are offensive today, they have all been modified in contemporary liturgies. *T. B'rachot* 6:18 reads as follows:

> Rav Judah says: A man must recite three benedictions each day:
> Blessed . . . who has not made me a gentile;
> Blessed . . . who has not made me a boor [that is, an ignoramus];
> Blessed . . . who has not made me a woman.
> A gentile—as it is written, "All the nations are nothing before Him" (Isaiah 40:17).
> A boor—because a boor does not fear sin (*M. Avot* 2:5).
> A woman—because women are not obligated to perform all the commandments.

The discussion of this tradition in the Babylonian Talmud objects to the blessing for not being made an ignoramus, since it sounds haughty ("And look who thinks he's so smart!"), and substitutes instead "who did not make me a slave." The versions of these blessings in the Cairo Genizah liturgies that follow the customs of the Land of Israel are phrased in positive and negative pairs. A typical text is:

> . . . who created me human and not an animal,
> a man and not a woman,
> an Israelite and not a gentile,
> circumcised and not uncircumcised,
> free and not a slave.

To avoid Christian censorship, some medieval manuscripts changed the first blessing to read simply "who has made me an Israelite." A thirteenth-century Spanish authority (Jacob ben Asher) writes that women, upon reciting these blessings, should say, ". . . who has made me according to His will."

Suffice it to say, these "identity" blessings have always been altered, if not entirely omitted, in Reform liturgies. They do not appear at all in the three editions of the *Union Prayer Book*. *Gates of Prayer* restored only the first two, phrased positively: "who has made me a Jew" and "who has made me to be free [*ben chorin*]." *Mishkan T'filah* retains these two and adds, in the first position, "who has made me in the image of God [*b'tzelem Elohim*]."

Finally, a word about the placement of these blessings: Since they form a separate unit, distinct from the *B. B'rachot* 60b blessings, they have often been placed at the end of the series (this is the usage in Sephardic prayer books). The Ashkenazic rite, however, places them right after the "rooster" blessing at the beginning of the series. *GOP* follows the Ashkenazic custom. *MT* follows the Sephardic custom and places these three blessings at the end. But *MT* reserves the final place for the blessings "who girds Israel with strength" and "who crowns Israel with splendor." These blessings, detached from their original context, are used to form a kind of coda to the entire series that focuses on the people Israel.

Laasok B'divrei Torah
Blessings before Torah Study

For Rabbinic tradition, *talmud Torah*—study of Torah—is *the* religious activity par excellence. It is through study and interpretation of Torah that we come to know God and what God requires of us. Indeed, for the Rabbis of the Talmud, *talmud Torah* is the most accessible way to *experience* God and the tangible traces of God's mind. As a Yiddish proverb puts it, *Toire iz di bester skhoire,* "Torah is the best occupation." For this reason, the first thing a Jew is supposed to do every morning (after getting up, getting washed, getting dressed, and so on) is to study Torah. And that is why the Morning Blessings in our siddur are immediately followed by blessings that introduce private Torah study.

The two blessings in our prayer book (C, pp. 42, 204, 296–297, 430; Sh, pp. 86, 178–179; W/F, pp. 42, 166) derive from *B. B'rachot* 11b. There the following quandary is posed: We are supposed to recite the *Sh'ma* (which, for the Rabbis means the full three paragraphs: Deuteronomy 6:4–9, 11:13–21, and Numbers 15:37–41; see below, pp. 40–43) every morning as soon as the sun rises, and this is to be preceded by a blessing for the divine gift to Israel of the Torah (today, *Ahavah Rabbah,* as we shall see below, pp. 48–50). But what if someone rose early to study Torah *before* reciting the *Sh'ma*? Clearly, that person would have to recite a *different* blessing before studying Torah. The text of that blessing, cited by Rav Judah in the name of Samuel, is "Blessed . . . who hallows us with mitzvot, commanding us to engage with words of Torah [*laasok b'divrei Torah*]." Note that this blessing affirms our *continual* obligation to be occupied with words of Torah.

The Talmud then informs us that Rabbi Yochanan would expand on this benediction, continuing as follows:

> Make pleasant, Adonai our God, the words of Torah in our mouths and in the mouths of Your people the household of Israel, so that we and our children and the children of Your

> people the household of Israel may all come to know/acknowledge Your name and be occupied with Your Torah. Blessed are You, Adonai, who teaches Torah to Your people Israel.

Noteworthy here is that words of Torah are meant to be sweet and pleasant in our mouths (hence the Eastern European custom of feeding children cookies with the letters of the Hebrew alphabet on them on their first day of school). Also, as we remarked before, it is through Torah study that one comes to know and acknowledge God.

The Talmud then notes yet a third option, in the name of Rabbi Hamnuna: "Blessed . . . who has chosen us from among the peoples and given us the Torah. Blessed are You, Adonai, who gives the Torah." This blessing is familiar to us because it is recited before we read from the Torah scroll in public—but it originates here, for private recitation. Its now-customary usage in the synagogue is post-Talmudic.

The Talmud generally prefers not to choose among liturgical formulations, but to endorse them all. That's what happens here, and that is why all three benedictions appear at this point in the traditional siddur before the study of passages from Torah, Mishnah, and Talmud. (While the Rabbis make a formal distinction between Scripture, which they call "Written Torah"—*Torah Shebichtav*—and their own traditions, which they call "Oral Torah"—*Torah Sheb'al Peh*—both are considered to be "Torah"; that is why Scripture, Mishnah, and Talmud are studied together liturgically.) In *Gates of Prayer* and *Mishkan T'filah,* only the first two blessings appear here, before a study text that has been conflated from the Mishnah and a passage that reworks the Talmud, as we shall now see.

Eilu D'varim

The Study of Torah Is Equal to Them All

WE HAVE NOTED that Torah study, both communal and private, forms a central part of Jewish liturgy because it is a crucial element of Jewish religious practice. Rabbinic tradition maintains that every Jew must study a bit of Torah every day: "One should always divide one's years into three parts, devoting one-third to the study of Scripture, one-third to the study of Mishnah, and one-third to the study of Talmud" (*B. Kiddushin* 30a). The Talmud concludes that the only certain way to fulfill this obligation is to do it daily. That is why the study of short passages from the Torah, from the Mishnah, and from the Talmud has been included in the morning liturgy since the time of *Seder Rav Amram* (before 875 CE).

Early on, there was variation in the precise passages studied. Many communities studied passages dealing with the daily morning sacrifices on the theory that if the actual sacrifices no longer could be offered, their *verbal narration* still could. (This remains the practice in traditional communities.) Another custom was to read the Priestly Benediction (Numbers 6:24–26), and *M. Pei-ah* 1:1, together with other Talmudic materials. The present custom of studying the two *Eilu D'varim* passages, *M. Pei-ah* 1:1 and a liturgical hybrid tradition based on *M. Pei-ah* 1:1 and *B. Shabbat* 127a, together with the Priestly Benediction, seems to be Franco-German in origin. The Tosafists (Rashi's students and grandsons) identify this as a French custom. Over time, both customs—Priestly Benediction + *Eilu D'varim*, and the sacrificial readings—were maintained.

The sacrificial readings were dropped from the outset in Reform prayer books. *Gates of Prayer*, which restored the Torah study passages to North American Reform practice, omitted the Priestly Benediction and gave a conflation of the *M. Pei-ah* and *B. Shabbat* hybrid texts, both of which extol the value of Torah study (and are conjoined here on that basis as well as because of their verbal similarity). *Mishkan T'filah* (C, pp. 44, 206, 298, 432; Sh, pp. 88, 180; W/F, pp. 44, 168) follows the text of *GOP* in this section. Here are the texts as they are found in the traditional liturgy:

These are the things [= obligations] that have no set measure
[= no upper limit]:
the corner of the field [= the obligation to leave the corner of the field for gleaning by the poor and needy];
the first fruits [of the new spring produce, which are brought to the Temple];
the pilgrimage offerings [brought up to Jerusalem on the festivals];
deeds of lovingkindness;
and the study of Torah. (*M. Pei-ah* 1:1)

These are the things of which a person enjoys their fruits [i.e., the interest] in this world, while the principal remains for him in the world to come:
honoring father and mother,
deeds of lovingkindness,
early arrival at the study house morning and evening,
hospitality to guests,
visiting the sick,
dowering the bride,
accompanying the dead [to burial],
devotion in prayer,
making peace between a man and his fellow,
and the study of Torah is equal to them all.
(a text found exclusively in the liturgy, based on a conflation of *M. Pei-ah* 1:1, items from *B. Shabbat* 127a, and items that do not occur elsewhere)[12]

Note that Rabbi Chaim Stern, in *GOP*, added at the end of his English rendering that "the study of Torah is equal to them all *because it leads to them all*," but that is not what this text actually claims. There is an ongoing dispute in rabbinic literature, beginning with the Mishnah, about which is greater, Torah study or deeds. One Talmudic tradition (*B. Kiddushin* 40b) indeed maintains that Torah study is greater *because* it leads to deeds, but not all of the texts giving primacy to Torah study (including this one) make that concession. For the Rabbis, Torah study is an intrinsic good and a supreme value in itself because, through it, one encounters God. And that is why Torah study remains an important part of Jewish worship.

Kaddish D'Rabanan

The Praise of God after Study

One of the traditional texts that *Mishkan T'filah* reintroduces into North American Reform liturgy is the *Kaddish D'Rabanan* (literally "Rabbis' *Kaddish*"), which is recited after *talmud Torah,* the study of Torah and rabbinic texts, both in the synagogue and in the *beit midrash* ("study house") (C, pp. 46–48, 208–210, 299–300, 434–436; Sh, pp. 90–92, 181–182; W/F, pp. 46–48, 170–172).

Many Reform Jews still think of the *Kaddish* as a mourner's prayer—since that is the sole form in which it was retained in the *Union Prayer Book*—but historically that was only one of its multiple liturgical functions (i.e., *Kaddish Yatom,* the Orphan's or Mourner's *Kaddish*), and a late one at that (see below, pp. 94–98). The major function of this prayer, in its several textual forms, in fact is to mark off and conclude the different parts of the service; it is recited at the end of each. *Chatzi Kaddish* ("Half *Kaddish*"), for example, marks off the end of the preliminary parts of the morning service before *Bar'chu,* the end of the Torah reading, and the end of the evening *Sh'ma* blessings before the *T'filah. Kaddish Shaleim* ("Full *Kaddish,*" not found in *MT*) marks off the end of the *T'filah. Kaddish D'Rabanan* marks off the end of a series of rabbinic study texts—here, *Eilu D'varim.*

Kaddish D'Rabanan is actually closest in function to (though not identical with) the original setting of this prayer of praise. We know from the Babylonian Talmud that the *Kaddish* originated as the praise of God recited after the public exposition of Torah (the "sermon") in both the synagogue and the rabbinic study house (see also below, p. 95). The name itself does not appear in the Talmud, nor do any of its textual forms. Instead we are told that "the world is sustained by . . . *Y'hei sh'meih raba d'aggad'ta*" ("Let His great name be praised—recited after the study of aggadah"; *B. Sotah* 49a). This is the congregational response in the *Kaddish* through which everyone may participate in its recitation—and that community participation is precisely what is being endorsed here.

The *Kaddish* is an example of the kind of prayer known in Christianity as a "doxology," a prayer of praise that recounts God's glory (*doxa*). In fact, this prayer is more than just the heaping up of adjectives of praise (*Yitgadal v'yitkadash sh'meih raba,* "Exalted and hallowed be God's great name"). It is also, and most importantly in Jewish tradition, a petition for the speedy coming of God's kingdom on earth (*v'yamlich malchuteih,* "May God's majesty be revealed") when all humans will acknowledge the truth of Israel's God and when Israel will be restored to her former glory. (This is also how it functions thematically as a prayer for mourners, who are encouraged thereby to look forward to the ultimate consolation of Israel.)

Kaddish D'Rabanan is distinguished by a special paragraph (*Al Yisrael v'al rabanan,* "For Israel and their rabbis/teachers") that invokes God's blessing upon "teachers [of Torah] and their disciples and all who engage in the study of Torah here and everywhere." Traditionally, this prayer is recited upon the completion of study wherever one happens to be. Here, it is used to conclude both the private morning Torah study and the Preliminary Morning Service; everything to this point in the service was originally recited privately, while what follows, from early on, was intended for the synagogue.

Whether the motivation for restoring *Kaddish D'Rabanan* in *MT* was the interest generated in this text by Debbie Friedman's popular adaptation and setting (C, pp. 47, 209, 300, 435; Sh, pp. 91, 182; W/F, pp. 47, 171) or simply the desire to conclude the study text of *Eilu D'varim* with the traditional invocation of blessing upon those who study Torah—or both—it is good to have this text back in our North American Reform liturgy, where it extols for all of us the value of Jewish study.

P'sukei D'zimrah
Verses of Song

> A person should stand to pray only in a reverent frame of mind. The pious men of old would wait an hour before praying, in order to direct their hearts to God. (*M. B'rachot* 5:1)

How should we prepare to pray? According to this Mishnaic ruling, we prepare by focusing, by turning our thoughts and intentions toward God. For almost two millennia, Jews have turned to the Book of Psalms as a way of focusing their hearts and minds on God: in distress, in jubilation, in thanksgiving, and in everyday circumstances, the psalms have provided a model and an encouragement to Jewish piety and given words and wings to our inchoate yearnings. Rabbinic prayers are redolent with the language of the psalms; whole verses are found on most pages of the prayer book. This is the reason why virtually every traditional worship service begins with a psalm verse or two—to frame the intended mood, to direct the heart.

The public morning service proper begins with a series of psalms, *P'sukei D'zimrah*, "Verses of Song," (or *Z'mirot*, "Songs," as this section is called by Sephardim), recited to help worshipers direct their hearts to God. As noted earlier, everything prior to this in the morning service was originally recited privately at home (which is why many traditional prayer books designate the *Birchot HaShachar* rubric as the "Preliminary Morning Service").

The custom of reciting *P'sukei D'zimrah* every morning goes back as far as the first rabbinic prayer books in the ninth and tenth centuries CE (Amram, Saadyah). It is based on a Talmudic interchange:

> Rabbi Yose said: May my portion be with those who recite the entire *Hallel* every day!
> —But isn't this blasphemous? [The *Hallel* psalms, 113–118, are only to be recited on festivals and new moons!]

—No, we refer here only to the Verses of Song [*P'sukei D'zimrah*].
(*B. Shabbat* 118b)

The Talmud never specifies *which* psalms comprise the "Verses of Song," but early post-Talmudic tradition identifies them as the last six psalms in the Psalter, 145–150, which are sometimes called the "Hallelujah" psalms, since all six, as they are recited liturgically,[13] end with this exclamation ("Praise God!"). These psalms form the core of the daily *P'sukei D'zimrah*. Other psalms of praise and psalm-like texts from elsewhere in Scripture have been added to them. The precise biblical texts and their order vary from rite to rite.

This recitation of various psalms has been made into a formalized liturgical structure by the addition, fore and aft, of rabbinic "framing" benedictions. (All public recitations from Scripture in Jewish liturgy are framed with rabbinic benedictions: consider also the Torah and haftarah readings, the readings of the Five *M'gillot*, the recitation of the *Sh'ma*, and the recitation of *Hallel*.) Here the introductory benediction, which will be discussed shortly, is *Baruch She-amar* ("Blessed is the One who spoke"; C, pp. 50, 212, 301, 438; Sh, pp. 94, 183; W/F, pp. 50, 174). The concluding benediction on weekdays is *Yishtabach shimcha* ("May Your name be praised"; C, p. 56; W/F, pp. 56). On Shabbat and the festivals, the concluding benediction is considerably longer and begins *Nishmat kol chai* ("The soul of everything alive"; C, pp. 219–223, 307–311, 446–450; Sh, pp. 101–105, 189–193; W/F, pp. 182–186).

Reform liturgies have generally abbreviated this part of the service, since it is only the prelude to the main prayers beginning with *Bar'chu*. *Mishkan T'filah* follows suit in this regard, giving us Psalms 100, 145 (i.e., *Ashrei*, which frames Psalm 145 with Psalms 85:5 and 144:15 before and 115:18 after), and 150 on weekdays (C, pp. 51–55; W/F, pp. 51–55; see also pp. 440–445; W/F, pp. 176–181 for festival mornings); and on Shabbat substituting Psalm 92 for 100 (C, pp. 214–219, 302–306; Sh, pp. 96–101, 184–188). (For more on these psalms and the concluding benediction, see below, pp. 130–133.)

Baruch She-amar: The Blessing before Verses of Song

Baruch She-amar, the blessing that precedes the recitation of psalms at this point in the service, appears in writing for the first time in the earliest post-Talmudic prayer codes, *Seder Rav Amram* and *Siddur Rav Saadyah.* Its content is the praise of God as trustworthy Creator of all; its style is hymnic and responsory, with each pair of lines (call-and-response) articulating the same thought:

> Blessed is the One who spoke and the world came to be. . . .
> Blessed is the One who continually authors creation.
> Blessed is the One whose whose word is deed;
> Blessed is the One who decrees and fulfills.

(The poetic sense here is that the Creator God's very act of speech or decree immediately brings about or fulfills what is intended; thus the English rendering in *Gates of Prayer*: "Blessed is the One whose word is deed, whose thought is fact.") The pious interjection *Baruch hu!* ("Blessed is the One!") at the end of the first line breaks up the poetic parallelism.

It is noteworthy, stylistically and rhetorically, that the name of God is not invoked at all in this poetic blessing; instead a pious euphemism is used: *Baruch she-* . . . , "Blessed is the One who . . . ." The second half of the traditional text in fact begins with the regular formula, *Baruch atah Adonai Eloheinu Melech haolam* and describes God as worthy of songs of praise. It concludes with the *chatimah, Baruch atah Adonai, Melech m'hulal batishbachot,* "Blessed are You, Adonai, Sovereign who is glorified through praise." In rhetorical and stylistic terms, the two parts of this text are distinct from each other, but together they form an impressive whole. The Reform version abbreviates the second part of the text (the beginning of the second blessing), thus eliminating any sense of overlength.

Baruch She-amar is a fitting poetic invitation to glorify God and to respond to the wonders of Creation by singing psalms of praise.

Psalm 145: *Ashrei,* Three Times a Day

> Rabbi Eleazar ben Abina said: Whoever recites "A song of praise by David" [*T'hilah l'David* = Psalm 145] three times daily is sure to inherit the world to come.
> Why is that? Because it is an alphabetical acrostic? Because

> it contains the verse "You open Your hand and satisfy every living being with favor"? For both reasons.
> (*B. B'rachot* 4b, abbreviated)

This Talmudic passage is the source for the custom of reciting Psalm 145 three times a day in rabbinic liturgy: once here in *P'sukei D'zimrah,* once toward the end of the morning service (on Shabbat, this is before the Torah is returned to the ark), and once at the beginning of the afternoon service. *Mishkan T'filah* omits the second recitation in the morning service but retains the other two (C, pp. 52–54, 215–217, 303–305, 338–341, 442–444; Sh, pp. 97–99, 607–609; W/F, pp. 52–54, 178–180), as did *Gates of Prayer*.

We noted above that the five concluding psalms in the Psalter, Psalms 146-150—sometimes called the "Hallelujah" psalms because each concludes with that word—form the core of the traditional *P'sukei D'zimrah.* (Of this group, *MT*, like *GOP* before it, retains only Psalm 150.) In order to segue into this group, Psalm 145 in liturgical recitation is also fitted out with an appropriate "Halleluyah" verse at the end, Psalm 115:18 (*Vaanachnu n'vareich Yah mei-atah v'ad olam, hal'luyah,* "We will bless You, God, now and always. Hallelujah!"). Psalm 145 is also fitted out liturgically with two additional verses at the very beginning. The last verse of Psalm 144 (v. 15) leads directly into it: *Ashrei haam shekacha lo, ashrei haam she-Adonai Elohav*, "Happy the people who have it so; happy the people whose God is Adonai." Preceding this is yet another verse that also begins with the word *ashrei* ("happy/fortunate/blessed"), Psalm 84:5, *Ashrei yosh'vei veitecha, od y'hal'lucha selah,* "Happy are those who dwell/sit in Your house; they forever praise You!" (By the way, this concordance-like association of biblical verses, based on shared key words, is typical of rabbinic liturgical construction. It is essentially midrashic in nature, which is to say that the Rabbis interpret Scripture through Scripture: shared words indicate to them that those verses were meant to illustrate and construe each other. Joining verses together liturgically is also a way of unlocking their joint power.) Psalm 84:5, similar to the *Mah Tovu* verses recited upon entering a synagogue, is understood to refer to people who are "sitting" in the synagogue before beginning their prayer (*B. B'rachot* 32b): they are the happy and blessed ones.

Returning to the Talmud passage with which we began, we may ask about the reasons why Psalm 145 is deemed there to be so special that it is deserving of a thrice-daily recitation. Cantor Bruce Ruben, paraphrasing the Talmudic tradition that we cited at the outset, writes: "Psalm 145 is an alphabetical acrostic. No doubt that helped make it popular, particularly in the centuries before printing, when few could afford a prayer book of their own. . . . Within the core of Psalm 145 the most famous verse is: *You open Your hand and satisfy every living being with favor* (v. 16). It asserts that God cares for every individual. Literally it reassures us that we are in good hands." [14] So the alphabetic acrostic makes this psalm easier to remember and to recite in public, while verse 16 points up the theme of God's ongoing providential guidance and care of the world, which the Rabbis always wished to underscore as a source of personal hope and moral expectation. The *ashrei* verses at the beginning stress that ultimate human happiness derives from our acknowledgment of, and closeness to, God. And the entire psalm rings out our praise and acknowledgment of the wondrous Creator and sustainer of life—altogether an appropriate text to sing throughout the day.

Psalm 150: Let All That Breathes Praise God!

Psalm 150 (C, pp. 55, 218, 306–307, 445; Sh, pp. 100, 188–189; W/F, pp. 55, 181) is the final, climactic psalm in the Hebrew Psalter.[15] It calls for the joyous—and noisy!—praise of God to resound from the divine sanctuary (i.e., the Temple) into the very heavens themselves, where God dwells. God is to be praised for mighty acts of creation, salvation, and deliverance (*g'vurot*) using every conceivable musical instrument—horns, strings, pipes, cymbals, and drums—a veritable symphony of praise. It is no wonder that this particular psalm has received so many musical settings, by both Jews and Christians, over the centuries.

Psalm 150 forms the fitting (and earliest) conclusion to *P'sukei D'zimrah*, the Verses of Song, which helps us prepare to pray. The traditional liturgy goes on to include yet other psalm-like passages after this (such as David's blessing of the people in I Chronicles 29:10–13, Nehemiah's praise of God in Nehemiah 9:6–11, and the Song at the Sea in Exodus 15), but these are additions to the basic core. *Mishkan T'filah* is right to end *P'sukei D'zimrah* here. How can we possibly top Psalm 150's final exhortation: *Kol han'shamah t'haleil Yah, Hal'lu Yah!* "Let *all* that breathes praise Adonai. Hallelujah!"

A final word is in order about the liturgical and musical performance of psalms in general. The psalms are meant for antiphonal recitation/singing; they are the original "responsive readings." What is tossed back and forth between prayer leader and congregation, however, is not alternating verses ("You say the *alef*-line and I say the *bet*-line"), as in most contemporary renderings of *Ashrei,* for example, but alternating *half*-verses. So the intended call-and-response sounds like this:

> LEADER: *Ashrei yosh'vei veitecha* ["Happy are those who dwell in Your house"].
> CONGREGATION: *Od y'hal'lucha selah.* ["They forever praise You!"]
> Or, in Psalm 150:
> LEADER: *Hal'lu El b'kodsho* ["Praise God in God's sanctuary"].
> CONGREGATION: *Hal'luhu birkia uzo.* ["Praise God in the sky, God's stronghold!"]

Biblical Hebrew poetry is constructed on the basis of "idea-rhymes," that is, the two halves of a verse basically say the same thing in different ways. The second half (the congregational response) intensifies the first half (the leader's initiation) by repeating and extending the same idea using different words or images. (Sometimes the verse subdivides into *three* stichs; then the second two together extend the first.) This is the intrinsic logic of a call-and-response pattern, as is the repeated refrain (like *Ki l'olam chasdo*; think also of work-crew songs). Many of the "responsive readings" in previous Reform prayer books to which some in our movement today have responded negatively are not really responsive readings at all in this sense of the word; they are simply texts that have somewhat arbitrarily been divided between reader and congregation. Try reading and singing psalms half-verse by half-verse in either Hebrew or English and see what a difference this makes!

Yishtabach Shimcha: The Weekday Closing Blessing after Verses of Song

We remarked above that the singing of psalms in the morning is made "liturgical" by being encased in rabbinic blessings, fore and aft. The closing blessing on weekdays is the relatively short (when compared with that on Shabbat and the festivals) *Yishtabach shimcha* (literally "May Your name be praised"; C, p. 56; W/F, pp. 56). This is a peroration to the psalms that precede it and sums up their import: may psalms of praise always be hymned—both in heaven and on earth—to God, who alone is worthy of that praise, as the divine Creator of all. On Shabbat and the festivals, the psalmic praise is more elaborate and so is its peroration, *Nishmat Kol Chai* (on which, see below, pp. 131–133).

Chatzi Kaddish

The Praise of God as Service Marker

AS MENTIONED above, many Reform Jews think of the *Kaddish* as a mourner's prayer, and this is only partly correct. The *Kaddish* has many forms and several distinct functions in a Jewish prayer service. At its core, the *Kaddish* is a prayer that praises God in extravagant terms (as noted earlier, the *Kaddish* is sometimes referred to as a "doxology"—a speaking of words of praise and glorification) and petitions for the speedy coming of God's kingdom, when all humanity will acknowledge the one true God—in other words, for the speedy coming of the messianic age.

We know from Talmudic literature that the *Kaddish* initially was a concluding messianic prayer, recited at the end of a sermon or exposition of Scripture in the rabbinic *beit midrash* ("study house") and in the synagogue (see *B. Sotah* 49a, *B. B'rachot* 3a, and *Midrash on Proverbs* 14:28). Sermons then as now concluded with words of hope, encouragement, and consolation—and the *Kaddish* extended those words in a grand praise of God. The fact that the language of this prayer is Aramaic, the vernacular language of study, rather than Hebrew, the classical language of liturgical prayer, testifies to its origin in the context of oral study. Particularly important to the Talmudic Rabbis was the congregational *response* to the words of the prayer leader, *Y'hei sh'meih raba m'varach l'alam ul'almei almaya*, "Blessed be God's great name to all eternity!"—these words of response were the way in which every person in the congregation actively identified with the sentiments of the prayer leader and participated in the prayer itself.

In the earliest post-Talmudic prayer literature, the *Kaddish* assumes several different forms and functions. It is recited immediately after the Torah reading (proximate to its original use; see Tractate *Sof'rim* 10). *Seder Rav Amram*, the first prayer code, knows of the *Kaddish* as a "service marker," that is, as an expression of praise that is recited at the conclusion of each part of the service: at the end of the preliminary prayers (after *P'sukei D'zimrah*), after the *T'filah*, and after the study of Talmudic texts.

Each of these functions is served by a slightly different textual form: the brief service marker by a short form called *Chatzi Kaddish* ("Half *Kaddish*" or "Reader's *Kaddish*"); the conclusion of the *T'filah* by a longer form called *Kaddish Shaleim* ("Full *Kaddish*"), which includes a petition for the acceptance of our prayers (*Titkabeil tz'lot'hon*, "May the prayers of Israel be acceptable"); and (as we saw above) the study of Talmudic texts by a long form called *Kaddish D'Rabanan* ("the Rabbis' *Kaddish*" or "Study *Kaddish*"), which includes a petition for the well-being of the rabbis and their students and all who study Torah (*Al Yisrael v'al rabanan*, "For Israel and their rabbis"). The additional custom of mourners reciting *Kaddish* at the end of (and subsequently, throughout) the service is later and originated in Ashkenaz (Franco-Germany) (see below, pp. 94–98).

The recitation of *Chatzi Kaddish* here (C, pp. 57, 208, 312, 451; Sh, pp. 90, 194; W/F, pp. 57, 187) marks the end of *P'sukei D'zimrah* and the preparatory prayer texts; what follows is the rabbinically prescribed service proper: the recitation of *Sh'ma* and its surrounding benedictions, and the *T'filah* ("Prayer")/*Amidah* ("Standing [Prayer]"). Earlier North American Reform prayer books, in the interest of brevity and non-redundancy, often omitted all forms of the *Kaddish* except for the Mourner's *Kaddish*. *Gates of Prayer* restored the *Chatzi Kaddish* here, at the end of *Kabbalat Shabbat* (before *Bar'chu*) in the Shabbat evening service (C, pp. 144, 263; Sh, pp. 26, 145), and after *Ashrei* (before the *T'filah*) in the afternoon services (C, p. 342; Sh, pp. 224). *Mishkan T'filah* additionally restores *Chatzi Kaddish* in the weekday evening service after the *Sh'ma* benedictions and before the *T'filah* (C, pp. 20; W/F, pp. 20), and the *Kaddish D'Rabanan* in the morning services after the study texts and before *P'sukei D'zimrah* (C, pp. 46–48, 208–210, 299–300, 434–436; Sh, pp. 90–92, 181–182; W/F, pp. 46–48, 170–172). *Kaddish Shaleim* after the *T'filah* remains omitted.

Bar'chu
The Call to Worship

From a purely halachic point of view, everything prior to this point in the morning service is considered to have been preliminary or preparatory: the *Birchot HaShachar* prayers originally were recited privately at home and the *P'sukei D'zimrah* psalms, recited upon arrival in the synagogue, are considered to be preparation for prayer. That is why this portion of the service was heavily abbreviated in earlier Reform prayer books and why it is still somewhat abbreviated in *Mishkan T'filah.* The mandatory, core liturgical rubrics are *K'riat Sh'ma Uvirchoteha* ("Recitation of *Sh'ma* and Its Blessings") and the *T'filah/Amidah,* the daily petitionary prayer sequence (from which the middle, petitionary section is omitted on Shabbat and replaced by a single benediction dealing with the sanctity of Shabbat).

To announce the "formal" beginning of the service and to call the congregation to assemble for public worship, the prayer leader exhorts those present, *Bar'chu et Adonai ham'vorach!* ("Praise Adonai to whom praise is due / who is worthy of praise!"; C, pp. 4, 58, 146, 226, 264, 313, 394, 452; Sh, pp. 28, 108, 146, 195; W/F, pp. 4, 58, 130, 188). The assembly, constituting itself as a worshiping congregation, then responds, *Baruch Adonai ham'vorach l'olam va-ed!* ("Praised be Adonai to whom praise is due, now and forever!"). (Classical Reform custom, as enshrined in the *Union Prayer Book,* did not always treat *Bar'chu* as a call-and-response. Often both the call and the response were read by everyone, in both Hebrew and English, and then sung together afterward.)

Traditionally, a minyan—quorum of ten adult males—is required to constitute a congregation for prayer. Without such a quorum, the assembled (men) must continue to pray privately, so *Bar'chu* and its response would be skipped over. (Ten is the smallest number of individuals the Rabbis thought could stand for the Jewish people as a whole, since each congregation represents the entire people of Israel at prayer). Reform congregations have held, and continue to hold, different views on this requirement. First of all, Reform Judaism affirms the value of gender egalitarianism, and thus women routinely are counted in the minyan. But public prayer—including *Bar'chu*—is often held without a minyan.

The call/invitation, *Bar'chu et Adonai!*, appears in the Mishnah, *B'rachot* 7:3, in a discussion about how groups of people should be invited to praise God after eating a meal together (reciting *Birkat HaMazon*, the Blessing after Eating, as a group)—whether the invitational call should be *N'vareich*, "*Let us* bless/praise," or *Bar'chu*, "Bless/Praise." Rabbi Akiva appeals as precedent to the custom of the synagogue, where the formula is *Bar'chu et Adonai*. Rabbi Ishmael demurs that the formula there should be *Bar'chu et Adonai ham'vorach*, "Praise Adonai *to whom praise is due*." The rationale for his version is explained in the Talmud of the Land of Israel (*B'rachot* 7:3, 11c): by adding *ham'vorach* ("to whom praise is due"), the prayer leader acknowledges that he, too, is obliged to praise God together with the entire congregation rather than rhetorically standing apart from it. The two Talmuds (*Y. B'rachot* 7:3, 11c, and *B. B'rachot* 50a), by the way, both understand that the synagogue custom referred to here is how one begins reciting the blessing before reading from the Torah (and, indeed, that custom is still in force today: that blessing begins, *Bar'chu et Adonai ham'vorach*, followed by the congregational response).

In addition to its use at the beginning of the public Torah reading, *Bar'chu* also came to be used in Babylonia to begin the prayer service proper before the recitation of the *Sh'ma*. It apparently was not used that way in the Land of Israel; it is not found before the *Sh'ma* rubric in Cairo Genizah texts that represent the liturgical customs of the Land of Israel. In its place we find either *Bar'chi nafshi et Adonai ham'vorach*, "Praise, O my soul, Adonai who is worthy of praise!" (based on Psalm 103:1), or the benediction that is given in *Mishkan T'filah* as an alternative on the left-hand page of the spread (pp. 5, 59, 227, 453):

Baruch atah, Adonai Eloheinu, Melech haolam,
asher kid'shanu b'mitzvotav v'tzivanu al mitzvat k'riat sh'ma
l'hamlicho b'leivav shaleim,
ul'yachdo b'leiv tov,
ul'ovdo b'nefesh chafeitzah.

Praised are You, Adonai our God, Ruler of the universe,
who hallows us with mitzvot, commanding us how to recite
the *Sh'ma*,
to declare wholeheartedly God's rule,
to declare earnestly God is One,
and to willingly worship God.

The rhetorical style here is that of the benedictions that are recited over the performance of mitzvot (*asher kid'shanu b'mitzvotav v'tzivanu*), and indeed the Rabbis understand the recitation of *Sh'ma* as mandated twice daily by the Torah (*b'shochb'cha uv'kumecha*, "when you lie down and when you get up"). But the Babylonian Talmud and the post-Talmudic literature that follows in its wake never in fact mandate such a benediction to be said before reciting the *Sh'ma*; this was only done (apparently) in the Land of Israel. So *Mishkan T'filah* restores this old custom from the Land of Israel as an alternative to the Babylonian custom of beginning public worship with *Bar'chu*.

K'riat Sh'ma

The Recitation of the *Sh'ma*

K'riat Sh'ma, the twice-daily recitation of the three biblical paragraphs Deuteronomy 6:4–9, Deuteronomy 11:13–21, and Numbers 15:37–41, was viewed by the Rabbis of the Mishnah and the Talmud as a biblical commandment: "Recite them [these words] . . . when you lie down and when you get up" (Deuteronomy 6:7 and 11:19). Hence the two Deuteronomy paragraphs in which this injunction appears were to be recited before going to bed at night and upon arising in the morning. The third paragraph, from Numbers (*parashat tzitzit*, "the paragraph about fringes"), came to be associated with the first two because it, too, deals with a physical reminder of God's commandments—the wearing of *tzitzit*, just like the *t'fillin* and the mezuzot in the Deuteronomy texts. (In *Mishkan T'filah*, the remaining biblical paragraphs of *K'riat Sh'ma* may be found on the following: C, pp. 10–13, 64–69, 152–155, 232–237, 267–268, 318–320, 400–403, 458–463; Sh, pp. 34–37, 114–119, 149–150, 200–202; W/F, pp. 10–13, 64–69, 136–139, 194–199.)

The Rabbis viewed the first paragraph as dealing with *kabbalat ol malchut shamayim*, "the acceptance of the yoke of the sovereignty of heaven," that is, God's rulership (*M. B'rachot* 2:2). Reform Jews commonly refer to this paragraph as "the *Sh'ma* and the *V'ahavta*," although in the Torah the two are continuous. In the prayer book, the sentence *Baruch shem k'vod malchuto l'olam va-ed*, "Blessed is God's glorious majesty forever and ever," appears as an interruption between the *Sh'ma* and *V'ahavta* verses. This sentence appears in *M. Yoma* 6:2 as the response of the congregation when the High Priest in the Temple on the Day of Atonement recited the name of God. In our context it also once functioned as a response, when it was customary in the Land of Israel to recite the biblical paragraphs of the *Sh'ma* responsively (*por'sin al/et Sh'ma* [*M. M'gilah* 4:3, 5–6], "slicing up the *Sh'ma*")—this was the congregational response to the reader's recitation of the first verse, in which the name of God appears twice. Because it now appears as an interruption of biblical verses, it is traditionally recited silently. In the radical Reform prayer book of the Berlin Reformgemeinde (1848), the *Sh'ma* and *Baruch shem* sentences (and the three *K'dushah* verses in the *T'filah*) were the only Hebrew responses in the entire liturgy. The congregation stood for the *Sh'ma* and *Baruch shem* sentences, which were recited by the service leader and sung by the choir and congregation. This custom was later taken over by Rabbi David Einhorn, in his prayer book *Olat Tamid* (1858), from which it was taken up into the *Union Prayer Book* (1894–95) and became the standard performance practice of classical Reform Judaism. Since the *Sh'ma* verse by itself came to be seen as a kind of creedal statement, emphasizing Jewish monotheism (as opposed to Christian trinitarianism), it was deemed appropriate to stand for its recitation. (The prominence given in this performance practice to the *Baruch shem* sentence, incidentally, accounts for how the traditional first paragraph of the *Sh'ma* came to be reconceived as two separate entities, "the *Sh'ma*" and "the *V'ahavta*" in popular Reform liturgical understanding—since the two parts of the paragraph were performatively separated by the *Baruch shem* sentence, they came to be conceptually separated as well.)

More recently, many Reform congregations have reverted to the traditional practice of remaining seated for the *Sh'ma* and of reciting *Baruch shem* silently (on this, more below). *Mishkan T'filah* singles out the *Sh'ma* verse for special treatment by presenting it as a two-page graphic that can be used for meditation or focus (C, pp. 10–11, 64–65, 152–153, 232–233, 400–401, 458–459; Sh, pp. 34–35, 114–115; W/F, pp. 10–11, 64–65, 136–137, 194–195).

The second paragraph of the *Sh'ma*, which the Rabbis characterized as dealing with *kabbalat ol mitzvot*, "the acceptance of the yoke of the commandments," has to do with reward and punishment for the observance or nonobservance of God's commandments. Specifically, if God's commandments are obeyed, the rains will fall at their proper times; disobedience, however—and particularly worshiping other gods—will be punished by drought, when God "locks up" the heavens. Radical Reformers in the nineteenth century (again, the Berlin group and Einhorn, for example) viewed this paragraph as both theologically and scientifically problematic: weather conditions do not respond to human moral behavior, on the one hand, nor does divine providence respond to every human activity in such a direct fashion. Hence, this paragraph was omitted from the more radical Reform prayer books, including the *Union Prayer Book*. (Rabbi Mordecai Kaplan had the same theological problems with this paragraph and substituted Deuteronomy 28:1–6 for it in his 1945 *Sabbath Prayer Book*, the first Reconstructionist prayer book.)

In more recent years, the new Reconstructionist liturgies reinstated the second paragraph of the *Sh'ma* as an option (while also retaining Kaplan's alternative passage), arguing that it can be interpreted along ecological lines: "If we continue to pollute the environment—and thus display contempt for the integrity of God's creation—pure rain will cease to fall, and the ground will cease to give forth its produce."[16] This rationale also was suggested in the first trial-draft of *Mishkan T'filah* (2002), which included the second paragraph as an option, noting that "traditional Reform thinking challenges Deuteronomic theology, that bad events which occur are a result of communal sinful behavior. We do accept responsibility for social and natural ecology: how we treat one another and our environment has a powerful, direct impact on society and the planet."

Nonetheless, the verses describing an angry God "sealing up the heavens" were printed in smaller type, acknowledging the theological difficulties with this image. The paragraph ultimately remained sufficiently problematic to require both a recommendation from the Siddur Editorial Committee and a vote by the CCAR Executive Committee. Both decided to uphold the earlier Reform deletion of the paragraph in its entirety: even though subject to mitigating non-literalist interpretations, the text itself remains difficult for a modern Jew to recite in the liturgy—although the second reading on page 235, "If we can hear the words from Sinai," by Rabbi Richard Levy, is in fact a contemporary interpretation of the second paragraph of the *Sh'ma*.

The third paragraph of the *Sh'ma* is variously referred to by the Rabbis as *parashat tzitzit*, since it deals with the obligation to wear fringes on the four corners of one's garment that are to serve as reminders of God's commandments, and as *Y'tziat Mitzrayim*, "the Exodus from Egypt," since at the end it refers to God as the One who redeemed the Israelites from Egypt. There is indirect evidence in the Mishnah (*B'rachot* 1:5) that this paragraph at some point may only have been recited in the morning, when one wore fringes, but not at night, when one did not—but the prevailing ruling in the Mishnah is that it, too, must be recited morning and evening. When the custom of wearing a tallit during morning prayers became less frequent among Reform Jews, this paragraph came to be dropped from the liturgy (again, the Berlin Reformers, Einhorn, and the *Union Prayer Book* were typical of this trend; the 1918 revision of the *UPB* reinstated a portion of the final part of the paragraph, beginning *L'maan tizk'ru*; the full conclusion was reinstated in *Gates of Prayer*, 1975). Now that many Reform Jews wear tallitot at morning prayers, *Mishkan T'filah* has restored the entire third paragraph as an option for those who wish to recite it—but only in the morning, since the tallit is not worn at night.

The three paragraphs of the *Sh'ma* together constitute an almost creedal statement of traditional Jewish faith—in the God whom we must love and obey, in God's providential attention to human action, in the God who delivers Israel from bondage. Jews respond by devoting themselves to the study of God's Torah throughout their waking hours.

Sh'ma Performance Practice: To Stand? To Sit?

One of the many distinctive features of *Mishkan T'filah* vis-à-vis earlier North American Reform prayer books is its disinclination to prescribe a single set of performance practices throughout the service (such as when to stand up, when to sit down, how a particular text is to be recited and by whom). This is justified as allowing "for maximum flexibility and with respect for varying congregational customs."

In particular, the diversity of practice in our movement today can be seen in the matter of the recitation of the *Sh'ma*: Does the congregation stand for the *Sh'ma*? If so, when and for how long? Does the congregation remain seated? Here we explore the origins and rationales for these diverse performance practices in the hope of helping to make better sense of our liturgical choices.

Interestingly, there appear to have been different performance practices from the outset for the recitation of the *Sh'ma* (the full three scriptural paragraphs: Deuteronomy 6:4–9, Deuteronomy 11:1–21, and Numbers 15:37–41, not just the *Sh'ma* verse). The Mishnah (*B'rachot* 1:3) records a dispute between the Houses of Hillel and Shammai as to whether "when you lie down and when you get up" (Deuteronomy 6:7) refers only to the time of day when *Sh'ma* is to be recited (Hillelites) or whether it also refers to physical posture (lying down at bedtime, standing up in the morning; Shammaites).

The Hillelite position was deemed normative, which means that no specific posture was prescribed. But in the early Islamic period (by the ninth century), we learn of divergent practices between the Jewish communities in the Land of Israel and in Babylonia. The Jews in Israel stood for the recitation of the *Sh'ma* (all three paragraphs), while the Jews in Babylonia remained seated. No explanation is given for the practice in the Land of Israel, but likely the standing posture enacts the importance of the liturgical act of affirming scriptural text (to this day, it is customary to stand for the recitation of the *Hallel* psalms on the festivals and for the public reading of the Ten Commandments and the Song at the Sea). The Babylonians apparently saw themselves as continuing the Hillelite practice; they accused the Palestinian Jews of being "Shammaites."

Since Babylonian practice became normative for all of the medieval rites, the traditional practice to this day is to remain seated while reciting the *Sh'ma*. One rises only for *Bar'chu* (the official beginning of public worship); the next time one stands is for the *T'filah*.

Reform practice on this issue has never been uniform. The first Reform congregation in Germany, the Hamburg Tempelverein, apparently retained the traditional practice; their prayer books (1818 and 1841) do not indicate otherwise. The prayer book of the radical Berlin Reformgemeinde (1848), on the other hand, instructed the congregation to rise for the *Sh'ma* verse and *Baruch shem* and then to be seated. These two texts were recited in German, then sung in Hebrew with the choir; the rest of the abbreviated service (excepting the *K'dushah* verses) was in German. The *Sh'ma* verse was singled out for special treatment because it came to be viewed as the "watchword of our faith," encapsulating the crucial difference between Judaism's strict monotheism and Christianity's trinitarianism. On the other hand, since Germans Lutherans stood for the recitation of their creed, so would German Jews.

As for the earliest Reform prayer books in North America, Leo Merzbacher's *Seder T'filah* for Temple Emanuel in New York (1855) and

Isaac Mayer Wise's *Minhag America* (Cincinnati, 1857) do not direct the congregation to rise for the *Sh'ma*. But David Einhorn's *Olat Tamid* (Baltimore, 1856–58), like the liturgy of the Berlin Reformgemeinde, does direct the congregation to rise[17] and singles out the *Sh'ma* verse and *Baruch shem* for decorous recitation in Hebrew by the rabbi, repeated by the congregation (the rest is in German). While Isaac Moses's original *Union Prayer Book*, volume 1 (1892), does not direct the congregation to rise for the *Sh'ma*, the "official" *Union Prayer Book* of 1894–95 (and its subsequent revisions: 1918–22, 1940–45) enshrines the practice of rising for the *Sh'ma* and *Baruch shem*, then sitting down (following Einhorn).

Gates of Prayer (1975) introduces an unprecedented performance practice. Rather than have the congregation stand for *Bar'chu*, then sit, then stand for *Sh'ma* and *Baruch shem*, then sit (the practice of the *Union Prayer Book*), this volume has the congregation rise for *Bar'chu* and *remain standing* through *Sh'ma* and *Baruch shem*, then sit. The rationale clearly is practical rather than ideological. In the earlier British Liberal *Service of the Heart* (1967), which was coedited by Rabbis Chaim Stern and John D. Raynor, the congregation stands at the very beginning of the service (when the rabbi enters?), sings a hymn, recites *Bar'chu*, sits, reads several prayers, then stands for *Sh'ma* through *V'ahavta*, sitting before *L'maan tizk'ru*. This practice, too, avoids the "up-and-down" feeling of the *Union Prayer Book*. Finally, the 1994 gender-sensitive revision of *GOP* has the congregation stand for the first time before *Chatzi Kaddish* and remain standing for *Bar'chu* (this reflects one traditional custom), which also avoids the "up-and-down" feeling.

Given this diversity of practice among recent Reform prayer books and the desire of some in our movement to restore elements of traditional performance practice, it is sensible for *Mishkan T'filah* to leave these options open to congregational choice.

The Morning *Sh'ma* Blessings

Yotzeir Or: "Creator of Light"

THE (TRADITIONAL) three biblical paragraphs of the *Sh'ma*, recited morning and evening, are framed fore and aft by benedictions; this is what makes their recitation liturgical. Just as the public Torah reading, haftarah reading, and *m'gilah* readings begin with a blessing praising God for giving us the Torah (the Prophets, the Scrolls) and conclude with a blessing restating this theme and, often, anticipating the fulfillment of God's promises of redemption,[18] so, too, does the recitation of the *Sh'ma* paragraphs begin with a Torah blessing (*Ahavah Rabbah* in the morning; *Ahavat Olam* in the evening) and conclude with a blessing affirming the truth of God's scriptural promises of redemption (*Emet V'yatziv* in the morning; *Emet Ve-emunah* in the evening). But prior to this in both the morning and evening services is a blessing that deals with the *occasion* for reciting the *Sh'ma*—"when you lie down and when you get up"—sunset (*Maariv Aravim*) and sunrise (*Yotzeir Or*).

The *Yotzeir Or* ("Creator of Light") blessing (C, pp. 60, 228, 313–315, 454; Sh, pp. 110, 195–197; W/F, pp. 60, 190) is similar in theme and attitude to the morning blessings that are recited upon awakening each morning. The theme is praise and gratitude for the gift of light and the renewal of Creation each day. Night/darkness/sleep are associated with disorder/danger/death. Light—and particularly the return of sunlight each morning—is associated with order, life, renewal, and the presence of God (the divine effulgence, or brightness). *Yotzeir Or* thus praises the Creator God "who each and every day renews the work of Creation" (in *Mishkan T'filah*: "You daily renew creation").

The traditional text of this blessing is quite long, because it also includes a description of the angelic hosts, who, according to ancient Jewish lore, begin again at sunrise each morning to intone their daily songs of praise to God (*Kadosh! Kadosh! Kadosh!*, "Holy! Holy! Holy!," as depicted in Isaiah 6, and *Baruch k'vod Adonai mimkomo*, "Blessed is the presence of God, shining forth from where God dwells," in Ezekiel 3)—the so-called

K'dushah D'Yotzeir ("the Sanctification in the *Yotzeir* Blessing"). Most (although not all) Reform liturgies have omitted this section of the blessing because of its length and its mythic focus on angels. The traditional Shabbat version of this blessing is even more elaborate than the weekday version, since premodern Jews were free to spend more time in synagogue on Shabbat and would pray in a more leisurely and extended fashion. The Shabbat version therefore incorporates the theme of the Shabbat, as the end and purpose of God's acts of creation, into this blessing that deals with the creation of the heavenly lights. These additions, too, have been pruned from most Reform prayer books; there is no difference in these prayer books between the daily and the Shabbat versions of the blessing.[19]

Mishkan T'filah retains the same abbreviated version of *Yotzeir Or* that appeared in the *Union Prayer Book* and in *Gates of Prayer* but has reinstated one traditional phrase: *Or chadash al Tziyon ta-ir v'nizkeh chulanu m'heirah l'oro*, "Shine a new light upon Zion, that we all may swiftly merit its radiance." This phrase appears in the Ashkenazic (Central and Eastern European) version of this prayer, but not in the Sephardic (Spanish-Portuguese) version.[20] The phrase draws a poetic connection between the renewal of sunlight every morning and the messianic "light" of Israel's redemption that God has promised to shine upon Zion in the future. The tenth-century scholar Saadyah ben Joseph, *Gaon* ("Eminence"), head of the academy of Sura in Babylonia, objected to the inclusion of this sentence as inappropriate to the theme of the blessing—praise for the physical light of day—but was trumped over time by the popular desire to express the hope for Israel's redemption whenever possible. Newly emancipated Reform Jews in the nineteenth century were anxious not to appear to their fellow countrymen as disloyal aliens, so they omitted all petitions for a return to Zion. Twenty-first century Reform Jews, at home in America and inspired by the modern State of Israel, feel free to reinstate this petition as an expression of solidarity with the Jewish state and our friends and relatives there. The phrase had previously been reinserted in all Israeli Reform prayer books.

This blessing is briefly discussed in the Babylonian Talmud, *B'rachot* 11a–b, where the first line is cited—*yotzeir or uvorei choshech, oseh shalom uvorei et hakol*, "Creator of light and darkness, who makes peace and fashions all things"—and it is noted that this is a slightly euphemized citation of Isaiah 45:7, "I [God] form light and create darkness; I make weal and create woe [*uvorei ra*]." The Rabbis, who took seriously the words that were used in prayer to invoke divine power, did not wish to invoke evil or woe upon themselves and thus changed the final word to something more neutral (just as modern reformers would later emend rabbinic liturgy to euphemize ideas that they found problematic!). Another biblical text cited is Psalm 104:24, *Mah rabu maasecha, Adonai . . .* , "How numerous are Your works, Adonai! In wisdom You formed them all, filling the earth with Your creatures!" In general, rabbinic prayers contain many biblical citations and use many biblical phrases, because biblical prayers are their models, and the Rabbis chose to invoke scriptural descriptions of God.

The *Yotzeir* benediction, recited every morning, appeals to the daily regularity of sunrise and sunset to demonstrate the existence of a cosmic order and to praise the Creator God who stands behind it and whose work it is.

Ahavah Rabbah: "Abundant Love"—The Torah Blessing

The blessing that immediately precedes the recitation of the *Sh'ma* verses (the second blessing in this liturgical series) is a Torah blessing. That is to say, both its theme and function are to praise God for having given the Torah—a portion of which is about to be recited—to the people Israel. So *Ahavah Rabbah* (C, pp. 62, 230, 316–317, 456; Sh, pp. 112, 198–199; W/F, pp. 62, 192) and its evening counterpart, *Ahavat Olam* (C, pp. 8, 150, 266, 398; Sh, pp. 32, 148; W/F, pp. 62, 192), at base are simply longer "versions" of the blessing that is recited before the public reading of the Torah, *asher bachar banu mikol haamim v'natan lanu et torato*, "who has chosen us from among the peoples and given us the Torah." The "version" before us here focuses in particular on the abundant love (*ahavah rabbah*) that God has showered upon us through the gift of Torah and the mitzvot it contains. The Jewish people's response to God's gift of Torah is to be constantly occupied with its study and with the performance of its dictates—"for they are our life and doing them lengthens our days," in the words of the evening text. The morning version contains the petition that just as in the past God has taught Torah to our ancestors, so may God teach Torah to us by "enlightening our eyes" to the meaning and value of divine instruction. The text continues with the wish that we may never be put to shame because we have trusted in God's salvation. This occasions the petition that Israel may be restored to its land from the places of its dispersion to "the four corners of the earth"—for our ancestors, this was to be *the* tangible sign of God's salvation. This petition has routinely been omitted from Reform prayer books since the very first ones in early nineteenth-century Germany (Berlin, 1817, and Hamburg, 1819); it was thought to call into question the loyalty of modernizing Jewish communities to their new homelands. *Mishkan T'filah* has restored the phrase as a gesture of solidarity with the State of Israel. (Interestingly enough, the first Reform congregational prayer book, Hamburg, 1819, rather than omitting this phrase entirely, substituted for it the more innocuous wording of the western Sephardic [Spanish-Portuguese] rite, "And bring upon us blessing and peace from the four corners of the earth.") *Mishkan T'filah* also doffs its *kippah* (so to speak) to the Sephardic rite by including in this paragraph the words *v'lo neivosh v'lo nikaleim v'lo nikasheil l'olam va-ed*, "Then we will never feel shame, never deserve rebuke, and never stumble," where previous Reform prayer books, following the Ashkenazic (German-Polish) rite of most of our grandparents, had only *v'lo neivosh l'olam va-ed*. Since this is not a substantive change, why bother? Because Shlomo Carlebach set these words (beginning with *V'ha-eir eineinu*) to music in the early 1970s, and his melody has become standard in many Jewish communities throughout the world. Carlebach had been a Chabad Chasid in his earlier years, and the text he set was the one that appears in the Chasidic prayer book. This Chasidic prayer book is sometimes called *Siddur HaAri* (= "The Siddur of Isaac Luria," the influential sixteenth-century kabbalist) and sometimes called *Nusach S'farad*, because it contains a mixture of Ashkenazic and Sephardic wordings and customs. (The actual Sephardic rite, on the other hand, is called *Minhag S'farad*.) One new alteration in *Mishkan T'filah* to the text of this blessing is the elimination of masculine hierarchical language describing God: the epithets *Avinu Malkeinu* ("our Father, our King") are deleted at the beginning of line 3 of the Hebrew text, as are the epithets *Avinu haAv harachaman* ("our Father, merciful Father") at the beginning of the sentence on line 5. Since these deleted words remain in the text of *Gates of Prayer*, congregations that sing this text to any of the traditional melodies will need to pay attention here and adjust their rote singing accordingly!

The conclusion, or *chatimah* (literally "seal"), of this blessing summarizes its theme: *Baruch atah, Adonai, habocheir b'amo Yisrael b'ahavah*, "Praised be You, Adonai, who chooses Your people Israel in love." The clause that transitions to this conclusion anticipates both this theme and the key word and significance of the *Sh'ma* verse that is about to be recited: *v'keiravtanu l'shimcha hagadol selah be-emet l'hodot l'cha ul'yached-cha b'ahavah*, "Truly, You drew us near to Your great Name, that we might acknowledge You, *declaring You One* in love."

The Babylonian Talmud, *B'rachot* 12a, is aware of two different verbal formulas for opening this blessing: *Ahavah rabbah* ("Abundant love") and *Ahavat olam* ("Everlasting love"), each transmitted by a different rabbinic master. The latter formula, *Ahavat olam*, is declared to be the preferred one because it approximates biblical language (Jeremiah 31:3—*V'ahavat olam ahavtich*, "And with an everlasting love have I loved you"). Following this cue in the Babylonian Talmud, the Sephardic rite begins both the evening and the morning versions of this blessing with the words *Ahavat olam*. The Ashkenazic rite, on the other hand, maintains both formulas, using *Ahavat olam* to begin the evening version of the blessing and *Ahavah rabbah* to begin the morning version; this way both Talmudic options are maintained while, at the same time, it is easier to tell the two versions apart when they are being referred to by their first words.

This Torah blessing then leads directly into the recitation of verses of Torah—*Sh'ma Yisrael*. At the same time, by framing this recitation, the blessing *redefines* it as an act of *talmud Torah*: the *study* of, and perpetual engagement with, words of Torah—the rabbinic religious activity and worship experience par excellence.

Emet V'yatziv: "True and Enduring"—The Blessing after Torah

Just as the public Torah and haftarah readings are followed by a blessing of praise acknowledging the truth of the divine words just proclaimed, so is the recitation of the *Sh'ma* (which traditionally comprises three biblical paragraphs). The blessing after the *Sh'ma* has come down to us in two versions, a longer one in the morning service (*Emet V'yatziv*, "True and Enduring"; C, pp. 70–72, 238–240, 321–322, 456; Sh, pp. 120–122, 203–204; W/F, pp. 70–72, 192) and a briefer one in the evening service (*Emet Ve-emunah*, "True and Trustworthy"; C, pp. 14–16, 156–158, 269–270,

404–406; Sh, pp. 38–40, 151–152; W/F, pp. 14–16, 140–142). The thematic content of both versions is the same and is already set forth schematically in early rabbinic literature:

> One who recites the *Sh'ma* must mention the Exodus from Egypt in *Emet V'yatziv*.
> Rabbi [Judah the Patriarch] says, "In it, one must mention God's sovereignty."
> Others say, "In it one must mention the smiting of the firstborn and the splitting of the sea." (*T. B'rachot* 2:1)
> [*Y. B'rachot* 1:9, 3d adds:]
> Rabbi Joshua ben Levi says, "One must mention them all and conclude, *Tzur Yisrael v'go-alo* [Rock of Israel and his/their Redeemer]."

As can be gleaned from this passage, the blessing is thematically composite; it includes many "bullet points." It begins, as we noted, by acknowledging the truth and reliability of God's words just recited from the Torah. Recall that the final paragraph of the *Sh'ma*, Numbers 15:37–41, concludes by invoking God as Redeemer, who delivered the people from Egypt. For the Rabbis, the Exodus from Egypt remains the most important paradigm for God's future and ultimate redemption of Israel. Thus, the mention of the Exodus from Egypt in the biblical passage—and in this blessing—will bring in its wake a petition for Israel's future redemption. The blessing's concluding formula (*chatimah*, "seal") praises God as Israel's Redeemer. *Tzur Yisrael v'go-alo* ("Rock of Israel and its Redeemer") is the wording in rabbinic sources from the Land of Israel and those Cairo Genizah texts that follow its prayer rite; the Babylonian formula—which appears in all of the other medieval rites—is *Go-eil Yisrael* ("Redeemer of Israel"), later changed to *gaal Yisrael* ("who redeemed Israel") so as to distinguish this blessing from the petition for Israel's redemption in the weekday *T'filah*, which concludes with the words *Go-eil Yisrael*.

In its traditional form, the morning version of this blessing, *Emet V'yatziv*, is quite lengthy (just like *Yotzeir Or*). Its several thematic points, nonetheless, are easily distinguished, and they precisely follow the dictates of the rabbinic passage cited above:

1. The truth and reliability of God's words in each of the three paragraphs of Torah just recited are acknowledged: God is affirmed as Israel's Sovereign for all generations (responding to the first paragraph of the *Sh'ma*); God's just and righteous commandments are binding upon us for all time (the second paragraph); God is affirmed as Israel's first, last, and sole Redeemer (the end of the third paragraph).
2. The theme of redemption becomes the focus of the second portion of the blessing. The redemptive scenario of the Exodus from Egypt is spelled out at length: God smote the Egyptian firstborn and saved those of the Israelites; God splits the sea and drowned the Egyptian cohorts while the Israelites crossed onto dry land. This leads climactically into an antiphonal recitation of two key verses from the Song at the Sea, Exodus 15:11 (*Mi chamochah*) and 15:18 (*Adonai yimloch*), and a final petition for Israel's ultimate redemption (*Tzur Yisrael, kumah b'ezrat Yisrael*, "Rock of Israel, rise in support of Israel").

Because of its length, printed prayer books often divide this blessing into several paragraphs to visually break up the text. This layout has often been followed in Reform prayer books as well, but with a difference: in addition to abbreviating the blessing, these prayer books often have presented it as a responsive reading in the vernacular. The verses from the Song at the Sea have usually been retained and sung in Hebrew—which is why Reform congregants often think of *Mi Chamochah* as a separate liturgical piece (that, indeed, is how it is treated in the page breaks of *Mishkan T'filah* and in the sidebars outlining the structure of the service). In fact, *Mi Chamochah* is simply the climax of the *Emet V'yatziv* benediction.

Reform abbreviations of this benediction generally have both omitted repetitions and excised the descriptions of God's vengeance upon the Egyptians (in the nineteenth and most of the twentieth century these were viewed as too unfriendly to non-Jews). The explicit petition for redemption at the end of the benediction was also abbreviated or excised, since it could be understood to suggest that Jews still viewed themselves as exiles awaiting a return to their land rather than as full citizens of their adoptive countries.

Emet V'yatziv and the evening *Emet Ve-emunah* are sometimes referred to as the *G'ulah* ("Redemption") benediction, since that is their ultimate theme. Franz Rosenzweig, the influential German Jewish philosopher and educator, in his *Star of Redemption*, famously characterized the three benedictions that surround the *Sh'ma* as a neat theological "package" articulating the main themes of the divine-human relationship in Jewish tradition: Creation-Revelation-Redemption. While the full pattern may not have been quite so deliberate at the outset (the "Creation" part results more from acknowledging and responding to the times of day when the *Sh'ma* is to be recited than from any schematic theological intention), there is no doubt that Rosenzweig's scheme well summarizes the thematic import of the *Sh'ma* and Its Blessings as this liturgical rubric has come down to us.

The Evening *Sh'ma* Blessings

The weekday evening service follows the same basic structure as the morning service, beginning with the recitation of the *Sh'ma* and Its Blessings, followed by the *T'filah*—except that it is considerably shorter. There are no lengthy additions to the traditional evening service (like preparatory prayer and psalms or a Torah reading), there is no reader's repetition of the *T'filah*, and the texts of the *Sh'ma* benedictions are considerably briefer.

As in the morning, the evening *Sh'ma* liturgy begins with *Bar'chu*, constituting the assembled worshipers as a praying community that stands for the Jewish people as a whole (traditionally, when a minyan, or quorum, of ten men is present). The traditional three biblical paragraphs of the *Sh'ma* are surrounded by benedictions, two before (as in the morning) and (unlike the morning) two afterward; this structure is already articulated in the Mishnah, *B'rachot* 1:4. The additional, concluding blessing in the evening is *Hashkiveinu*, a prayer for divine protection while we sleep. The three other *Sh'ma* blessings are structurally and thematically comparable in both their longer morning and briefer evening versions. The first blessing in each case responds to the time of day at which it is recited—sunrise or sunset. So the morning version, *Yotzeir Or*, praises God for creating the light of day, while the evening version, *Maariv Aravim*, praises God for bringing on the evening twilight (the Hebrew word *erev* refers to a "mixture" of light and darkness, just as the English word "twilight" refers to the period "twixt," that is, between light and darkness). The second blessing, which immediately precedes the recitation of the biblical texts, acclaims God as the giver of Torah to Israel, the beloved people (*Ahavah Rabbah*, "Abundant Love," in the morning; *Ahavat Olam*, "Everlasting Love," in the evening). The third blessing, which immediately follows the biblical texts, praises God whose words of Torah are true and whose promises of redemption are trustworthy, since they have already been demonstrated in the paradigmatic deliverance from Egyptian bondage (*Emet V'yatziv*, "True and Enduring," in the morning; *Emet Ve-emunah*, "True and Trustworthy," in the evening).

Maariv Aravim: "Bringer of Twilight"

The evening *Maariv Aravim* (literally, "who mixes the twilight") blessing (C, pp. 6, 148, 265, 396; Sh, pp. 30, 147; W/F, pp. 6, 132) praises God for having created the cosmic order—the regular changing of the times and seasons as the celestial bodies rotate in their courses. God eternally "rolls light away from darkness and darkness from light" (this phrase already occurs in the Babylonian Talmud, *B'rachot* 11b). It is noteworthy that although this is an evening blessing, it does not leave us (figuratively, at least) "in the dark"; rather the dark is seen as part of a constantly recurring cycle of light and darkness that demonstrates the wisdom of its divine Creator.

Because this benediction is relatively short, it has rarely been further abbreviated in Reform liturgies (unlike its morning counterpart), although individual prayer-book editors have taken literalist offense at some of its poetic imagery and pruned the text accordingly. The *Union Prayer Book*, for example, in all of its editions, omitted the phrase "rolling light away from darkness and darkness from light"—although it is unclear at this distance whether the imagery was deemed objectionable or simply redundant. *Mishkan T'filah* (like *Gates of Prayer* before it) gives the full traditional text.

Ahavat Olam and *Emet Ve-emunah*: "Everlasting Love" and "True and Trustworthy"— The Blessings Surrounding Torah

The two blessings that directly frame the *Sh'ma* recitation are thematically and functionally the same in the evening and in the morning. The two versions differ only in their length and in their actual wording: the evening wordings are more compact and pithy than their morning equivalents.

The blessing that immediately precedes the *Sh'ma* acclaims God who, out of an everlasting love for the people Israel, has given us the Torah, with which we are to occupy ourselves during every waking moment, and excerpts from which—the *Sh'ma* paragraphs—we are about to proclaim. As we noted above (p. 50), the Babylonian Talmud (*B'rachot* 12a) is familiar with two ways to begin this blessing: either with the phrase *Ahavah rabbah* ("Abundant Love") or with *Ahavat olam* ("Eternal/everlasting love"). While there is no substantive difference between the two, the Talmud prefers the latter because it derives from a biblical verse: "And with an everlasting love have I loved you" (*V'ahavat olam ahavtich*—Jeremiah 31:3; for the Rabbis, when it comes to prayer language, biblical is better). In the wake of this Talmudic dispute, the Ashkenazic rite splits the difference, assigning the former language to the morning version of this blessing, and the latter language to the evening version. (The Sephardic and Italian rites, on the other hand, opt with the Talmudic decision to use the latter language both morning and evening, although the wording of the rest of the morning blessing in those rites corresponds roughly to that in the Ashkenazic rite.) Most Reform prayer books (like *Mishkan T'filah*, C, pp. 8, 150, 266, 398; Sh, pp. 32, 148; W/F, pp. 8, 134) have retained the full traditional wording of the evening version, since it is relatively brief, while abbreviating somewhat the longer morning version.

The blessing that immediately follows the *Sh'ma* recitation (= the third in the series) affirms God's trustworthiness, the truth of the words of Torah just recited, and the reliability of the divine promise of redemption alluded to in the final words of the *Sh'ma* ("I am Adonai, your God, who brought you out of the land of Egypt to be your God"). Early rabbinic tradition (*T. B'rachot* 2:1) prescribes that this blessing include mention of the Exodus from Egypt (picking up on the theme of this last *Sh'ma* verse), God's sovereignty, the destruction of the Egyptian firstborn, and the splitting of the sea—and indeed all of these "bullet points" appear in the traditional versions, although the specific wordings are different in the morning and the evening. The morning version in the Ashkenazic rite also includes an explicit petition that God speedily redeem Israel again, just as happened when Israel went forth from Egypt: "Rock of Israel, rise in support of Israel" (*Tzur Yisrael, kumah b'ezrat Yisrael*). The morning version of this blessing has been considerably shortened in most Reform prayer books, on account of its repetitive style, while both morning and evening versions have been pruned of language that might appear to gloat over the death of the Egyptians and the destruction of Israel's enemies generally. *Mishkan T'filah* also makes these trims, for the same reasons; its evening text (C, pp. 14–16, 156–158, 269–270, 404–406; Sh, pp. 38–40, 151–152; W/F, pp. 14–16, 140–142) follows that of *Gates of Prayer* and the *Union Prayer Book*.

***Hashkiveinu*: "Grant That We Lie Down in Peace"—The Evening Prayer**

Hashkiveinu, the second benediction after the *Sh'ma* (the fourth and final blessing in the series), is recited only in the evening service (C, pp. 18, 160, 271, 408; Sh, pp. 42, 153; W/F, pp. 18, 144). It is a prayer for divine protection throughout the night—that we may lie down in peace and awaken in the morning unharmed. A moving and comforting image in the prayer is of God spreading over us a canopy of peace and protection while we are lying asleep, unaware of the dangers of the world around us, since "the Guardian of Israel neither slumbers nor sleeps" (Psalm 121:4). This image is reinforced in the expanded *chatimah* (closing benedictory formula) that is used only on Shabbat: "Blessed are You, Adonai, Guardian of Israel, whose shelter of peace is spread over us, over all Your people Israel, and over Jerusalem." On weekdays, the *chatimah* is simply, "Blessed are You, Adonai, Eternal Guardian of Israel" (C, p. 18; W/F, pp. 18). Two equally old and appropriate *chatimot* thereby have been preserved by distributing them between weekday and Shabbat use. Traditionally, this prayer is offered again (together with a longer prayer for protection overnight and a series of thematically relevant biblical verses) after the *Sh'ma* has been recited on one's bed immediately before going to sleep.

Hashkiveinu has usually been part of Reform liturgy, although it was omitted, for example, from the *Union Prayer Book* of 1895 and its 1918 revision in the Shabbat evening service—possibly because, as a bedtime prayer, it was deemed inappropriate for a public worship service. When the text has been included in Reform prayer books, some of its traditional language has been either deleted or reinterpreted (as occurs, for example, in the weekday evening service in the first two editions of the *UPB,* where it is included at the end of the *T'filah*). Most troubling has been the phrase "and remove Satan from before us and behind us." We should note, first of all, that the traditional Jewish Satan is not the same as the Christian Devil, not an independent force of evil. Rather Satan—or *hasatan,* since the term is not a proper name, but a noun of function deriving from the vocabulary of legal proceedings—is the adversary, or the prosecuting attorney in the divine courtroom (this is the meaning in Job 1:6, where the term first occurs). As such, this mythically personified function becomes equivalent to whatever negatively impacts on us in the world. Early Reform prayer books kept the Hebrew original but "demythologized" it in their vernacular translations or paraphrases. Thus in the earliest Reform congregational prayer book (Hamburg, 1819) "Satan" becomes *Unglück*, "misfortune," "unhappiness." The newly revised *UPB* of 1940 includes the prayer only in its fourth Sabbath eve service and there omits the offending phrase in both the Hebrew and the English. (It also uses the weekday *chatimah* on Shabbat, thereby avoiding the appearance of particularism or even Jewish nationalism.) *Gates of Prayer* restored the Hebrew text in its entirety (including the *chatimah* for Shabbat) but rendered the problematic phrase about Satan in English as "subdue our inclination to evil" (p. 133). *Mishkan T'filah* again omits this problematic phrase in the Hebrew—and additionally removes the gendered and hierarchical divine epithet *Malkeinu*, "our King," substituting *Shomreinu*, "our Protector" (keeping the same number of syllables for already-existing musical settings of this text).

Introduction to the *T'filah*
The Core of the Jewish Worship Service

THE *T'FILAH* (the "[Petitionary] Prayer") is the centerpiece of every Jewish worship service; there is, quite literally, no service without it. *Hat'filah* ("The Prayer") is the name this rubric bears in classical rabbinic sources. More commonly today it is called the *Amidah* (an abbreviation of *T'filat Haamidah*, the "Standing Prayer"), since traditionally it is recited in a standing posture. This name originated in Sephardic communities; Ashkenazim most often referred to the prayer sequence as the *Sh'monah Esreih* or *Sh'moneh Esreih* ("Eighteen," the number of blessings it originally contained on weekdays).

The essence of the *T'filah*, and its liturgical logic, is petitionary prayer. This is the part of the service where the worshiper prays for his or her needs and those of the Jewish people. The Rabbis instituted this liturgy to take the place of the now-destroyed Temple service (*B. B'rachot* 26b); they refer to it homiletically as *haavodah shebalev*, "the [Temple] service of the heart" (*Sifrei D'varim* 41; *B. Taanit* 2a; *Y. B'rachot* 4:1, 7a). Initially, this *was* the "service," period! That is why, traditionally, it is to be recited three times a day, corresponding to the times of the morning and late afternoon sacrifices. Since there were only *two* daily sacrifices in the Temple service, scholars still puzzle over why there are *three* daily prayers—whether this might conform to a Temple-era private prayer practice of pious individuals (see Daniel 6:11 and Psalm 55:18, *erev vavoker v'tzohorayim*: "evening, morning, and noon"—the setting, rising, and high point of the sun in its daily course) or to something else. On Shabbat and the festivals, an additional (*Musaf*) *T'filah* traditionally is recited, corresponding to the additional Temple sacrifice offered on these occasions. Many—but not all—Reform prayer books and communities have omitted the *Musaf* service on Shabbat and the festivals because of its intimate connection to the Temple rituals and the hope for their restoration, and in order to shorten the liturgy.

The *T'filah* takes the rhetorical form of a sequence of blessings, originally eighteen (now, nineteen[21]) on weekdays and seven on Shabbat and the festivals. The sequence is divided into three parts: it begins with blessings of praise, continues with the petitions proper, and concludes with an expression of gratitude and the Priestly Benediction, followed by a prayer for well-being (the more exact meaning of *shalom*). The Rabbis characterize this three-part structure of the *T'filah* as praise-petition-thanksgiving (*B. B'rachot* 34a), or as beginning and ending with praise and reciting petitions in the middle (*Sifrei D'varim* 343; *Y. B'rachot* 2:4). On Shabbat and the festivals, the middle petitionary section is omitted; petitions are deemed to be inappropriate on these days of rest and joy, since they remind people of their daily troubles (*Midrash Tanchuma, Vayeira*, 1)—and because God, too, needs a day off! In place of the petitionary section on Shabbat and the festivals is a single benediction, *K'dushat HaYom* ("Sanctification/Sanctity of the Day"), which offers praise to God for the special day and its holiness.

Rabbinic prayers are never offered without proper preparation. Meditation on psalms or psalm verses (as we saw in the case of *P'sukei D'zimrah*, which precedes the morning service proper) is often recommended as the way to prepare to pray. That is also the case with the *T'filah*. The Babylonian Talmud (*B'rachot* 4b) indicates that the verse *Adonai, s'fatai tiftach ufi yagid t'hilatecha*, "Adonai, open up my lips, that my mouth may declare Your praise" (Psalm 51:17; C, pp. 74, 164, 242, 273, 323, 344, 468; Sh, pp. 46, 124, 155, 205, 226; W/F, pp. 74, 204), should be recited at the very beginning of the *T'filah* and that the verse *Yih'yu l'ratzon imrei fi v'hegyon libi l'fanecha, Adonai tzuri v'go-ali*, "May the words of my mouth and the meditations of my heart be acceptable to You, Adonai, my Rock and my Redeemer" (Psalm 19:15; C, pp. 100, 180, 260, 283, 335, 360, 492; Sh, pp. 62, 142, 165, 217, 242; W/F, pp. 100, 228), should be recited at the end. Thus, our prayers will be framed by appropriate words from Scripture that simultaneously open our hearts to pray and invoke divine favor on behalf of our words and aspirations. While the concluding verse, *Yih'yu l'ratzon*, has figured prominently in Reform liturgies (sometimes only in English translation), the opening verse has sometimes been omitted, as in the three editions of the *Union Prayer Book*. Only with *Gates of Prayer* was this verse reclaimed for North American Reform liturgy. Several melodies and musical settings have made it well known in recent decades.

As noted above, Talmudic literature sees the *T'filah* as made up of three sections: the first three benedictions, which are deemed to be expressions of praise; the last three benedictions, which are deemed to be expressions of gratitude; and the middle twelve (thirteen) benedictions, which are petitionary (*Y. B'rachot* 2:3; *B. B'rachot* 34a). In point of fact, there are implicit petitions in the first two benedictions of praise and explicit petitions in two of three final benedictions (only the middle one, *Hodaah*, is simply an expression of gratitude). The first benediction, *Avot V'Imahot*, serves to establish a connection at the very outset between the petitioner/worshiper and Deity by invoking the God of the ancestors, whose descendants reap the benefit of their good deeds, piety, and intimacy with God. The implicit petition here is that God remember the meritorious behavior of our ancestors and benefit their descendants on that account. The second benediction, *G'vurot*, which invokes God's power to redeem, release, restore, and revive, implicitly requests that this power be exercised on our behalf. The third benediction, *K'dushat HaShem*, invoking God's sanctity, consists only of praise.

The petitionary sequence that follows on weekdays can be subdivided into two groups, the first requesting aspects of well-being that can be personal as well as communal (understanding and discernment, the ability to repent and change, forgiveness, redemption, healing, prosperity), the second detailing the yearned-for scenario of Israel's communal redemption (ingathering of the exiles, restoration of Israel's judicial and political leadership, punishment of evildoers and rewarding of the faithful, rebuilding of Jerusalem, and renewal of the Davidic monarchy), followed by a concluding petition for the acceptance of our prayers.

The three concluding blessings, recited every day, then ask for the acceptance of our verbal worship and the restoration of the sacrifices, express gratitude for divine benefactions, and finally request God's blessing of peace and well-being (traditionally, the last blessing is a communal response to the Priestly Benediction, Numbers 6:24–26, with which the Temple service had concluded). The first and last of these blessings are, in fact, petitions. We now explore each of the *T'filah* blessings in greater detail.

The Weekday *T'filah*

First Benediction: *Avot V'Imahot*— Invoking the Merits of Our Ancestors

> Rav Judah said: A person should not petition for his needs in either the first three benedictions or the last three benedictions [of the *T'filah*], but rather in the middle ones. For Rabbi Chanina said: In the first ones, he resembles a servant who is praising his master; in the middle ones, he resembles a servant who is requesting a gift from his master; in the last ones, he resembles a servant who has received a gift from his master and takes his leave. (*B. B'rachot* 34a)

This tradition from the Babylonian Talmud characterizes the three-part rhetorical structure of the daily *T'filah* in highly functional terms. When approaching the Master of the universe to appeal for divine help in maintaining your very livelihood, you can't simply begin with the "ask." As in all hierarchical relationships, etiquette instead requires an "indirect" approach: you must first acknowledge your situation of dependence but may also wish to appeal to the history of your relationship by way of rationale—past acts of service, past favors granted that warrant present assistance.

While some might find this Talmudic analogy disturbing or distasteful on account of the social hierarchies that it encodes and the instrumental conception of prayer that it assumes, it nonetheless provides a plausible context for understanding the rhetorical intent of the *T'filah*'s first benediction, *Avot* (now, *Avot V'Imahot*; C, pp. 76, 166, 244, 274, 324, 346, 470; Sh, pp. 48, 126, 156, 206, 228; W/F, pp. 76, 206). How, indeed, does one approach the Master of the universe? How does one begin to pray as a Jew if not by explicitly identifying oneself *as a Jew*, as a descendant of Abraham, Isaac, and Jacob, Sarah, Rebecca, Rachel, and Leah? "Remember us? We are family!"

Thus the *T'filah* begins by invoking the God of our ancestors, "the great, mighty, and awesome God" (citing Deuteronomy 10:17 and Nehemiah 9:32), who remembers those acts of devotion and covenantal loyalty (*chesed, chasadim*) performed by our ancestors in generations past and, in acknowledgment of their deeds, will bring redemption to their descendants. (The expressions *g'milut chasadim, gomeil chesed/chasadim* refer to the reciprocation of acts of loyalty.) Already in this opening benediction the theme of redemption—the major petitionary theme of the traditional *T'filah*—is sounded. The traditional text (following the old Babylonian formulations[22]) reads *umeivi go-eil livnei v'neihem*, "and will bring *a Redeemer* to their descendants"—referring to the belief in an individual messianic figure who will initiate the Jews' redemption and return to the Land of Israel, the rebuilding of the Temple, and the inauguration of a new world age. The very first Reform prayer books already were uncomfortable with this somewhat mythic image, preferring instead to pray for redemption (*g'ulah*) in a generalized sense—which could also be understood in non-supernaturalist terms as the ongoing political and social amelioration of the situation of the Jews and other oppressed minorities. The European Reform prayer books retained the traditional Hebrew text (*go-eil*) but rendered the term in German as *Erlösung*, "redemption." Only in America was the Hebrew text altered to *g'ulah* (first by Isaac Mayer Wise in *Minhag America*, 1857).[23] The only other significant and lasting Reform emendation to the text of this prayer is fairly recent: the addition of the *Imahot* (Matriarchs) to the *Avot* (Patriarchs)—that change began in the mid- to late 1970s and was near universal a decade later. Among official Reform liturgical publications it is first reflected in the gender-neutral edition of *Gates of Prayer* (1994), where the order of the Matriarchs is chronological: Sarah, Rebecca, Leah, Rachel. *MT* changes that order to Sarah, Rebecca, Rachel, Leah, reflecting the order as it appears in the few traditional prayers that include the Matriarchs (such as the *Mi Shebeirach* prayer for the sick), and as had come to be standard by this time in Conservative and Reconstructionist prayer books.

The benediction's traditional *chatimah* (conclusion or "seal") praises God as *magein Avraham*, "Shield of Abraham," drawing on the imagery of Genesis 15:1, where God says to Abra(ha)m, *Al tira Avram; anochi magein lach*, "Fear not, Abram; I am a shield to you." The addition of Sarah to this *chatimah* posed the question of what phrase should be used to characterize God's protecting relationship with her. The phrase used in some Reform liturgies, *ufokeid Sarah*, "and Caretaker of Sarah," draws on comparable biblical imagery in Genesis 21:1, *V'Adonai pakad et Sarah*, "God took providential note of Sarah" (with reference to the birth of Isaac). *Mishkan T'filah*, following the gender-sensitive edition of *Gates of Prayer* (1994), instead uses *v'ezrat Sarah*, "and Helper of Sarah," drawing on language in the benediction's immediately preceding phrase that transitions into the *chatimah—melech ozeir umoshia umagein*, "Sovereign, Helper, Savior, and Shield."

Because Jewish worship is communal, even when we may be praying alone, we always use the first person plural, "we." The first benediction of the *T'filah* draws out and makes explicit that "we" of whom, before God, we are always a part: we are the children of our parents and grandparents, the descendants of Abraham and Sarah, the people who stood at Sinai—*Am Yisrael*, the Jewish people.

Second Benediction: *G'vurot*—God's Mighty Acts

G'vurot means "powers" or "mighty acts." The second benediction of the *T'filah* (C, pp. 78, 168, 246, 275, 325, 348, 472; Sh, pp. 50, 128, 157, 207, 230; W/F, pp. 78, 208), called by this name in the Mishnah (*Rosh HaShanah* 4:5), invokes God's power over life and death—in the realms of both nature (rainfall and the turn of the seasons) and humanity (health, welfare, liberation, life after death). The recurring theme in this benediction is God's power to revive the dead as the ultimate act of salvation. For the Rabbis, resurrection of the dead was intimated in the rebirth of nature each year through the renewing power of rainfall and dew. That is why this benediction contains seasonal inserts—*mashiv haruach umorid hagashem*, "who causes the wind to shift and rain to fall," during the autumn and winter, beginning with Sh'mini Atzeret and ending on the first day of Pesach, and (in the Sephardic rite, but not in the Ashkenazic rite) *morid hatal*, "who rains dew upon us," during the spring and summer months, beginning with the first day of Pesach and ending on Sh'mini Atzeret—these relate, of course, to the agricultural seasons in the Land of Israel. *M. Taanit* 1:1 refers to the winter seasonal insert as *g'vurot g'shamim*, "the power of rainfall."

The powerful images invoked in this benediction all depict acts of divine salvation: God sustains and feeds the living, upholds those who have fallen, heals the sick, sets free the captive, and keeps faith with those who sleep in the dust (the dead) by causing salvation to sprout—a vegetation metaphor for resurrection.[24]

The idea of resurrection of the dead was controversial at the turn of the Common Era and into the first several centuries. It first appears in biblical literature—Daniel and additions to Isaiah—around the time of the Maccabean Wars in the early second century BCE, minimally as a solution to the problem of those righteous dead who did not survive to enjoy the Maccabean victory. Both Josephus (*Jewish War* 2:8; *Antiquities* 18:1) and the Gospels (Mark 12:18; Matthew 22:23; Luke 20:27) maintain that this belief was affirmed by Pharisees but denied by Sadducees. *M. Sanhedrin* 10:1 rules that anyone who holds that the idea of resurrection is not to be found in the Torah has, oneself, no portion in the world to come.[25] Some scholars have held that the prominent rhetorical position assigned to this belief in the second benediction of the *T'filah* was intentionally polemical, but this cannot be known for sure, and prayer texts in any event are frequently "overdetermined" with respect to their intent (that is, they "intend" many things simultaneously).

The belief in resurrection, at any rate, became an integral part of rabbinic tradition. It became controversial once more at the outset of modernity, running up against scientific materialism, on the one hand, and the enlightened modern Christian emphasis only on the immortality of the soul, on the other.[26] For this reason, the phrase *m'chayeih (ha)meitim*, "who resurrects the dead," was omitted from most (but not all) Reform prayer books, particularly in North America. (In Europe, it was often retained in the Hebrew but paraphrased in the translation.) The substitute formula *m'chayeih hakol*, "who gives life to all," first appears in Rabbi Samuel Adler's 1860 revision of Rabbi Leo Merzbacher's 1855 Reform prayer book for Temple Emanuel in New York. The *chatimah* of the *Union Prayer Book*, *notei-a b'tocheinu chayei olam*, "who implants eternal life within us," was adapted from Rabbi David Einhorn's *Olat Tamid* (1856–58).

More recently, many North American liberal Jews have chosen to revert to the traditional formula, which can be understood metaphorically or affirmed in a transrational, transcendent fashion (see, for example, Neil Gillman's book *The Death of Death: Resurrection and Immortality in Jewish Thought*, 2000). A survey of Reform congregants' worship desiderata, conducted by the CCAR in the mid-1990s, which helped to generate the guidelines for editing what became *Mishkan T'filah*, recommended:

> The CCAR should take note of the greater appreciation now being given to the traditional texts and should consider, for example, the paragraphs of the Shema which have been deleted in GOP, resurrection of the dead, and other elements of the traditional siddur which Reform has dropped. . . . Consideration should be given to the possibility of alternatives within the same prayer (e.g. *mechayyeh hakol* next to *mechayyeh meitim*).

These guidelines indeed were followed in producing the final version of *Mishkan T'filah*. By including both the traditional and the revised formulas in this blessing of the *T'filah*, the prayer book allows worshipers to make their own choices.

A second common Reform emendation of this blessing has been to omit the seasonal insertions about rain and dew. This was done initially to break the connection with the agricultural season in the Land of Israel, on account of political sensitivities (lest the Jews appear to themselves and to others to be a kind of "fifth column" in their European places of citizenship), but also in order to have a uniform text all year round that would be easier to recall and recite. Isaac Mayer Wise, in his 1857 *Minhag America*, included the composite phrase *morid hatal mashiv haruach umorid hagashem*, which Wise renders in English as "The dew falls, the winds blow, and the rain descends, to sustain life with grace,"[27] to be recited all year round in place of the seasonal inserts. Again, in light of the contemporary attachment of North American Reform Jews to the Land of Israel, it was deemed appropriate by the editors of *Mishkan T'filah* to restore the traditional seasonal inserts—including the Sephardic one, *morid hatal*, which is now recited by most Israeli Jews regardless of their rite of origin, and has been included in the Israeli Liberal prayer book *HaAvodah Shebalev* ("Service of the Heart") as well as in the new Israeli prayer book currently in process.[28]

Mishkan T'filah and *M'chayeih Hameitim*

A perfect example of the desire to include in *Mishkan T'filah* more passages from the traditional liturgy and to reconsider earlier Reform deletions is the treatment of *m'chayeih hameitim*, the affirmation of God's resurrection of the dead, in the second benediction of the *T'filah*. This belief, as we have noted, was controversial in its origins, went on to become a hallmark of classical rabbinic theology that was given liturgical prominence in the daily *T'filah*, then became controversial again in the nineteenth and twentieth centuries among modern Western Jews. This section aims to set in historical context both the rabbinic belief in resurrection and its liturgical expression so as, once again, to make sense of our contemporary liturgical choices.

The early Israelites believed in a shadowy afterlife in the underworld (Sheol, somewhat like the Greek Hades), without any reward or punishment after death. The individual joined his or her ancestors; immortality was attained through one's descendants. The problem of ultimate reward and punishment for individuals became acute later, in the Hellenistic era, which had a fuller concept of individual, as opposed to corporate, identity. The late biblical book of Daniel, which dates from the period of the Maccabean Wars (167–163 BCE), frets about the problematic situation of those righteous martyrs who fought for Judean victory against the Syrians but did not live to experience its fruits. The solution? "At the time of the end . . . many of those who sleep in the dust of the earth shall awake, some to everlasting life, and some to shame and everlasting contempt" (Daniel 12:2). This is likely the earliest articulation of the concept of resurrection in Jewish literature.

At the end of the Second Commonwealth period, a belief in bodily resurrection in order to receive reward or punishment after death was a hallmark of Pharisaic religious conviction, opposed by the Sadducees (both Josephus, the Roman-Jewish historian, and the Gospels attest to this). The Mishnah (ca. 200 CE), the earliest rabbinic text, carries forward that Pharisaic belief and indeed excoriates anyone who holds that the belief in resurrection cannot be found in the Torah; such a person has no share in the world to come (*M. Sanhedrin* 10:1).

The belief in resurrection figures prominently in the second benediction of the rabbinic *T'filah*. The theme of this benediction is God's power over life and death: God causes the rain and dew to fall, reviving plant life. By analogy, God will keep faith with "those who sleep in the dust" (the language comes from the Daniel passage quoted above) and bring them back to bodily life in the messianic age, for both reward and punishment. The expression *m'chayeih (ha)meitim*, "Reviver of the dead," occurs four times in the traditional wording, as emphasis.

By the nineteenth century, this religious concept had become problematic. Enlightened Protestants in Western Europe affirmed the immortality of the soul, but not the bodily resurrection of the dead (although the latter was, in fact, a traditional Christian belief as well). Bodily resurrection was neither scientific nor spiritual. By the time of the Reform rabbinical conferences in the middle of the nineteenth century, most of the Reformers also had spiritualized this belief. (To tell the truth, medieval Jewish rationalists like Maimonides also held this opinion, although they often held it to themselves.) Abraham Geiger expressed this stance as follows:

> Many religious concepts have taken on a more spiritual character and, therefore, their expression in prayer must be more spiritual. From now on the hope for an afterlife should not be expressed in terms that suggest a future revival, a resurrection of the body; rather, they must stress the immortality of the human soul.[29]

Nonetheless, *none* of the German Reform prayer books—including Geiger's *Israelite Prayerbook for Public Worship throughout the Entire Year*—ever changed the wording of the benediction in Hebrew! Presumably, it was felt that the Hebrew expression *m'chayeih hameitim* could be understood figuratively. In some (though not all) of these same prayer books, however, the German rendering of the phrase is paraphrastic. Geiger (1854), for example, renders:

> Your supernal power, O God, gives life, preserves, and renews it. You revive vegetation when it freezes, and, when it dies, you let new growth spring up. You raise up the fallen, send healing to the sick, and keep faith with those who sleep in the dust. Indeed, Your supernal power inspires the dead with the promise that their salvation will sprout in a new, eternal life! Be praised, O God, who gives life here and there [i.e., in this existence and the next].[30]

It should also be noted that the most radical German Reform prayer book, that of the Berlin Reformgemeinde (1848 and many revisions), simply eliminated the Hebrew text of the *T'filah* (except for the *Kedushah* responses) and provided an abbreviated German paraphrase that, in this benediction, invokes God's grace to the *souls* of the dead.

North American Reform prayer books, on the other hand, frequently (though not always) changed the Hebrew text of this benediction, as well as supplying a vernacular paraphrase. As we noted above, Rabbi Samuel Adler's 1860 revision of Rabbi Leo Merzbacher's prayer book for Temple Emanuel, New York, substitutes the phrase *m'chayeih hakol*, "who gives life to all things"; this is later taken up in *Gates of Prayer* (1975), and remains the default text in *Mishkan T'filah*. The first edition of Rabbi Isaac Mayer Wise's *Minhag America* (1857) retains the traditional text, since it strives to be the prayer book for all American Jews; by the 1872 revision, however, Wise eliminates *m'chayeih hameitim* and substitutes (in only the last two iterations) *V'ne-eman atah lachayim v'lameitim: Baruch atah Adonai, m'chayeih nishmot hameitim*, "Faithful are You to the living and the dead: Praised be You, O Lord, who revives *the souls of* the dead" (empasis added). Rabbi David Einhorn's radical *Olat Tamid* (1856–58), which became the model for the *Union Prayer Book* (1894–95), introduces the phrase *(ha)notei-a b'tocheinu chayei olam*, "who implants within us eternal life" (which, incidentally, derives from the traditional blessing recited after the public Torah reading); this is taken up into all three editions of the *Union Prayer Book*. (Einhorn also renders *m'chalkeil chayim b'chesed / podeh nefesh avadav mimavet b'rachamim rabim*, "who graciously sustains the living / who, in great mercy, redeems *the souls of* His servants from death.")

In recent years, many have questioned Reform liturgical literalism as too quick to emend the traditional text. Is it not possible to understand the expression *m'chayeih hameitim* as a metaphor? Can it not, as a metaphor, be a source of comfort to those in mourning and a source of hope to others? Still others ask, "Is there nothing beyond God's ability? In that case, God can reverse death." Yet others point to the feminist-inspired desire for a more embodied spirituality as another contemporary motivation. For all these reasons, *Mishkan T'filah* supplies both options, *m'chayeih hakol* and *m'chayeih ha-meitim*, letting worshipers exercise informed choice in addressing their religious needs.

Whichever version one chooses to recite, this prayer powerfully connects us with our own sense of fragility and mortality, on the one hand, and our hope for divine sustenance and meaning beyond the grave, on the other.

Third Benediction: *K'dushat HaShem*—God's Holiness and the *K'dushah* ("Sanctification")

The third benediction of the *T'filah*, the last of the "opening benedictions" or "blessings of praise" recited on every occasion, invokes God's holiness. *M. Rosh HaShanah* 4:5 refers to this blessing by the name *K'dushat HaShem*—literally "the holiness of the (divine) name," but actually "the holiness of God," since *HaShem* is a euphemism for God (whose four-letter name was to be treated with great respect and pronounced only by the High Priest in the Temple courtyard on Yom Kippur). This brief benediction, beginning with the words *Atah kadosh v'shimcha kadosh*, "You are holy, Your name is holy," can be found in *Mishkan T'filah* in the evening services (C, pp. 80, 170, 276, 474; Sh, pp. 52, 158; W/F, pp. 80, 210). Traditionally, it is also recited in the morning and afternoon services when praying without a minyan, and during the silent *T'filah* it is offered privately by each worshiper before the congregational *T'filah* is led by the reader or cantor (*sh'liach tzibur*, the congregation's representative before God). (Most Reform prayer books eliminated the silent private *T'filah* recitation as redundant, retaining only the congregational *T'filah*, recited out loud.) In the morning and afternoon services when a minyan is present, the congregational *T'filah* replaces this short blessing with the more extended and public *K'dushah* ("Sanctification"), which is recited antiphonally by the reader and the congregation (C, pp. 82, 248, 326–328, 476; Sh, pp. 130, 208–210; W/F, pp. 82, 212).

The Hebrew root *kuf-dalet-shin* (as in the adjective *kadosh*, "holy"; the verb [*l'*]*kadeish*, "to sanctify"; and the nouns *kiddush*, "sanctification" and *k'dushah*, "holiness") means "set apart" or "separate." The German Lutheran theologian and phenomenologist of religion Rudolf Otto, in his book *The Idea of the Holy* (1917), famously rendered "the holy" as "the wholly Other." In biblical and rabbinic thought, only God is intrinsically holy—different, other, set apart. Those things that are rendered holy—"sanctified," "consecrated"—such as sanctuaries, priests, and (ideally) the people Israel itself (*K'doshim tih'yu*, "Be holy!" [Leviticus 19:2]), are so by virtue of their close association with or "dedication" to God.

Marking out or invoking God's holiness liturgically means acknowledging God's special "difference"—and striving to participate in it. This is the import of the communally recited *K'dushah*, in which the worshipers repeat—and aim to participate in—the words of the angelic praise of God reported in Isaiah's Temple vision (Isaiah 6:5):

Kadosh! Kadosh! Kadosh Adonai tz'vaot!
M'lo chol haaretz k'vodo!

Holy! Holy! Holy is Adonai who commands multitudes!
God's presence fills all the earth![31]

From late Second Temple times onward, Isaiah's vision of God seated on a celestial throne and surrounded by a host of divine beings ("angels") who ceaselessly and antiphonally proclaim the divine holiness (other-ness, set-apart-ness) has served as the model for Jewish pietists and mystics who have striven to attain the same vision and/or to participate in the angelic chorus of divine praise. This, in fact, is what the rabbinic liturgical *K'dushah* is all about, and this is why it is only recited when a *minyan* is present. To replicate "down below" the actions of the angelic chorus in heaven, and thereby to join in with them, requires that there be "down below" a corresponding Israelite chorus—traditionally, ten adult males making up a congregation that liturgically represents the entire Jewish people. Similarly, the customs of bowing to the left and to the right on reciting the words [*v'kara*] *zeh el zeh* ("and they called one to the other") and of rising up on one's toes three times when reciting the word *kadosh* are each physical enactments of, and participation in, the angelic activities being narrated. (In recent years, some Reform Jews have been reclaiming these traditional practices.)

The second verse recited in the congregational *K'dushah*, Ezekiel 3:12, *Baruch k'vod Adonai mimkomo* ("Blessed is the presence of Adonai in God's place"[32]), also derives from a prophet's vision of the divine realm, in this case Ezekiel's vision of God on God's moving throne (or "chariot"). Here, too, the worshiper seeks to participate in a vision of God and thereby draw near to God's holy presence.

The third verse is Psalm 146:10 (which concludes that psalm):

Yimloch Adonai l'olam,
Elohayich Tzion l'dor vador,
Hal'luyah!

Adonai shall reign forever—
Your God, O Zion—to all generations.[33]
Hallelujah [= Praise Yah]!

This verse simply proclaims God's eternal majesty and rulership over all things, a fitting conclusion to the *K'dushah* as well.

Since most Reform prayer books eliminated the silent, private *T'filah* and retained only the congregational recitation, the actual third benediction has been found only in the evening services (as in *Mishkan T'filah*, following the usage of *Gates of Prayer* and the *Union Prayer Book* before that). The morning and afternoon services, on the other hand, retain only the public *K'dushah*. While elaborate descriptions of angels were regarded as mythological and embarrassing by rationalist Reformers and mostly excised from the liturgy, the *K'dushah* recitation itself was highly valued, since (among other reasons) God's sanctity and awesomeness were attributes earnestly affirmed in the bourgeois Protestant environment in which the Reform Movement originated. Additionally, the communal singing of the *K'dushah* verses was (and remains) a dramatic, participatory highlight of the service beloved in, and thus carried over from, traditional practice. So, too, even when, as in the *Union Prayer Book*, it was not Reform custom to stand for the *T'filah*, it always remained customary to stand for the *K'dushah*.

The *K'dushah* concludes the first portion of the *T'filah*. The middle portion, as we shall see, differs between weekdays and Shabbat or holidays.

The Weekday Petitions

There are thirteen petitions in the weekday *T'filah* (C, pp. 84–90; W/F, pp. 84–90). The first cluster of petitions—(1) *Daat*, for knowledge/discernment, (2) *T'shuvah*, for the ability to repent and return to God, and (3) *S'lichah*, for divine forgiveness—have antecedents in the psalms (Psalm 51, for example) and in the prophetic literature (Hosea, Jeremiah, Ezekiel). The focus here is both personal and communal. The Talmud of the Land of Israel (*Y. B'rachot* 2:4) construes the sequencing of these petitions according to the following logic: the attainment of knowledge and discernment will prompt us to repentance, which will in turn make us worthy of divine forgiveness and redemption. An adaptation of this tradition, by Rabbi Judith Z. Abrams, appears in *Mishkan T'filah* (C, p. 102; W/F, p. 102). By and large, these petitions have been retained with no verbal changes in Reform prayer books.

Following these is the petition (4) *G'ulah*, for redemption. Because the entire second half of the *T'filah*'s petitionary section deals with the scenario for Israel's future redemption, some scholars have suggested that the petition here was intended to request personal, rather than communal, redemption. I am inclined to view that distinction as artificial and unwarranted in the rhetorical context of the *T'filah* as a whole, in which requests for personal and communal well-being are effectively merged. This blessing was omitted from some Reform prayer books, including the *Union Prayer Book*, precisely because it was understood to be a petition for national, corporate redemption according to the traditional messianic scenario of the *T'filah*'s second half.

The next two petitions deal with human welfare: (5) *R'fuah*, for healing, and (6) *Birkat HaShanim*, for prosperity (literally "the blessing of the [agricultural] years;" requesting a year of good rainfall and crop harvest). It is common to insert into the healing benediction a personal request for the healing of a loved one or friend. There are seasonal inserts for rainfall and dew in the petition for prosperity, just as there are seasonal inserts into the *G'vurot* blessing at the beginning of the *T'filah*. Reform prayer books have sometimes altered the wording of both of these blessings—in the first instance, to stress healing from physical pain and disease rather than divinely inflicted plagues (*makot*), and in the second instance, to remove the impression that Jews in the West were still tied to the agricultural calendar of the Land of Israel and that the weather was a physical manifestation of divine pleasure or displeasure. *Mishkan T'filah* adds wording from the Sephardic rite to the petition for healing, so that it mentions wounds and pain in addition to the Ashkenazic rite's "plagues" (translated in *MT* as "illness"). *MT* also eliminates the seasonal changes in the wording of the petition for agricultural prosperity.

The following six petitions traditionally detail the scenario for Israel's messianic redemption: (7) *Kibutz Galuyot*, for the ingathering to the Land of Israel of the dispersed exiles; (8) *Mishpat,* for the restoration of Israel's court system and autonomy; (9) *Birkat HaMinim,* a curse upon heretics, slanderers, and informers; (10) *Tzadikim,* an invocation of blessing, by contrast, upon the righteous; (11) *Boneh Y'rushalayim,* for the rebuilding of Jerusalem; (12) *Birkat David,* for the restoration of the Davidic dynasty; and (13) *Shomei-a T'filah,* for the hearing of prayer and granting of our requests. The first five of these petitions have often been omitted or reworded in Reform prayer books, usually to generalize and universalize them so that they request redemption for all humanity; *MT* follows in this tradition. The third of these petitions, for punishment of apostates, slanderers, and evildoers, has frequently been omitted enirely; when it is retained (as in *MT*), it is refashioned into a prayer for vanquishing wickedness rather than wicked people ("Hate the sin, not the sinner"). In recent decades, the prayer for the rebuilding of Jerusalem (often omitted earlier) has been retained, but given a more contemporary interpretation. Its companion, the prayer for the restoration of the Davidic dynasty (these two were initially a single benediction in the rite of the Land of Israel, but were recited separately in Babylonia), is revised as a general plea for justice and deliverance.

The petitionary section of the *T'filah* concludes with a generic prayer for the acceptance of all of our specific prayers (*Shomei-a T'filah*). This prayer also figures independently in the *S'lichot* liturgy on Yom Kippur and in the month preceding it as a good, all-purpose summary and conclusion.

First Closing Benediction: *Avodah*—For the Acceptance of Worship

The weekday, Shabbat, festival, and High Holy Day *T'filot* all conclude with the same three benedictions: (1) *Avodah,* for the acceptance of worship (C, pp. 92, 174, 254, 279, 330, 354, 484; Sh, pp. 56, 136, 161, 212, 236; W/F, pp. 92, 220); (2) *Hodaah,* gratitude/acknowledgment (C, pp. 94, 176, 256, 280–281, 331–332, 356, 486; Sh, pp. 58, 138, 162–163, 213–214, 238; W/F, pp. 56, 222); and (3) *Shalom,* for peace/well-being (C, pp. 96/98, 178, 258, 282, 334, 358, 488/490; Sh, pp. 60, 140, 164, 216, 240; W/F, pp. 96/98, 224/226). As was noted above, the first and third of these are petitions, while the second is an expression of thanksgiving.

Avodah refers to an act of service or worship. It is the same Hebrew word that was used for the act of sacrificial worship in the Temple. The Rabbis, who called their *T'filah* of eighteen benedictions "the service of the heart" (*haavodah shebalev*), explicitly took over that Temple terminology and applied it to regular prayer. *M. Tamid* 5:1 relates that after reciting the *Sh'ma* in the Temple, the priests would recite a benediction *al haavodah*, "for the [acceptance of] worship [= the sacrifices]," and would bless the assembled people with the biblical *Birkat Kohanim* ("Priestly Benediction," Numbers 6:24–26). These two elements subsequently were taken over into the synagogue service at the end of the *T'filah*. (In the traditional morning service, *Birkat Kohanim* precedes the recitation of *Sim Shalom*.) Thus, the rabbinic *T'filah* concludes the way the Temple service would have concluded. In this vein, the traditional *Avodah* text refers multiple times to the sacrificial worship and the hope for its restoration:

> Look favorably, Adonai, upon Your people Israel and their prayers;
> *Restore the [sacrificial] worship to the sanctuary of Your house;*
> *Accept with love and favor the fire-offerings of Israel and their prayers.*
> And may the worship of Your people Israel ever be acceptable to You.
> May our eyes behold Your merciful return to Zion.
> Blessed are You, Adonai, whose Presence returns to Zion.

This text was problematic for most early Reformers because of its explicit petition not only for a return to Zion but also for a restoration of the sacrificial cult in the Temple. Most (but not all) Reform prayer books over the past two centuries have excised the italicized lines above as well as the penultimate line and have emended the *chatimah*. The more neutral phrase that is substituted in most Reform prayer books for *hamachazir Shechinato l'Tzion*, "whose Presence returns to Zion," is *she-ot'cha l'vadcha b'yirah naavod*, "whom alone we serve in reverence." This is the text of the *Union Prayer Book*, as well as of its North American predecessors, Leo Merzbacher's *Seder T'filah* (1855), Isaac Mayer Wise's *Minhag America* (1857), and David Einhorn's *Olat Tamid* (1858). As Jakob Petuchowski (*Prayerbook Reform in Europe*, p. 231) points out, this custom goes back to the 1841 revision of the Hamburg Temple Prayer Book. The Hamburg Reformers did not invent this text, but knew it from the Ashkenazic festival and High Holy Day liturgies, where it appears as the *chatimah* for this benediction. What they could not have known in 1841 is that this is, in fact, the old *chatimah* from the rite of the Land of Israel, now known to us from the fragmentary prayer books in the Cairo Genizah that follow this rite. When the early medieval Ashkenazic festival and High Holy Day liturgies took over *piyutim* (hymns, liturgical poems) from the Land of Israel, they took over as well the old Eretz Yisraeli formulations of the *chatimot* that went with them—so wordings from the Land of Israel are preserved in the medieval Ashkenazic rite! The standard *chatimah, hamachazir Shechinato l'Tziyon,* on the other hand, derives from the old Babylonian rite. When, in the early 1970s—the flush years of American Jewry's re-identification with the State of Israel—Rabbi Chaim Stern was editing *Gates of Prayer,* he reincorporated the traditional, Babylonian *chatimah* and preserved the old Eretz Yisraeli (*UPB*) one as well in some of the services. Stern also composed a new transition to the traditional *chatimah*:

> *El karov l'chol korav, p'neih el avadecha v'choneinu.*
> *Sh'foch ruchacha aleinu.*
>
> God who is near to all who call, turn lovingly to Your servants.
> Pour out Your spirit upon us.

Stern (*Gates of Understanding* I, p. 191) comments, "We have omitted the trad. references to sacrificial worship, substituting a thought (based on Pss. 145:18, 25:16) on the theme of God's nearness to all who seek Him with sincerity." *Mishkan T'filah* retains both the *GOP* and the *UPB* texts, using the former on the right side of the two-page spread and the latter as an alternative on the left side.

Because of a number of well-loved musical settings of this benediction, its Hebrew text (particularly in the *UPB* version) is well known to most Reform Jews.

Second Closing Benediction: *Hodaah*—Gratitude

We noted above that the three daily sections of the *T'filah* are often characterized as comprising (1) praise, (2) petition, and (3) thanksgiving (and that the petitionary section is replaced on Shabbat, the festivals, and the High Holy Days with a single benediction dealing with the sacred occasion). In the course of our study we have noted that the benedictions of praise in fact contain implicit petitions (we praise the God of the ancestors *and thereby* invoke God's aid to their descendants; we praise the mighty God *and thereby* invoke God's power to save us). We have also noted that only the second of the three concluding benedictions is an expression of gratitude; the other two in fact are petitions (for God's acceptance of our worship and for God's blessing of peace/well-being). Those structural observations bring us at last to a consideration of the benediction that expresses our gratitude to God.

The two words in the English language that cannot be spoken enough are "Thank you." That pertains as well to our stance vis-à-vis God. The rabbinic tradition that we cited at the beginning of our account of the *T'filah* likens the person who concludes his or her prayer to a servant who has received from his master the gift that he has requested and now departs with an expression of gratitude (*B. B'rachot* 34b). In fact, the gifts that are enumerated in this blessing are the ones that we often take most for granted—until we lose them: "our lives which are Your hand, our souls which are in Your care, Your miracles that we experience every day, and Your wondrous deeds and favors at every time of day: evening, morning, and noon." These "daily miracles"—the so-called little things—in reality *are* the big things. In that recognition lies the heart of Jewish piety. Not only does Jewish tradition urge each of us to "set Adonai before me at all times," in the words of Psalm 16:8, but also to say "Thank you" to God at all times (what else are the occasional *b'rachot* recited over eating, waking up, and so forth, about?). It is not accidental that Rabbi Chaim Stern, when pondering a rubric title for the brief daily morning benedictions (*Birchot HaShachar*) in *Gates of Prayer*, chose the phrase *Nisim B'chol Yom* (translated in *Mishkan T'filah* as "For Daily Miracles"), which derives from the *Hodaah* benediction; the themes and attitudes of both are identical.

It is worth pointing out that the first words of our benediction, *Modim anachnu lach*,[34] are translated in *Mishkan T'filah* as "We acknowledge with thanks" (a variant on the *Union Prayer Book*'s "We gratefully acknowledge"). The reason is that the verb *l'hodot* means both "to thank" and "to acknowledge" and that the text continues: "that You are Adonai, our God and the God of our ancestors, forever"—this is to be understood as a declaration of fact, hence an acknowledgment on the part of those who are praying.

There are two occasional insertions into this blessing. The first is during each of the eight days of Chanukah (C, p. 556; Sh, p. 264; W/F, p. 292), and the second is for Purim (C, p. 557; W/F, p. 293). Both of these are indicated in *Mishkan T'filah* in the appropriate place of the weekday *T'filah* (C, p. 94; W/F, p. 94), as well as, for Chanukah, of the various Shabbat *T'filot* (C, pp. 176, 256, 281, 332, 356; Sh, pp. 58, 138, 163, 214, 238); Purim can never fall on Shabbat. Chanukah and Purim are both postbiblical festivals (or, "post-Torah," since the Book of Esther is, of course, biblical). They each celebrate what the tradition views to have been a miraculous divine salvation of the Jewish people, at the time of the Maccabees (the sons of the priest Matityahu/Mattathias) and at the time of Esther and Mordecai. Liturgically, these holidays are marked in the *T'filah* by including in the *Hodaah* benediction a specific expression of gratitude "for the miracles and for the redemption" (*al hanisim v'al hapurkan*) of the Jews on these two occasions. In our own day, it has become customary in many Jewish circles to incorporate into this benediction on Yom HaAtzma-ut (Israel Independence Day) as well an expression of gratitude "for the miracles and for the redemption" of the Jewish people experienced through the founding of the State of Israel (C, p. 555; W/F, p. 291).

The *Hodaah* benediction in the *T'filah* is thus the quintessential liturgical expression of gratitude to God—both on special occasions and every day, since God's miracles indeed are "with us daily, at all times—evening, morning, and noon."

A rabbinic tradition notes that in the world to come, all of the prayers and all of the sacrifices will be rendered obsolete—except for the prayer of gratitude and its sacrificial counterpart, the offering of thanksgiving, which will endure forever (*Midrash on Psalms* 56:4). This is an exceptionally wise tradition: even envisioning an ideal era without want, when there will be no need for petitionary prayers, there will *always* be a need to express our gratitude. If that is to be true in the messianic future, so much the more so is it true in the world of here and now.

Third Closing Benediction: *Shalom*—Peace/Well-Being

M. Tamid 5:1 relates that the priests serving in the Jerusalem Temple would recite the *Sh'ma* together each morning and after this would "bless the people with three blessings: *Emet V'yatziv* ['True and enduring'], *Avodah* ['Worship'], and *Birkat Kohanim* ['Priestly Benediction']." The first of these would seem to correspond generally to the rabbinic blessing that follows the recitation of the *Sh'ma* in the morning (the first words are the same), and the second to the *Avodah* benediction in the *T'filah*, the first of its closing benedictions.[35] The third is the biblical Priestly Benediction, Numbers 6:24–26 ("May God bless you and keep you . . ."). The traditional *T'filah* closes with this threefold benediction at morning and afternoon services (it is omitted in the evening service because there is no reader's repetition, during which it would be recited). Most Reform prayer books omit this from the *T'filah* at all services, for reasons to be discussed below, but often use it to close the entire service. The last three words of the Priestly Benediction, in Hebrew, are *v'yaseim l'cha shalom*, "and may you find peace"; in the *T'filah*, these words are followed by a final rabbinic blessing whose first words respond to the end of the Priestly Benediction: *Sim shalom . . . aleinu v'al kol Yisrael amecha*, "Grant peace . . . to us and to all Your people Israel."[36] By concluding public prayer with a petition for peace and well-being (the Hebrew word *shalom* means both), the Rabbis not only summarize in one request everything that has come before,[37] but also link the structure of their worship with that of the now-destroyed Temple.

This connection to, and recollection of, the Temple worship, which was valued so highly by the early Rabbis and so many generations of premodern Jews, was precisely what bothered early Reformers of Jewish worship in the nineteenth and twentieth centuries. The Priestly Benediction, which in fact is still delivered by the priests in traditional congregations at the additional (*Musaf*) service on Shabbat and the festivals (among Ashkenazic Jews today, only on the festivals), continued to be viewed as an appropriate conclusion for the service proper but was to be delivered by the rabbi or service leader. The liturgical role of hereditary priests in the congregation was viewed as outmoded, an unwanted throwback to Temple times; all priestly prerogatives were abandoned together with the prayers for the restoration of the Temple worship. The *Sim Shalom* benediction, on the other hand, was highly valued and often universalized, both in the vernacular rendering and in the Hebrew. Consider, for example, the beloved English version in the *Union Prayer Book*: "Grant us peace, Thy most precious gift, O Thou eternal source of peace, and enable Israel to be its messenger unto the peoples of the earth"; and the *UPB* Hebrew changes: *al kol yirei sh'mecha* ("to all who revere Your name"), instead of *al kol Yisrael amecha* ("to Israel Your people"), and *oseh hashalom* ("Maker of peace") instead of *ham'vareich et amo Yisrael bashalom* ("who blesses Your people Israel with peace").[38] *Gates of Prayer* restored the standard versions as "more traditional" options, and *Mishkan T'filah* follows *GOP* in this regard.

With the Priestly Benediction and the final petition for peace, we have come to the end of the public, statutory prayer. What follows is the opportunity for individual, private prayer.

The Private Prayer after the *T'filah: Elohai N'tzor*—"My God, Guard My Speech from Evil"

From its very inception, the *T'filah*, or *Amidah*, has been understood as a communal prayer, even while the traditional obligation to recite it three times a day falls upon each individual Jew (male and female). That is why it is phrased in the first-person plural, even when recited by an individual not in the company of a minyan. But the Rabbis of the Talmud recognized that people have private prayer needs as well and wish to express those needs whenever they are praying the *T'filah*. Thus, when praying for healing (*r'fuah*) in the daily petitionary section of the *T'filah*, individuals are encouraged to include a private prayer naming the person(s) in need of healing for whom they are specifically concerned.[39] Other personal prayers should be uttered at the very end of the *T'filah*—presumably so that they will not otherwise interrupt or confuse the communal prayer.[40]

Both Talmuds give instances of personal prayers uttered by individual Rabbis after they finished praying the communal *T'filah* (*B. B'rachot* 16–17b; *Y. B'rachot* 4:2); altogether there are fifteen of these prayers, ten in the Babylonian Talmud and five in the Talmud of the Land of Israel. These are given as pious models of personal prayer. In the earliest post-Talmudic prayer codes (those of Amram and Saadyah), however, only the last of these in the Babylonian Talmud is given—as a prayer that should be recited verbatim by individuals at the end of the *T'filah*.[41] This is the prayer attributed to Mar the son of Rabina: *Elohai, n'tzor l'shoni meira us'fatai midabeir mirmah . . .* , "My God, guard my speech from evil and my lips from deception. . . ." From Amram, this is taken up into all of the medieval prayer codes and prayer books and from there into the Reform prayer books, where it was often abbreviated and partially paraphrased or rewritten. Here is the original:

> My God, keep my tongue from evil and my lips from deceitful
> speech.
> To those who curse me, let my soul be silent;
> May my soul be to all like the dust.
> Open my heart to Your Torah and let my soul pursue Your
> commandments.
> [And deliver me from mishap, from the evil impulse, from an
> evil woman,
> and from all evil that threatens to come into the world.[42]]
> As for all who plan evil against me,
> swiftly thwart their counsel and frustrate their plans.
> Act for the sake of Your name; act for the sake of Your power;
> act for the sake of Your holiness; act for the sake of Your Torah.
>
> *That Your beloved ones may be delivered,*
> *save with Your right hand and answer me* (Psalm 60:7).[43]
> *May the words of my mouth and the meditations of my heart be*
> *acceptable to You, Adonai, my Rock and my Redeemer* (Psalm 19:15).

Many Reform prayer books have chosen to give a vernacular paraphrase of this text rather than to translate it literally. The version in the *Union Prayer Book* (newly revised edition, 1940) is a classic—and popular—example:

> O God, keep my tongue from evil and my lips from speaking guile. Be my support when grief silences my voice, and my comfort when woe bends my spirit. Implant humility in my soul, and strengthen my heart with perfect faith in Thee. Help me to be strong in temptation and trial and to be patient and forgiving when others wrong me. Guide me by the light of Thy counsel, that I may ever find strength in Thee, my Rock and my Redeemer.

Mishkan T'filah (C, pp. 100, 180, 260, 283, 335, 360, 492; Sh, pp. 62, 142, 165, 217, 242; W/F, pp. 100, 228), on the other hand, provides the full Hebrew text and a faithful translation.

As we noted above (p. 60), *B. B'rachot* 4b indicates that a psalm verse should both precede and conclude each recitation of the *T'filah*: Psalm 51:17 (*Adonai, s'fatai tiftach*, "Adonai, open up my lips . . .") at the beginning, and Psalm 19:15 (*Yih'yu l'ratzon imrei fi*, "May the words of my mouth . . .") at the end. Since the private prayer of Mar the son of Rabina is to be recited *after* the *T'filah*, Sephardim recite the psalm verse *Yih'yu l'ratzon before* that prayer, technically concluding the *T'filah* with the psalm verse, while Ashkenazim recite the psalm verse at the end of Mar's prayer. North American Reform custom generally has singled out this verse for musical treatment, either in English or in Hebrew. It provides an appropriate conclusion for the *T'filah* as a whole, as well as for personal prayer.

Weekday Torah Service

Most Reform Jews are familiar with the Torah service on Shabbat mornings.[44] The Torah is also read on Shabbat afternoons and on Monday and Thursday mornings. The full weekly reading is done in traditional synagogues on Shabbat mornings; this is the main reading of the week, since Shabbat is to be given over to worship, study, and rest. Reform congregations on Shabbat mornings generally read only a segment of the weekly portion, since the full portion tends to be quite long.[45] The brief first section of the following week's Torah portion is read on Shabbat afternoon and on Monday and Thursday mornings (traditionally, it is the same section at each of these services). The custom to read from the Torah during the week as well as on Shabbat is a very old one. The Rabbis ruled that three days should not pass without an opportunity for people to hear the Torah read out loud (*B. Bava Kama* 82a).

The public reading of the Torah is the dramatic centerpiece of the Jewish worship service. The elaborate ritual that accompanies this—with the Torah scroll being removed from the ark and paraded through the congregation while biblical psalm verses and other texts are chanted, both before and after the reading—symbolically recalls the revelation at Sinai.[46] The performance practices of parading the scroll through the congregation and of calling up members of the congregation to recite the Torah blessings, both of which break down the "fourth wall" between the bimah and the congregation, were curtailed in nineteenth- and early twentieth-century Reform congregations (particularly in North America), in the name of order and decorum, but subsequently have been reinstated, at least partially, over the past half-century, to further congregational participation in the worship service.

The verbal liturgy that surrounds the Torah reading (the so-called Torah Service) correspondingly is less elaborate on weekday mornings (C, pp. 104–117; W/F, pp. 104–117) and Shabbat afternoons (which are both identical) than on Shabbat mornings. The liturgy itself is composed mostly of strings of biblical verses. On weekdays and Shabbat afternoons, the traditional liturgy begins with the Torah's description of the Ark of the Covenant—which makes tangible the presence of God in the midst of the people—moving before the Israelites as they proceed through the wilderness (*Vay'hi binsoa haaron*, "When the ark would travel"). Moses acclaims God's presence with the words, "Arise Adonai, and let your enemies be scattered! Let all those who despise You flee from before You!" (Numbers 10:35). In the same way, the ark that houses the Torah scrolls and the scroll itself are associated with the presence of God in the midst of the worshiping congregation. This is followed immediately by Isaiah 2:3, *Ki miTziyon*: "For from out of Zion will come the Torah, and the word of Adonai from Jerusalem." The interjection "Blessed is God who in holiness gave the Torah to the people Israel" is rabbinic in origin. Since the sixteenth century, this has been followed in traditional liturgies by a passage from the *Zohar* (*Vayak'heil*, 206a), where a prayer is recommended for recitation before the open ark: *B'rich sh'mei d'marei alma*, "Praised be the name of the Master of the universe." Then the scroll is removed, and the reader intones Psalm 34:4, *Gadlu l'Adonai iti*: "Exalt Adonai with me, let us extol God's name together." As the Torah moves through the congregation (reminiscent of the Ark of the Covenant moving with the Israelites in the wilderness), the congregation sings David's praise to God from I Chronicles 29:11, *L'cha Adonai*: "Yours, Adonai, is the greatness, might, splendor, triumph, and majesty. . . ." *Mishkan T'filah*, like most Reform rites, omits at the beginning the verses from Numbers about the Ark as well as the passage from the *Zohar*.

It is customary on weekdays and Shabbat afternoons for three people to be called up to the Torah (*aliyah laTorah*) to recite the blessings. In a traditional synagogue, this will be a priest (*kohein*), a Levite (*Leivi*), and a regular Israelite male (*Yisrael*). Reform ritual, having long ago abandoned these remnants of the Temple's cultic hierarchy, simply calls up (at most) three people. No distinction is made on the basis of gender. In the traditional liturgy, there is an elaborate introduction calling up the priest to recite the first blessings; what remains of this in *Mishkan T'filah* is the reader's invitation, *Havu godel*: "Let us declare the greatness of our God and render honor to the Torah." *MT* then gives a Sephardic custom, for the one who receives an *aliyah* to bless the congregation, "May God be with you!" to which the congregation responds, "May God bless you!"

These same texts appear in the Shabbat morning service. Following the reading, a *Mi Shebeirach* blessing is offered for the person called up to the Torah, as well as prayers for healing—just as on Shabbat morning.

When the Torah scroll is lifted up, displayed to the congregation, and then wrapped (*hagbahah* and *g'lilah*), it is customary to recite *V'zot ha-Torah*: "This is the Torah which Moses placed before the people of Israel, God's word through the hand of Moses." The first part of this utterance is Deuteronomy 4:44, and the second part is Numbers 9:23. This was often omitted in Reform prayer books, as it is understood to affirm the literal revelation of the text of the Torah, but was reinstated as an option in *Gates of Prayer.*

The texts recited or sung as the Torah is put back in the ark are identical on weekdays to those recited on Shabbat morning. The prayer leader first urges the congregation, *Y'hal'lu et shem Adonai*, "Let us praise the name of Adonai!" (Psalm 148:13), and the congregation responds with the next verse, *Hodo al eretz v'shamayim*, "God's majesty is above the earth and heaven" (Psalm 148:14), as the Torah again proceeds through the congregation. The weekday psalm for this *hakafah* ("encircling procession") is Psalm 24, *L'Adonai haaretz um'loah*, "The earth and all its fullness are God's." This psalm ends with a reference to a divine procession, presumably into the Temple: *S'u sh'arim rasheichem*, "Lift up your heads, O ye gates, that the Sovereign of glory may enter!" On Shabbat, Psalm 29 is recited at this point, *Havu l'Adonai b'nei eilim*, "Ascribe to Adonai, O divine beings"; this psalm, which describes God's power on display in a thunderstorm is associated by the Rabbis with the giving of the Torah at Sinai amid thunder and lightning, and hence accompanies the Torah procession through the congregation. While the restoration of the *hakafah* when the Torah is removed from the ark has become customary by now in most Reform congregations, the same cannot be said for the second *hakafah* as the Torah is returned to the ark, so most Reform prayer books do not give the *hakafah* psalms at this point. Neither of them appears in *Mishkan T'filah.*

As the Torah is being put back into the ark, Numbers 10:36, *Uv'nucho yomar*, "And when it [the Ark] alighted, he [Moses] would say: Return, O Adonai to the myriads of Israel!" is traditionally recited; this forms a bookend with the previous verse, recited when the Torah is removed from the ark. This, too, is generally omitted from Reform prayer books on account of its somewhat magical associations. The biblical texts conclude with Proverbs 4:2, 3:18, 3:17, and Lamentations 5:21: *Ki lekach tov* ("For I have given you good instruction"), *Eitz chayim hi* ("It is a tree of life"), and *Hashiveinu Adonai eilecha* ("Return us to You, Adonai"; this verse had been omitted in the *Union Prayer Book*, on account of its penitential tone). Noteworthy here is the way in which biblical verses are recontextualized and thereby given new and extended meanings.

Concluding Prayers

Aleinu

ALL SERVICES CONCLUDE with the same two prayers: *Aleinu* and Mourner's *Kaddish* (*Kaddish Yatom*, literally "Orphan's *Kaddish*").[47] That is why these two prayers are located at the back of *Mishkan T'filah* (C, pp. 585–599; Sh, pp. 281–295; W/F, pp. 321–335), just as they were in *Gates of Prayer* (pp. 613–630). Most traditional siddurim reproduce them at the end of each service, as was also done (for most, though not all, services) in all editions of the *Union Prayer Book*. But given the amount and variety of liturgical materials in both *GOP* and *MT* and the number of optional variants for these two prayers, it was deemed more appropriate to print them only once, at the back of the book.

The prayer that begins with the words *Aleinu l'shabei-ach*, "Let us now praise," has a complicated and controversial history, both in medieval Europe and in the modern period. It originated in late antiquity as part of the Rosh HaShanah liturgy (where its full, extended text is still found today, and where it is chanted, in the Ashkenazic rite, according to one of the oldest European Jewish melodies known to us, one of the so-called *manginot miSinai*, "melodies from Sinai"). The topic of the prayer signals its origin: it articulates the *Malchuyot* ("Divine Kingship/Sovereignty") theme that is so prominent on Rosh HaShanah and in conjunction with which the shofar is blown. In Talmudic literature, Rosh HaShanah is "the birthday of the world," the anniversary of Creation, and the day on which God's kingship is proclaimed and acknowledged—in the present by the people Israel; in the messianic future by all human beings.[48] This dissonance between present reality and future messianic expectation is movingly depicted in *Aleinu*: at present it is *our* duty to praise the God of all while the gentiles worship gods that cannot save them, but in the messianic future all humanity will acknowledge that the God of Israel is the one true God—*Bayom hahu yih'yeh Adonai echad ush'mo echad* (Zechariah 14:9): "On that day [to come], Adonai will [truly] become One, and God's Name will be One" because God will be acknowledged by all.

The most dramatic and crucial portion of the Rosh HaShanah liturgy takes place traditionally in the *T'filah* of the *Musaf* (additional) service[49] when the shofar is blown in three sets of blasts over three sets of ten biblical verses each, dealing with the themes of *Malchuyot* (the proclamation of God's rulership over all the earth), *Zichronot* ("Remembrance," invoking God's past acts of providential intervention on behalf of biblical ancestors and the people Israel, and the divine promises of future providential intervention), and *Shofarot* (invoking associations with the blowing of the shofar when God, in the past, was revealed and gave the Torah at Sinai and, in the future, will again redeem the people Israel). Each of these series of blasts is introduced by (1) a poetic introduction to one of the themes; (2) the series of ten thematically relevant scriptural verses; and (3) a section-specific petition asking God to speedily manifest divine rulership over all humanity, take providential note of the people Israel, and sound the great shofar to announce Israel's deliverance. The text *Aleinu l'shabei-ach*, which we now recite daily at the end of every service, is the poetic introduction to the ten verses of *Malchuyot*; indeed, the two scriptural verses with which it ends—*Adonai yimloch l'olam va-ed*, "Adonai will reign forever and ever" (Exodus 15:18), and *V'hayah Adonai l'Melech al kol haaretz. Bayom hahu . . .*, "Adonai will become Sovereign of all the earth. On that day . . ." (Zechariah 14:9)—are the first and the penultimate verses of the ten.[50]

How then did this quintessential Rosh HaShanah prayer get taken into the daily service? The new custom developed in the Rhineland between the twelfth and fourteenth centuries. The liturgist and halachist Ephraim of Bonn mentions *Aleinu* as the sweet-sounding prayer chanted by the martyrs of Blois, France, in 1171 as they were being slaughtered, but the custom of daily recitation in fact may be older.[51] Certainly the narratives that link it to Jewish martyrdom in the period of the Crusades gave it additional popularity and salience. The first paragraph in particular puts in bold relief the medieval Jewish defiance of, and sense of superiority to, non-Jews, and ultimately aroused much Christian ire—so much so that the prayer was frequently censored in western Christendom from the fifteenth century onward. The offending portion of the text reads as follows:

. . . who has not made us like the nations of other lands
Nor placed us like the families of the earth;
Who has not made our lot like theirs
Nor our destiny like that of all their multitudes.
For they prostrate themselves to vanity and emptiness
And pray to a god who cannot save,
While we bow down, prostrate ourselves, and acknowledge
The Supreme King over all kings, the Holy One, praised be He!

The italicized lines are the ones that were censored out of Ashkenazic prayer books because they caused offense to the Church (but they have remained, for example, in the Sephardic and Middle Eastern prayer books, where Church censorship was never an issue).[52]

Because the prayer remained a bone of contention with Christian authorities in the German states well into the eighteenth century[53] and because of its uncomfortable comparison of Jews and gentiles, both early and later Reformers frequently omitted it, abridged it, or paraphrased it. The *Union Prayer Book*, for example, omitted the Hebrew entirely (except for the two lines *Vaanachu kor'im* and *Bayom hahu*, which were treated as musical responses) and gave an emended English text of the first paragraph.[54] *Gates of Prayer* gave four different options for dealing with this text, including restoring the traditional version (but maintaining its censored form). Each of these four options is retained in *Mishkan T'filah*, where, instead of succeeding each other in linear fashion, they are juxtaposed with each other on a two-page spread (C, pp. 586–587; Sh, pp. 282–283; W/F, pp. 322–323).[55]

The first right-page text in *MT* (option one of the four options; C, p. 586; Sh, p. 282; W/F, p. 322) is the Hebrew version of the *UPB*'s English text (the latter is the second left-page text—option four; C, p. 587; Sh, p. 283; W/F, p. 323), accompanied by a more literal translation. This version deletes the offending lines about a Jewish "special destiny" and replaces them with the text that traditionally follows *Vaanachnu* (the first four lines of the text that begins *Shehu noteh shamayim v'yoseid aretz*, "For You spread out the heavens and established the earth"—C, p. 588; Sh, p. 283; W/F, p. 323). The second right-page option (option two; C, p. 586; Sh, p. 282; W/F, p. 322) is the traditional text. While *GOP* gave this text as the first option (p. 615), the editors of *MT* ultimately felt uncomfortable doing that, since its extreme particularism still makes many Jews (and others) uncomfortable. Option three in *MT* (at the top of C, p. 587; Sh, p. 283; W/F, p. 323) corresponds to *GOP*'s fourth option (p. 620). It also deletes the offending two lines but replaces them with a creative text based on the rhetoric and vocabulary of those deleted lines. Jewish difference is now defined in positive terms: our lot is to proclaim and bear witness to God's singularity, and our destiny is to advance the coming of God's rule over all humanity (giving voice to the Reform idea of the mission of Israel). This Hebrew text first appeared in *Service of the Heart*, the British Liberal prayer book edited by Rabbis Chaim Stern and John Rayner that was published in 1967 and served as the model for the North American *Gates of Prayer* (1975).

In *MT*, the entire *Aleinu* prayer is spaced over three two-page spreads (C, pp. 586–587, 588–589, 590–591; Sh, pp. 282–283, 284–285, 286–287; W/F, pp. 322–323, 324–325, 326–327). This is done primarily to offer a number of options for each portion of the text. Since the first portion historically has been the most controversial, as we have noted, *MT* gives more options (four) for that than for any other portion, including giving two options on the right-hand page (C, p. 586; Sh, p. 282; W/F, p. 322) of the first spread (a practice followed nowhere else in *MT*!).

The text that begins *Shehu noteh shamayim*, "For You spread out the heavens" (top of C, p. 588; Sh, p. 284; W/F, p. 324), is actually the immediate continuation of the (traditional) text given at the bottom of the first right-hand page (C, p. 586; Sh, p. 282; W/F, p. 322). The placement of this text on a separate page allows it to be used following *any* of the options on the previous two-page spread (C, pp. 586–587; Sh, pp. 282–283; W/F, pp. 322–323). Thus, the page break at this point is partly for functional reasons. But it also reflects what has come to be standard performance practice in the Reform Movement since the nineteenth century—the congregational (earlier, choral) singing of the line *Vaanachu kor'im* ("We bend the knee") as the climax of this section of the prayer.[56] This line is not sung in more traditional Ashkenazic prayer practice, nor is it singled out for special emphasis; it simply leads directly into the next line, accordingly to the original rhetorical intent of the prayer: "We bow . . . before the supreme King over kings, the Holy One, praised be He, who spread out the heavens and established the earth."[57] So the thematic content of the first section of the traditional *Aleinu* prayer (beginning on the bottom of C, p. 586; Sh, p. 282; W/F, p. 322, and continuing through the middle of C, p. 588; Sh, p. 284; W/F, p. 324) is that in the present age, it is only the Jewish people who acknowledge the one true God, the Maker of heaven and earth, whose power, majesty, and glory are revealed "in the heavens above and on the earth below." Indeed, it is the special covenanted destiny of the Jewish people to acknowledge the true God while other nations pursue false gods who cannot save. This section of the prayer rhetorically finishes with a citation of Deuteronomy 4:39, "Know then this day and take it to heart that Adonai is surely God in the heavens above and on the earth below. There is none else."

The second, and concluding, portion of *Aleinu* begins with the words *Al kein n'kaveh* ("Adonai our God, how soon we hope"; middle of C, p. 588; Sh, p. 284; W/F, p. 324) and ends with *Bayom hahu* ("On that day"; C, p. 590; Sh, p. 286; W/F, p. 326). It expresses the hope that in the messianic future all humanity will acknowledge the God whom Israel alone now worships. This portion, too, concludes with a biblical verse, Zechariah 14:9, "Adonai will become Sovereign over all the earth. On that day Adonai will become One and God's Name [i.e., reputation, acknowledgment] will be One." (Recall that in its original context as the introduction to the verses of *Malchuyot*—Divine Sovereignty—in the Rosh HaShanah liturgy, *Aleinu* passes directly into the citation of ten verses of Scripture, of which Zechariah 14:9 is the ninth; the tenth and last is Deutereonomy 6:4, *Sh'ma Yisrael.*) This part of *Aleinu* includes the line *l'takein olam b'malchut Shaddai*, "perfecting the world under rule of God," which is one of the literary sources for the Hebrew phrase *tikkun olam*, which expresses the contemporary Reform value of mending/repairing/perfecting the world through acts of social justice. The actual usage in the prayer, however, does not refer to human action so much as to divine action: God in the messianic age will cause other nations to acknowledge the sole divinity of the one true God, worshiped in the present only by Israel, and this in itself will bring about a kind of repair in the world—the expression here does not refer to human acts of social justice. That meaning derives, in an extended fashion, from other uses of the phrase *tikkun haolam/tikkun* in classical and medieval rabbinic and kabbalistic literature.

The top left-page alternative of the concluding section of *Aleinu* in *MT* (C, p. 589; Sh, p. 285; W/F, p. 325) is an adaptation of the familiar English version ("May the time not be distant . . .") from the *UPB* (as found in *GOP*, p. 617, bottom). The original version of this text was written by Rabbi David Philipson and appears in his 1891 prayer book for Congregation Bene Israel (now Rockdale Temple) in Cincinnati, *Services for Sabbaths and Holidays* (p. 37), from where it was adapted for the first edition of the *Union Prayer Book* (1894–95). The bottom left-page alternative in *MT* is an abbreviation of the second part of the Hebrew text on the facing page, with a free English rendition. Next is a creative prayer by Rabbi Elyse D. Frishman (top, C, p. 591; Sh, p. 287; W/F, p. 327; following is the traditional last line of *Aleinu*, which is usually sung by the congregation (this, too, a Reform performance practice dating from the nineteenth century).

Aleinu is a fitting prayer with which to conclude every service, since it expands on the vision of a world perfected and redeemed—a vision held before our eyes as we leave the sanctuary and go out again into the world with the incentive to work to make it so.

Meditations before the Mourner's *Kaddish*

Meditations on life and death, read or shared aloud in the spoken language of the congregation, immediately before the recitation of the Mourner's *Kaddish* is a modern, Reform innovation; the traditional service has no real equivalent at this point.[58] Even in Reform prayer books, the custom is relatively late; it seems to appear for the first time in various American congregational prayer books of the 1870s and 1880s[59] and is already a staple of all editions of the *Union Prayer Book* (1894–95; 1918–22; 1940–45). The ten options given in *Mishkan T'filah* (C, pp. 592–597; Sh, pp. 288–293; W/F, pp. 328–333) derive from various sources, some venerable in the North American Reform community and some quite contemporary.

The first (C, p. 592; Sh, p. 288; W/F, p. 328) is a contemporary poem, "Epitaph," by American poet Merrit Malloy.[60] This poem had circulated over the past decade or so in a number of photocopied occasional services before its inclusion in an "official" Reform prayer book. Its message is that our beloved dead can best be memorialized when we share with others the love that we still bear them.

The second (C, p. 593; Sh, p. 289; W/F, p. 329) is a well-known reading by Rabbi Samuel S. Cohon from the 1940 revision of the *UPB* (p. 73, #2; while this text was adapted considerably in *Gates of Prayer*, pp. 627–28, #12, *MT*'s version is much closer to the original). It counsels trust in God in the face of death, rather than yielding to despair.

The third (C, p. 593; Sh, p. 289; W/F, p. 329) is a familiar meditation from *GOP* (p. 627, #10). It was originally written by Rabbis Ted G. Falcon and Howard B. Zyskind and appeared in their *A Common Service*, edited by Rabbi Alvin J. Reines (1972), and was slightly revised for *GOP*. While acknowledging our mortality, it affirms that "something of us can never die," since "with our lives we give life." God is not mentioned here, and the stance is equivocal.

The fourth reading (C, p. 594; Sh, p. 290; W/F, p. 330) is a portion (section 48) of the longer poem-cycle "Song of Myself" by Walt Whitman (published originally in *Leaves of Grass*, 1855). The stance is that of an American transcendentalist—voicing a cosmic Self and a "freethinker's sermon."

The fifth reading (C, p. 594; Sh, p. 290; W/F, p. 330) is part of a verse-play, *Agamemnon*, by the twentieth-century American poet, playwright, and literary scholar William Alfred. It reflects on the terrible paradox of the human condition: that all of us must eventually lose what we love—and yet, love we must.

The sixth reading (C, p. 595; Sh, p. 291; W/F, p. 331), by Rabbi Richard Levy, is familiar from *GOP* (p. 625, #7). Its theme, too, is that "we do best homage to our dead when we live our lives most fully, even in the shadow of our loss," and that "every life finds purpose" in the Source of life.

The seventh reading (C, p. 595; Sh, p. 291; W/F, p. 331), *Yeish Kochavim*, is a poem by Hungarian-Palestinian (i.e., pre-state) poet Hannah Senesh. Upon her emigration to Palestine, Senesh joined a kibbutz, trained as a Haganah fighter, and parachuted back into Yugoslavia to help save Hungarian Jews from the Nazis. She was captured, tortured, and executed. This poem and her *Ashrei Hagafrur* ("Blessed Is the Match") are often used to commemorate Yom HaShoah. The burden of this poem is that those whose physical lights have already gone out nonetheless continue to light the way for us. (There is also a popular musical setting of this text by Cantor Jeff Klepper and Rabbi Daniel Freelander.)

The eighth reading (C, p. 596; Sh, p. 292; W/F, p. 332), by Rabbi Israel

Bettan, also derives from the *UPB* (pp. 74–75, #4). The revised version here is that of *GOP* (p. 623, #2). Its theme, too, is that "grief is a great teacher, when it sends us back to serve the living" and that "even when they are gone, the departed are with us, moving us to live as, in their higher moments, they themselves wished to live."

The ninth reading (C, p. 596; Sh, p. 292; W/F, p. 332), a meditation by Rabbis Chaim Stern and Henry Cohen, derives from *GOP* (p, 628, #13). It is a reflection on Jewish lives lost during the Holocaust and on the struggle for faith after the Holocaust.

The tenth and final reading (p. 597), by Rabbi Peter Knobel, is a *Yizkor* prayer that honors both Jewish and American lives sacrificed to greater causes—freedom, security, ideals.

The selections close with a text by Rabbi Robert I. Kahn, adapted from *GOP* (p. 622), that there introduces the section of readings "Before the *Kaddish*." Here it leads directly into the recitation of the *Kaddish*. It asks us to turn our thoughts to those who have died and to "meditate on the meaning of love and loss, of life and death."

Many voices are heard in these selections: some Jewish, some not; some theistic, some not; some male, some female—all urging us to affirm that life ultimately is meaningful and that our losses can be transformed through caring for all those around us.

The Mourner's *Kaddish*

The last prayer at every service (except for a closing song or benediction) is the *Kaddish* recited by mourners (C, p. 598; Sh, p. 294, W/F, p. 334). In Hebrew, it is called *Kaddish Yatom*, literally "Orphan's *Kaddish*," because it was first recited by a son on behalf of his deceased father; this was later expanded to include as well one's mother, brother, sister, son, daughter, and spouse—the seven relatives for whom recitation of *Kaddish* is mandated in Jewish law. The prayer is mostly in Aramaic, the vernacular language of rabbinic study, rather than Hebrew. The word *kaddish* is an adjective and means "holy" or "sanctified." Several paragraphs of the prayer begin with a series of synonyms for the praise of God—"May God be praised, exalted, sanctified," and so on.

Any discussion of the Mourner's *Kaddish* usually begins with the observation that the prayer itself includes no mention of death and, indeed, has nothing to do with death. While homiletical explanations for this often are proffered, the actual reason is that the *Kaddish* was not originally a mourner's prayer at all. It was initially recited at the conclusion of a public exposition of Torah (*d'rashah*; hence the use of Aramaic, the language of popular discourse) and expressed the fervent hope for the speedy coming "in your lifetime, in your days, and in the lifetime of all (now living) Israelites" of God's messianic kingdom—when the world would finally be set right, all people would acknowledge the true God, and Israel would be restored to its land and governance (see *B. Sotah* 49a, *B. B'rachot* 3a, and *Midrash on Proverbs* 14:28). The theme, then, is the same as that of *Aleinu*; that is why these two prayers together nicely round out the service.

How the *Kaddish* prayer came to be associated with mourners is an interesting story. As we noted in our treatment of the *Chatzi Kaddish* (pp. 35–36), the *Kaddish* assumes several different forms and functions in early post-Talmudic literature. In the eighth century it is mentioned as being recited immediately after the Torah is read (Tractate *Sof'rim* 10). This same source, from the Land of Israel, also notes that at the conclusion of the additional (*Musaf*) service on Shabbat, the congregation exits the synagogue to greet the mourners (who wait outside and do not enter the building during the Shabbat services on account of their mourning); the congregation blesses them with the benediction for mourners (*Birkat Aveilim*; this blessing is no longer recited and its exact formulation is lost to us). This is followed by the recitation of the *Kaddish* (the exact form of the text is not specified), as a prayer of comfort and hope for the speedy coming of God's kingdom. *Seder Rav Amram*, the first prayer code (Babylonia, before 875 BCE), knows the *Kaddish* as a service marker, recited at the conclusion of each portion of the service (as is the case today in a traditional service), but relates nothing about a mourner's *Kaddish*. That custom, it turns out, develops later, in the Rhineland.

The late homiletical text *Seder Eliyahu Zuta* (eighth century, from the Land of Israel) and, more extensively, the Franco-German liturgical code *Machzor Vitry* (late eleventh century) both give variants of a legend according to which a famous rabbi (Yochanan ben Zakkai, according to *Seder Eliyahu Zuta* 17; Akiva, according to *Machzor Vitry* 144) meets a man gathering either sticks or thorns. The man turns out to be the spirit of a dead man; he is gathering kindling to stoke the fires of punishment that will purge his sins. He informs the rabbi that his punishment will cease if the infant son about to be born to his pregnant wife becomes so learned in Torah that he will be able to lead the congregation in prayer—specifically in those prayers that require a congregational response: *Bar'chu* and the *Kaddish*. The rabbi then determines to teach Torah to the infant son of the deceased man so that he will be able to lead the congregation in prayer and thereby release his father's soul from Purgatory. The account in *Machzor Vitry* concludes by noting that "for this reason, it is customary at the end of the Sabbath for the prayers to be led by a man whose father and mother are deceased, so that he may recite *Bar'chu* or *Kaddish*."

The idea here is that by leading the congregation in prayer at the end of the Sabbath, when the dead are thought to return to their punishment (even the dead get a day off for Shabbat, the foretaste of the redeemed world!), the orphan is able thereby to redeem his parents' souls from purgation. This, then, is the origin of the custom of having mourners recite the *Kaddish*—actually, of leading the congregation so that they respond, *Amein. Y'hei sh'meih raba m'varach l'alam ul'almei almaya*, "Amen. Blessed be God's great name to all eternity." It is the significance of the communal activity in its *relational* aspect as much as, if not more than, the recitation itself that is initially deemed to be efficacious; this is why, in more traditional communities, the entire service—certainly in the afternoon or evening—will be led by a person observing the *yahrzeit*, or anniversary, of a parent's death.[61]

The custom of reciting *Kaddish* for one's deceased close relatives, and the other memorial customs developed in medieval Ashkenaz, became so deeply rooted in Jewish culture and personal observance that there was never any thought of attenuating most of them in the modern world. In fact, the prayer book of the earliest ongoing Reform congregation (Hamburg, 1819) elaborates on the Mourner's *Kaddish* in such a way as to actually make it a mourner's prayer for the dead. Borrowing from the Spanish-Portuguese Sephardic memorial rite (*Hashkavah*) and the Ashkenazic burial *Kaddish*,[62] the Hamburg prayer book added the following paragraph (in Aramaic):

> For Israel, for the righteous, and for all those who have departed from this world according to the will of God, may there be abundant peace and a good portion in the world to come,

> and grace and compassion from the Maker of heaven and
> earth, and let us say: Amen.

This paragraph (sometimes with minor alterations) was taken over into virtually every Reform prayer book in Europe and North America up to the second half of the twentieth century. It figures prominently in all editions of the *Union Prayer Book*, though most Reform Jews were not capable of reciting it in Aramaic. (Often, the English paraphrase, "The departed whom we now remember have entered into the peace of life eternal . . . ," would be substituted at this point.) *Gates of Prayer* (1975) eliminated it entirely, restoring the traditional text of the Mourner's *Kaddish* (the text that was known to those Reform Jews who had come from a more traditional upbringing).

In the Hamburg prayer book, the *Kaddish* is introduced by another Hebrew paragraph, taken from the Spanish-Portuguese Sephardic *Hashkavah* ritual that draws on a variety of Talmudic texts as follows:

> All Israel have a place in the world to come, as it is written,
> *Your people are all righteous; they will possess the land forever*
> (Isaiah 60:21). [*M. Sanhedrin* 10:1]
>
> Happy is the person whose labor has been in Torah and has
> thereby given pleasure to his Creator. He grew up with a good
> name and departed the world with a good name, and concerning him did the wise King Solomon say, *Better a good name
> than precious oil and the day of death than the day of birth*
> (Ecclesiastes 7:1). [*B. B'rachot* 17a]
>
> Learn much Torah and you will earn much reward—and know
> that the reward for the righteous is in the world to come.
> [*M. Avot* 2:21]

This is the first instance in a Reform prayer book of what would become the meditation, or series of meditations, in the vernacular before the *Kaddish* (see above, p. 92).

Traditionally, only the mourners rise and recite the *Kaddish*; this is a way of acknowledging them publicly. The same custom is found in nineteenth-century Reform prayer books (although the prayer leader would lead them in the recitation). The Reform custom of having the entire congregation rise and recite the *Kaddish* seems to be relatively late. Some explain it as a post-Holocaust custom, in which the entire congregation recites *Kaddish* on behalf of those who have no descendants to recite for them. But the custom appears before the end of the Second World War and might also have been motivated by a desire not to embarrass any mourners who were not capable of reciting the *Kaddish* on their own (this is the only prayer to be transliterated—in Ashkenazic pronunciation—in the *Union Prayer Book*, and only in the 1940 revision). A custom gaining popularity in many Reform congregations today is to ask the mourners to rise first (often as the names of the deceased are read) and then to ask the rest of the congregation to join them; this does justice to both concerns.

The persistence and emotional attachment to the Mourner's *Kaddish* (and to Jewish mourning customs in general) results from the tangible link that contemporary Jews thereby enact to both their immediate families and their extended family, the entire Jewish people and its traditions.

Closing Hymns

Adon Olam, Yigdal, Ein K'Eloheinu

ONE OF THE EARLIEST practical liturgical reforms of the nineteenth century was the consistent inclusion of opening and closing hymns (often in the vernacular) at each service, on the model of Protestant church services. But there were also native Jewish precedents for this practice: the Erev Shabbat service in the Ashkenazic rite, for example, ends with *Adon Olam*, the Italian rite concludes this service with *Yigdal*, and the Persian rite concludes it with *Ein K'Eloheinu*.[63] All three of these hymns commonly appear in Reform prayer books as concluding hymns. There is also much unison congregational singing in the liturgical customs of Spanish-Portuguese (Sephardic) Jews, and this was consciously borrowed by early Reformers (indeed, all the cantors of the Hamburg Temple—the first ongoing German Reform congregation—up through the first decade of the twentieth century were Sephardim, the Hebrew pronunciation used there was Sephardic, and many of the melodies used throughout the nineteenth century for Hebrew texts were Spanish-Portuguese[64]).

The Hebrew hymns (*piyutim*) that have been sung at the end of the service in Reform congregations since the early nineteenth century all derive from the traditional liturgy but were not written as "closing hymns"; indeed, they were not composed for any particular liturgical "location." Since the sixteenth century, *Adon Olam* and *Yigdal* both appear at the beginning of the morning service, as part of the preparation for prayer, in many rites. *Ein K'Eloheinu* appears before *Aleinu* in the Shabbat additional (*Musaf*) service and in this same position in the daily morning service in all rites except for Ashkenaz.[65] We will briefly examine each of these hymns in turn.

Adon Olam ("Eternal God"[66]; C, p. 625; Sh, p. 325; W/F, p. 361) is variously proposed to have been written by the Babylonian *gaon* Sherira (906-1006) or one earlier, or by the Spanish poet Solomon ibn Gabirol (1021-1070). In fact, we do not know who wrote it, where, or when—except that the style (rhyme and regular meter) is definitely that common in the Judeo-Muslim world. Ismar Elbogen notes that it began to appear in manuscript siddurim shortly before the advent of printing, in the late fifteenth century.[67] This very moving poem extols the unique, eternal, and transcendent God who is at the same time the immanent Redeemer and Helper of every individual. The last stanza, "Into Your hand I entrust my spirit / when I sleep and when I wake, / and with my spirit, my body also; / Adonai is with me and I shall not fear"—a powerful statement of personal faith—suggests that the poem might have been written to be recited at bedtime (and, indeed, it concludes the recitation of the *Sh'ma* on one's bed every night and is often recited on one's deathbed). The poem has between two and five additional lines in the Sephardic rites; some of them are clearly later additions.

Yigdal Elohim Chai ("May the living God be exalted"; C, p. 628, Sh, p. 324; W/F, p. 364) is a poetic setting of Maimonides's Thirteen Principles of Faith (originally formulated, in prose form, in his commentary to the *Mishnah*—written in the decade between 1158 and 1168—to Tractate *Sanhedrin*, chapter 10).[68] The poem is generally ascribed to the fourteenth-century Italian poet Daniel ben Judah. This poem, too, is rhymed with regular meter, and it has thirteen verses—each elaborating one of the thirteen principles. These are (1) God's existence; (2) God's unity and singularity; (3) God's incorporeality; (4) God's eternality; (5) God as Creator of all; (6) God's gift of prophecy and prophets to Israel; (7) Moses as the greatest of the prophets; (8) the Torah as God's unique revelation to Israel; (9) the singularity and immutability of God's Torah; (10) God's omniscience; (11) God's providence, rewarding the upright and punishing the wicked; (12) the future coming of the Messiah to inaugurate the divine redemption of Israel; (13) God's resurrection of the dead at the time of the future redemption. Many Reform prayer books (including *Gates of Prayer* and *Mishkan T'filah*) have altered the last two verses, since their assertions have been rejected by most Reform theology: instead of the coming of a personal messiah, these revisions substitute *p'dut olam*, "an everlasting redemption, when all that lives and breathes will witness God's deliverance"; instead of a physical resurrection of the dead, they substitute the less specific *chayei olam nata b'tocheinu*, "God has implanted eternal life within us." (The latter phrase comes from the blessing recited after the Torah reading; it was also used by Rabbi David Einhorn as a substitute for *m'chayeih hameitim* in his prayer book and taken over from there into the *Union Prayer Book*; see above, p. 69.)

Ein K'Eloheinu ("There is none like our God"; C, p. 626; Sh, p. 322; W/F, p. 362) is the oldest of these three hymns; it is already found in *Machzor Vitry* (twelfth century). Its style, too, is the simplest: there is no rhyme or meter, merely the repetition of the same four epithets for God in each verse, with only the first word varying from verse to verse. The hymn is recited daily (at the end of the morning service) in the Sephardic rite, but only on Shabbat (before *Aleinu* in the additional service) in the Ashkenazic rite. The first word of the first three verses forms the acrostic *Amen*, followed by *baruch* and *atah* as the first words in the next two verses—a helpful reminder of the order of the verses. It is customary among Ladino-speaking Jews to sing most of the traditional hymns in either or both Hebrew and Ladino (Judeo-Spanish), often going back and forth between the two languages. This custom is acknowledged in one of the settings of *Ein K'Eloheinu* given in *Mishkan T'filah* (C, p. 631; Sh, p. 327; W/F, p. 367).

Weekday Afternoon and Evening Services

As previously noted above, the weekday afternoon and evening services are briefer than the weekday morning service and contain only the basic service elements. The afternoon service is composed only of the *T'filah*, which is recited three times daily. (It is, in fact, the rabbinic requirement to pray the *T'filah* also in the afternoon that generates this service.) The only textual difference from the morning *T'filah* is that, in the Ashkenazic rite and the Reform prayer books (like *Mishkan T'filah*) that basically follow it, the final *T'filah* blessing, for peace, is shorter and begins with the words *Shalom Rav* instead of *Sim Shalom*. This is a variant version that appears only in the Ashkenazic rite.

The *T'filah* is preceded by *Ashrei* (Psalm 145 with additional verses), by way of preparation to pray, as well as *Chatzi Kaddish*, and followed by the standard closing prayers (*Aleinu* and Mourner's *Kaddish*). Unlike in *Gates of Prayer*, there are no separate pages in *MT* devoted to the weekday afternoon service, but the table of contents lists this service and gives page numbers for where each of its components, in order, may be found in the volume.

The weekday evening service is composed of the evening recitation of the *Sh'ma* and Its Blessings (in their shorter, evening form already discussed) and the evening *T'filah*, which, like its afternoon counterpart, uses the shorter version of the final blessing, for peace, that begins with the words *Shalom Rav*. Because the evening service is recited at nightfall, when everyone wants to get home for dinner and sleep rather than lingering in the synagogue, there is, traditionally, no reader's repetition of the *T'filah*; it is recited silently by every individual. Reform practice has often been for the first three blessings to be recited together out loud, with the rest recited silently. The *T'filah* is again followed by the standard closing prayers, *Aleinu* and Mourner's *Kaddish*. Many Reform Jews will be familiar with the weekday evening service from having attended shivah minyanim. It is found at the very beginning of *MT* (C, pp. 2–20; W/F, pp. 2–20), after which the reader is directed to the weekday *T'filah* and closing prayers, all of which appear later in the book in separate sections.

Since we have mentioned here the alternative version of the final *T'filah* blessing in the Ashkenazic afternoon and evening services (*Shalom Rav* instead of *Sim Shalom*), we should ask the obvious question: Why do we have a different textual version here for a standard prayer? This question actually is phrased inside out, from a historical perspective. We learn from the differences between the Talmud of the Land of Israel and the Babylonian Talmud, as well as from the textual evidence of prayer books that were preserved in fragmentary form in the Cairo Genizah, that there were from the outset different ways of formulating what is essentially the same benediction or prayer with respect to matters of theme and topic. The traditions of the Land of Israel and Babylonia formulated and selected different wordings to be more or less standard. Indeed, within the tradition of the Land of Israel there are often two or more text types of the same *T'filah* benediction (not taking into account the different poetic versions that exist of these benedictions). It happened, then, that some of the medieval rites, in order to preserve some of these "alternate" versions, chose to distribute them among various daily or occasional services.

In our case, the Ashkenazic rite of Germany and, later, Poland (but not any of the other rites!) chose to preserve two different wordings of the *Shalom* benediction: a longer form for the main, morning service and a shorter one for the briefer afternoon and evening services. The *chatimah*, or "seal" of the benediction—the concluding benedictory formula that summarizes its theme—is the same for both versions, *Baruch atah Adonai, ham'vareich et amo Yisrael bashalom*, "Praised are You, Adonai, who blesses Your people Israel with peace."

And while we are speaking about alternative textual versions, this was originally the Babylonian *chatimah*; the one from the Land of Israel is *Baruch . . . oseih hashalom*, "Praised . . . Maker of peace." This Eretz Yisraeli *chatimah* was also taken up into the Ashkenazic rite for the festivals and High Holy Days together with liturgical poems (*piyutim*) from the Land of Israel that it accompanied. And that is how, when some of the nineteenth-century editors of Reform prayer books, like Rabbis Isaac Mayer Wise, David Einhorn, and Samuel Adler, were looking for a less "particularistic" *chatimah* for this benediction than the traditional (Babylonian) one, they seized upon the more generic wording that they knew from the Ashkenazic High Holy Day and festival liturgies—*oseih hashalom*—without knowing that this came, in fact, from the old rite of the Land of Israel!

The daily liturgy forms the core of the liturgy for the entire year. The services for Shabbat, the festivals, and the High Holy Days are simply variants of and additions to the daily liturgy, prompted by the specific themes and concerns of those special days on the Jewish calendar. This will become clear in our discussions of the Shabbat and festival services that follow.

Shabbat

Introduction to Shabbat Services

SHABBAT IN JEWISH TRADITION is a time for rest, for refreshment of body and soul, and for Torah study. It is also a time for fellowship in community. All of these themes and purposes are reflected in the Shabbat liturgy. The evening service at the beginning of Shabbat (Erev Shabbat) is preceded by *Kabbalat Shabbat*, an elaborate ritual for welcoming Shabbat that goes back to the Safed community of kabbalists in the sixteenth century. It is filled with celebration and song. This leads directly into the evening service proper, which follows the same structure as the weekday evening service but contains special prayers and readings for Shabbat, as will be noted below.

The morning service for Shabbat, which is the liturgical centerpiece of the day, is longer than the daily morning service (since, traditionally, no one is hurrying off to work after the service). In keeping with the desire and need to study on Shabbat, it contains a fuller Torah service, a longer Torah reading, and a reading from the prophetic literature as well (haftarah). This is followed by a *d'var Torah* (a brief homiletical exposition of the Torah reading) or a fuller sermon. Traditionally, this leads into the additional (*Musaf*) service, which is composed solely of an additional *T'filah* recitation, with appropriate textual variations, and corresponds to the additional Shabbat sacrifice offered in the Temple. Most (but not all) Reform prayer books have abandoned this service.

The afternoon service for Shabbat is the same as that for weekdays, with the addition of a brief Torah reading from the beginning of the following week's *parashah* (the same reading, with the same Torah liturgy, that is performed on Monday and Thursday mornings during the following week).

The evening service at the end of Shabbat (*Motza-ei Shabbat*) is essentially a weekday evening service, with additional psalm readings at the beginning and end of the service, requesting protection during the week, and the insertion of the *Havdalah* benediction, distinguishing between the holy Shabbat and the ordinary weekdays to follow, into the first intermediate blessing of the weekday *T'filah. Havdalah* is recited again over a cup of wine and a newly lit candle at the end of the service. *Mishkan T'filah* includes the *Havdalah* ceremony over the cup of wine (C, p. 610; Sh, p. 306), but not the *Havdalah* insertion into the first intermediate blessing in the weekday *T'filah.*

Erev Shabbat *Kabbalat Panim*
Welcoming the Congregation before Welcoming Shabbat

BEGINNINGS AND ENDINGS are important—as in life, so in liturgy. How does one enter a place of worship? How does one enter the act of worship? The readiness is all. Preparation is the key. That is why, according to the Mishnah (*B'rachot* 5:1), "the pious ones of old would wait an hour before praying, in order to direct their hearts to God."

We, too, need to transition into prayer, particularly on Erev Shabbat, when we come to the synagogue after being preoccupied with the daily concerns of the past week. That is why *Mishkan T'filah* precedes the Erev Shabbat service with a series of personal and communal meditations to help each of us (and all of us together) to prepare ourselves for worship, to focus on the big issues in our lives rather than just the small stuff.

MT here also implicitly reflects some of the work of Synagogue 3000, specifically some of the research and thinking that went into Ron Wolfson's *The Spirituality of Welcoming*.[69] Wolfson stresses the importance of being a welcoming congregation, of greeting people, of making each individual feel valued and "at home." Bringing people together, creating a community, must take place at the outset of a service before, as well as while, beginning to pray. This is most often achieved musically, through singing together. Merri Arian, who was the director of music at Synagogue 3000, writes:

> How we begin the prayer experience is important. We need to recognize where the congregants are coming from—a missed train, a late babysitter, a hassled week at work, a week of being indoors with a sick child. They need to be welcomed into the prayer experience. . . . When carefully planned, the music at the beginning of the service can do just that.[70]

This is the reason why *MT* gives a two-page spread of "entry" songs (C, pp. 128–129; Sh, pp. 10–11) before *Kabbalat Shabbat*. The entire preparatory section—meditations, songs, candle lighting, and *Kiddush*

(C, pp. 120–129; Sh, pp. 2–11)—is called *Kabbalat Panim*, "Welcoming" (literally "receiving/acknowledging faces"). It is about community-building and getting ready to worship together.

The two traditional rituals that appear in this section—candle lighting and *Kiddush* over a cup of wine—initially were performed only in the home, where the Shabbat meal would be eaten. But the custom of reciting *Kiddush* in the synagogue on Erev Shabbat is already known in the Babylonian Talmud (*P'sachim* 100b–101a) and is justified by the claim that travelers often stayed in the synagogue over Shabbat and ate their meals there. Candle lighting traditionally is done before Shabbat begins. While mindful of the prohibition against lighting a fire on Shabbat, the Rabbis nonetheless held that a lamp should be burning at home throughout Shabbat, so that the evening meal is not eaten in darkness, which would diminish one's Shabbat joy (*oneg Shabbat*).[71] Kindling the Shabbat lights in the synagogue as part of the Erev Shabbat service is a relatively late Reform custom: it appears for the first time in the 1940 revision of the *Union Prayer Book* and coincides with the popularity of the after-dinner Friday evening service in North American Reform congregations. The blessing over the Shabbat light(s) is first found in *Seder Rav Amram* (before 875 CE), although its formal analogue, the blessing over the Chanukah candles, already appears in the Babylonian Talmud (*Shabbat* 23a).[72]

The familiar text of the *Kiddush* over a cup of wine also appears for the first time in *Seder Rav Amram*. This is the Babylonian formulation; the wording in the old rite of the Land of Israel, known to us through fragmentary prayer books in the Cairo Genizah, is a bit different. *MT* (C, pp. 122–123; Sh, pp. 4–5) gives the full traditional text for the ritual. The name, *Kiddush* ("Sanctification"), is short for *Kiddush HaYom* or *K'dushat HaYom* ("Sanctification of the Day")—it signifies that, through the verbal act of reciting this formula, we mark out the beginning of the sacred day (Shabbat or festival) and take upon ourselves those observances and restrictions that make it distinctive and set apart (*kadosh*). Only the final paragraph (*asher kid'shanu b'mitzvotav v'ratzah vanu*) is actually the *Kiddush* benediction. The short blessing over wine that precedes it (*borei p'ri hagafen*) is recited whenever wine is drunk. On Friday evenings both of these blessings traditionally are preceded by verses from Genesis 1:31–2:3, which recount the primal sanctification of the seventh day by God at the end of the six days of Creation. (These verses were omitted in the *Union Prayer Book*, likely because of their mythic character—lest they should be construed literally.) Theologically speaking, the *Kiddush* benediction praises God for having sanctified the Jewish people through the gift of Shabbat (and the sacred calendar). Shabbat serves as a twofold reminder of God's mighty deeds—the act of Creation and the redemption from Egypt. Thus, at the very beginning of Shabbat we proclaim its cosmic and historic significance.

Traditionally, *Kiddush* in the synagogue is recited after the *T'filah* and before *Aleinu*. Many Reform congregations save it for the very end of the service, leading into the *Oneg Shabbat* reception, when congregants can eat and drink. *MT* chooses to give the *Kiddush* at the very beginning of the service, right after candle lighting, in order to group together these two rituals that are also performed at home and that welcome the entry of Shabbat.

Kabbalat Shabbat
Welcoming the Sabbath

Overview

Kabbalat Shabbat ("Welcoming the Sabbath"; C, pp. 130–141; Sh, pp. 12–23) is one of the latest rituals included in the traditional liturgies of all Jewish communities. It dates to the sixteenth century and is one of the many ritual innovations developed and introduced by kabbalists who gathered in Safed, in the northern Galilee region of the Land of Israel, under the inspiration of Rabbi Isaac Luria (whose acronym is Ha-AR"I; "the Lion"; the letters stand for ***A****doneinu* [= "Our Master"] **R**abbi **Y**itzchak).

The *Kabbalat Shabbat* ritual that we are familiar with today consists of two elements: the singing or recitation of seven psalms, corresponding to the seven days of the week,[73] and the singing of *L'cha Dodi*, a kabbalistic hymn composed by Rabbi Solomon Alkabetz in Safed that welcomes the Sabbath as the bride of Israel (but, as we will spell out below, this hymn has deeper kabbalistic meanings as well). The first six psalms, 95–99 and 29, describe the power of God as Creator of the world; all creation sings God's praises. This, of course, corresponds to and is meant both to recall and to enact the Creation story at the beginning of the Torah. The seventh psalm, 92, is *Mizmor shir l'yom haShabbat*, "A song for Shabbat," and represents the seventh day of Creation, the Sabbath itself. The brief Psalm 93, "Adonai is sovereign, God is robed in grandeur," concludes the ritual. Although technically an eighth psalm, the Rabbis treated this as an appendage to Psalm 92, since it exalts the reign of God over nature that is established at the end of the six days of Creation. *L'cha Dodi* is sung between the sixth and seventh psalms, so as to heighten the anticipation of the arrival of Shabbat (which is enacted with the recitation of Psalm 92).

Today's *Kabbalat Shabbat* ritual differs in many respects from its earliest versions, which are described in sixteenth-century mystical-pietist manuals. Today's ritual is performed in the synagogue, directly before the Friday evening service (which technically begins with *Bar'chu*); it is experienced by most worshipers as actually being *part* of that service. The early *Kabbalat Shabbat* rituals (and there were several different ones) took place outside, in the hills surrounding the town of Safed, with an unimpeded view of the sun sinking in the west. The Friday evening service in the synagogue was a totally separate entity that took place at a later hour. Gradually, as the *Kabbalat Shabbat* ritual spread and became more popular, it was moved (still outside) into the synagogue courtyard, after which everyone would go inside for the evening prayers. Finally, the ritual was moved into the synagogue, where it takes place now. The only remnant of its earlier performance outside is when the congregation rises for the last stanza of *L'cha Dodi* and turns to face the western door, where the sun is setting, exclaiming *Bo-i chalah! Bo-i chalah!* ("Enter, O bride! Enter, O bride!").

Today's ritual contains seven psalms; but this (Ashkenazic) custom is not found in the early sixteenth-century mystical-pietist manuals, which were composed by Sephardic Jews. These manuals list only Psalms 29 and 92 (and 93). There were also other versions of *L'cha Dodi* early on, besides the one by Solomon Alkabetz that has become traditional.[74] The early rituals were accompanied by various physical activities that are no longer performed. Here are excerpts from several manuals that describe the early *Kabbalat Shabbat* ritual(s):

> Every Sabbath eve they go out into the field or to the courtyard of the synagogue and welcome the Sabbath. Everyone dresses in his Sabbath garments. They recite the Psalm " [Ascribe] to the Lord, O heavenly beings" [Ps. 29] and the Sabbath hymn [*L'cha Dodi*], followed by the "Psalm for the Sabbath day" [Ps. 92].[75]

> A number of groups go out on the eve of the Sabbath [into an open field] while it is yet day, dressed in white clothes, and welcome the Sabbath. They recite the Psalm "[Ascribe] to the Lord, O heavenly beings" [Ps. 29] and the hymn *L'cha Dodi*, as well as the "Psalm for the Sabbath day" [Ps. 92]. Then they say, "Come, O bride."[76]

> This is the order of *Kabbalat Shabbat*: Go out into an open field and recite: "Come and let us go into the field of holy

> apple trees"[77] in order to welcome the Sabbath Queen. . . . Stand in one place; it is preferable if you are able to do so on a high spot, one which is [clear] as far as one can see in front of him, and for a distance of four cubits behind him. Turn your face to the West where the sun sets, and at the very moment that it sets close your eyes and place your left hand on your chest and your right hand upon your left. Direct your concentration—while in a state of awe and trembling as one who stands in the presence of the King—so as to receive the special holiness of the Sabbath.
>
> Begin by reciting the Psalm: "[Ascribe] to the Lord, O heavenly beings" [Ps. 29], singing it entirely in a sweet voice. Following this, recite three times: "Come, O bride, Come, O bride, O Sabbath Queen." Next, recite: "A psalm, a song for the Sabbath day" [Ps. 92] in its entirety, followed by "The Lord is King; He is robed in majesty" until "for all time" [Ps. 93]. Then open your eyes and return home.
>
> Enter and wrap yourselves in a fringed prayer shawl. . . . Circle the table—prepared with the Sabbath loaves—walking around it several times until you have repeated everything which you had recited while in the field.[78]

This ritual is based, in part, on a Talmudic precedent (*B. Shabbat* 119a): "Rabbi Chanina would wrap himself in his tallit and stand toward evening on Fridays, saying, 'Come, let us go out and welcome Queen Sabbath [*Bo-u v'neitzei likrat Shabbat hamalkah*].' Rabbi Yannai would dress himself on Friday afternoon and say, 'Come, O bride! Come, O bride! [*Bo-i chalah! Bo-i chalah!*]'"

Reform prayer books, historically, have been somewhat wary of the *Kabbalat Shabbat* ritual, both because of its kabbalistic origins and because it lengthens the Shabbat eve service. It is omitted entirely in the earliest Reform prayer books (Berlin, 1816 and 1817; Hamburg, 1819). It also does not appear in the several editions of the *Union Prayer Book* (1895, 1918, 1940), although Psalm 92 is retained. The 1940 revision, which offers five service options for Friday night (one for each Shabbat of the month), begins each of them with one of the *Kabbalat Shabbat* texts: Psalm 92, an abbreviated *L'cha Dodi*, Psalm 97, Psalm 98, and an abbreviated Psalm 95.

Gates of Prayer (1975) restores *Kabbalat Shabbat* as a liturgical unit in its first Friday evening service. It provides the full texts of Psalms 29 and 92–93 and *L'cha Dodi*, and abbreviated texts of Psalms 95–99. *Mishkan T'filah* gives fuller texts of Psalms 95–99, although still abbreviated.

Kabbalat Shabbat provides the opportunity to welcome the Sabbath with song and music, and that is how it is enacted today in most Reform congregations.

Psalms 95–99, 29

As we pointed out above, the *Kabbalat Shabbat* ritual consists of two parts: the singing or recitation of seven psalms (in the Ashkenazic rite) and the singing of the hymn *L'cha Dodi*. The seven psalms represent the seven days of Creation, and thus the whole is a kind of enactment of the Creation story in the first chapter of Genesis, culminating in the arrival of Shabbat. Psalms 95–99 and 29 (C, pp. 130–37; Sh, pp. 12–19), representing the six workdays of Creation, precede the singing of *L'cha Dodi* (C, pp. 138–39; Sh, pp. 20–21), while Psalm 92, "A song for Shabbat" (C, p. 140; Sh, p. 22), and Psalm 93 (C, p. 141; Sh, p. 23) follow it.

Within the Psalter, the five psalms 95–99 form a continuous thematic group: they declaim in song the praise of God, who created, and hence rules over, heaven and earth. Psalm 95 begins with the exhortation, "Come, let us sing joyously to Adonai, raise a shout for our Rock and Deliverer!" Psalms 96 and 98 begin identically: "Sing to Adonai a new song!" Psalms 97 and 99 also begin identically: "Adonai reigns!" Thus Israel and all creation sing out to God and acclaim/acknowledge the sovereignty of the Creator of heaven and earth, whose work of Creation is finished on the seventh day. Psalm 95:4–5 exults that "in God's hands are the depths of the earth; the peaks of the mountains are God's. God's is the sea, God made it; and the land, which God's hands fashioned." This theme continues in Psalm 96:5–6, 11–12: "Adonai made the heavens. Glory and majesty are before God; strength and splendor are in God's temple. Let the heavens rejoice and the earth exult; let the sea and all within it thunder, the fields and everything in them exult." And in Psalm 97:1–2: "Let the earth exult, the many islands rejoice! Dense clouds are around God, righteousness and justice are the base of God's throne." And in Psalm 98:7–8: "Let the sea and all within it thunder, the world and all its inhabitants; let the rivers clap their hands, the mountains sing joyously together." And in Psalm 99:1: "Adonai, enthroned on cherubim, is sovereign, peoples tremble, the earth quakes."

As we can see in this last verse, the Creation theme leads directly into (and indeed justifies) the sovereignty theme: because God created the world, God appropriately rules over and judges the world: "For God is coming to rule [= judge] the earth; God will rule the world justly and its peoples with equity" (Psalm 98:9; cf. the almost identical wording at Psalm 96:13). "Mighty ruler who loves justice, it was You who established equity, You who worked righteous judgment in Jacob" (Psalm 99:4). The theme of God's judgment and justice is also amplified closer to home: "O you who love Adonai, hate evil! God guards the lives of God's loyal ones, saving them from the hand of the wicked. Light is sown for the righteous, radiance for the upright. O you righteous, rejoice in Adonai and acclaim God's holy name" (Psalm 97:10–12). It is easy to get caught up in the breathless praise of God here when these psalms are sung to stirring and rhythmic melodies.

Psalm 29 is also breathless and dramatic. Here the power of God is on display in a thunderstorm: "The God of glory thunders, Adonai, over the mighty waters . . . breaks cedars . . . kindles flames of fire . . . convulses the wilderness . . . and strips forests bare." Again, the theme is God's power both to tame the wild, chaotic forces of nature and to release them: "Adonai sat enthroned at the Flood; Adonai sits enthroned, sovereign forever"—"while in God's temple all say 'Glory!'" The inclusion of this psalm in *Kabbalat Shabbat* is thus based on the common theme of the Creator God enthroned over the forces of nature. There is, however, yet another association between this psalm and the Sabbath day. Early rabbinic midrash (biblical interpretation) connected the images of the thunderstorm in this psalm with the thunder and lightning through which the Torah was given to the Israelites at Sinai. Psalm 29 is treated as an "intertext" to the narrative in Exodus 19 (*M'chilta D'Rabbi Yishmael, Amalek*, 3; *Bachodesh*, 1). That is why this psalm traditionally is also sung when the Torah is being paraded through the congregation on Shabbat morning, before it is returned to the ark. There is yet another rabbinic tradition that the Torah was given to Israel on Shabbat (*B. Shabbat* 86a–87b), which further serves to link the recitation of Psalm 29 to this day of the week.

The recitation of Psalm 29 provides a vivid and dramatic prelude to the singing of the Shabbat hymn *L'cha Dodi*, which immediately follows.

L'cha Dodi: Greeting the Bride

The centerpiece and emotional high point of the *Kabbalat Shabbat* ritual unquestionably comes when the entire congregation joins in the singing of the hymn *L'cha Dodi* ("Come, My Beloved!")—the moment of greeting the Sabbath bride. This hymn—for which there are more melodies than for any other Jewish liturgical text—was composed by the sixteenth-century Safed kabbalist Solomon Alkabetz, whose brother-in-law Moses Cordovero was the primary kabbalistic teacher in Safed before the arrival in 1569 of Isaac Luria. Alkabetz's name is inscribed in the poem as an acrostic: the first letter of the first word of each of the first eight stanzas together spell out "Sh'lomoh HaLevi." Each stanza is preceded by the following refrain:

> *L'cha dodi likrat kalah, / p'nei Shabbat n'kab'lah*
> Beloved, come to meet the bride; / let us greet Shabbat.

This primary image of the poem, going out to greet the Sabbath bride, derives from the two previously-cited Talmudic traditions (above, p. 114).

Of the nine stanzas in this hymn, the first two describe the Sabbath, drawing on several well-known midrashic traditions (see below). The next six address the ruined and abandoned city of Jerusalem, urging her in the words of the prophet Isaiah to arise and shine, for the light of her redemption has come and the glory of God is revealed over her. Finally, the last stanza directly addresses the Sabbath bride, bidding her exultantly to enter among the faithful of God's treasured people.

But the deeper intent and meaning of the hymn is found at the level of its kabbalistic symbolism. In kabbalistic terms, the bride in this hymn is not Shabbat at all, but *Shechinah* ("Indwelling [Divine] Presence") or *Malchut* ("Majesty"), the most immanent of the ten *s'firot*, or dynamic aspects of the divine energy-flow, which is represented as feminine. Similarly, the *dod*, "beloved," whom the poet urges to go out and greet the bride, is not the people Israel, but *Tiferet* ("Glory"), the seventh *s'firah*, which is depicted as masculine. The kabbalistic symbolism of the poem thus depicts the union of the masculine and feminine aspects of the Godhead, a moment of cosmic equipoise and redemption that takes place on Shabbat. In their kabbalistic meaning, each of the verses deals with an aspect of this movement toward union within the divine realm. So, for example, with regard to the first verse:

Shamor v'zachor b'dibur echad, / hishmianu El ham'yuchad,
Adonai echad u'shmo echad, / l'shem ul'tiferet v'lit'hilah.

"Keep" and "remember": a single command / the Only God caused us to hear.
Adonai is One, God's Name is One; / glory and praise are God's.

The first line of this verse references a well-known midrash, or rabbinic biblical interpretation (*M'chilta D'Rabbi Yishmael, Bachodesh,* 7). The Ten Commandments appear twice in the Torah: once at Exodus 20:2–14 and again at Deuteronomy 5:6–18. The Shabbat commandment is worded slightly differently in each of these versions. In Exodus, it begins "Remember [*zachor*] the Sabbath day to keep it holy," while in Deuteronomy it begins, "Keep [*shamor*] the Sabbath day to keep it holy." The Rabbis explain (away) this verbal variation by noting that God, unlike humans, is capable of saying two things at the same time, thus both of these variants originated simultaneously in the same miraculous divine utterance. (In Alkabetz's poem, the Deuteronomy variant *shamor* precedes the Exodus variant *zachor* because, for purposes of the name-acrostic, *Sh'lomoh,* he needs to begin the verse with a *shin,* not a *zayin*!). At the kabbalistic level of interpretation, however, this midrash suggests that the two "versions," *shamor* and *zachor,* represent female and male, *Shechinah* and *Tiferet,* which come together on Shabbat to form one divine unity.

Similarly, in the second verse, Shabbat is described as the font of all blessing—just as blessing and divine energy flow to the lower worlds through the channels of the *s'firot,* the divine source, from top to bottom. (Shabbat here again represents the most immanent of the *s'firot, Shechinah.*) Drawing on a midrashic tradition (*B'reishit Rabbah* 10:9), Shabbat is characterized here as not only the very end of the process of Creation (chronologically, the seventh day), but also the very beginning and purpose of the entire process of Creation ("last in deed; first in [divine] thought/plan"). Again, this suggests the purposefulness of the process of emanation of the ten *s'firot*, from the hidden and transcendent *Ein Sof* ("Boundless") to the most immanent *Shechinah*.

The Safed kabbalists were intensely messianic in their expectations—and in the intent of their ritual practices. Just as Shabbat is the propitious time for the divine union on high, it is also the propitious time for the redemption on earth—the return to Jerusalem of her exiled children. But, for the kabbalists, the earthly process in fact is isomorphic (that is, has the same structure) with the divine process and symbolically refers to it. So the next six stanzas of the poem refer both to the earthly and the heavenly unifications.

The climax of the poem is the final stanza, which ecstatically depicts the union of the bride and the groom: *Bo-i chalah! Bo-i chalah!* ("Enter, O bride! Enter, O bride!"). The congregation rises for this stanza and faces the entrance (on the western wall), where the sun is setting and Shabbat is entering.[80]

Reform prayer books historically have often omitted the entirety of the *Kabbalat Shabbat* ritual, including *L'cha Dodi*—both for reasons of length and because of its kabbalistic origins and symbolism. Those prayer books that have included *L'cha Dodi* have often abbreviated the poem, omitting in particular those verses that mention the restoration of Jerusalem and the return of her children. (The abbreviated version is usually confined to verses 1, 2, 5, and 9.) Both *Gates of Prayer* and *Mishkan T'filah* have included the full text. There are many musical traditions for the singing of *L'cha Dodi*, including varying the melody and increasing the tempo as the poem rises to its climax.

L'cha Dodi remains a beloved hymn throughout the Jewish world. It draws on both biblical and rabbinic imagery; while perfectly accessible at the surface level, it depicts a vibrant divine realm below the surface.

Psalms 92–93: The Psalms for Shabbat

After *L'cha Dodi*, the *Kabbalat Shabbat* ritual concludes with the singing or recitation of Psalms 92 and 93. Psalm 92 bears the title *Mizmor shir l'yom haShabbat*, "A psalm. A song for Shabbat," and is identified in the Mishnah (*Tamid* 7:4) as the psalm that the Levites sang in the Temple on Shabbat. Rabbinic interpretation in the same Mishnah passage reads this title as meaning "A psalm for the time that is to come, for the day that will be entirely Shabbat rest and eternal life." That is, the psalm points to the messianic future, which will be an eternal Shabbat (that is why Shabbat is referred to in rabbinic lore as a foretaste of the world to come; *B. B'rachot* 57b; *M'chilta D'Rabbi Yishmael, Shabta*, 1). Indeed, long before the *Kabbalat Shabbat* ritual was created by kabbalists in the sixteenth century, this psalm was regularly recited at the beginning of the Erev Shabbat service in most of the medieval prayer rites (the custom is first mentioned by Maimonides in the twelfth century). Psalm 92 is also recited prominently during the *P'sukei D'zimrah* ("Verses of Song") section at the beginning of the Shabbat morning service, as we shall see below.

Psalm 92 begins:

> *Tov l'hodot l'Adonai / ul'zameir l'shimcha elyon.*
> *L'hagid babokeir chasdecha, / ve-emunat'cha baleilot.*
> It is good to praise Adonai; / to sing hymns to Your name, O Most High,
> to proclaim Your steadfast love at daybreak, / Your faithfulness each night.

It is clearly this note of praise and thanksgiving characterizing the psalm as a whole that accounts for its early identification with Shabbat. While weekday prayer is full of petitions, Shabbat is a day for praising God.[81] The psalm mentions the musical instruments—ten-stringed harp and lyre—that accompany the human voice in its songs of divine praise. The psalmist responds with awe and wonder to the mysteries of God's Creation as well as God's providence, which ultimately brings about the punishment of the wicked and reward of the righteous: "Surely your enemies, Adonai, / surely Your enemies perish; / all evildoers are scattered" (Psalm 92:10), while "the righteous bloom like a date-palm; they thrive like a cedar in Lebanon" (*Tzaddik katamar yifrach / k'erez baL'vanon yisgeh*; this latter verse has received many popular musical treatments).[82]

The brief Psalm 93 (actually an *eighth* psalm, but sometimes treated in rabbinic commentary as an extension of Psalm 92) follows. Like Psalms 95–99, which begin the *Kabbalat Shabbat* ritual, it describes God enthroned above Creation. According to the Mishnah (*Tamid* 7:4), this psalm was recited by the Levites in the Temple on Fridays. A rationale for this custom is provided in the Babylonian Talmud, *Rosh HaShanah* 31a: God sits enthroned above Creation once the work has been completed at the end of the sixth day. At that time "Adonai is sovereign, God is robed in grandeur. . . . The world stands firm; it cannot be shaken." Kabbalistic commentary identifies the time when "God is sovereign" as the messianic era, when God's rule will be universally acknowledged.

While many Reform prayer books eliminated the *Kabbalat Shabbat* ritual entirely, virtually all of those began the evening service with the singing of Psalm 92, following the older, pre-kabbalistic custom. (Psalm 93 sometimes was omitted as well.)

Chatzi Kaddish is recited after *Kabbalat Shabbat*, marking the end of this prelude to the Shabbat evening service. Traditionally, this is followed by ritual Torah study relevant to the beginning of Shabbat: *M. Shabbat* 2 (*Bameh madlikin*, "With what [wicks] may we light [the Sabbath lamp]?") and brief traditions from *B. Shabbat* 12a and *B. B'rachot* 64a, followed by *Kaddish D'Rabanan* (the "Rabbis' *Kaddish*" or "Study *Kaddish*"), recited after Talmud study. This latter material is omitted from Reform prayer books. *Mishkan T'filah* instead concludes *Kabbalat Shabbat* with the song *Shalom Aleichem*, followed by *Chatzi Kaddish*.

Shalom Aleichem
A Mystical Greeting of the Shabbat Angels

Most of us are familiar with the song *Shalom Aleichem*, which *Mishkan T'filah* places at the end of the *Kabbalat Shabbat* liturgy (C, p. 142; Sh, p. 24). *Gates of Prayer* used this as an opening song for Erev Shabbat Service X (p. 270), and it also appears at the back of both of these prayer books in the section of song texts. In the traditional siddur it is part of the Erev Shabbat home ritual, recited immediately upon returning from the synagogue before the Shabbat evening meal. Both the text and the custom derive from Lurianic kabbalistic circles in the sixteenth century, as one of their many creative ritual elaborations (the *Kabbalat Shabbat* ritual itself being another Lurianic ritual innovation, as we have seen).

The basis for this custom is Talmudic; it derives from the following traditions (*B. Shabbat* 119b):

> Rav Chisda said in Mar Ukba's name:
>
> Whoever prays on the eve of Shabbat and recites *Vay'chulu* ["The heavens and the earth were finished" (Genesis 2:1)], the two ministering angels who accompany him place their hands on his head and say to him, *Your iniquity is taken away and your sin is purged* (Isaiah 6:7).
>
> It was taught:
>
> Rabbi Yose the son of Rabbi Judah said:
>
> Two ministering angels accompany a man on the eve of the Sabbath from the synagogue to his home, one a good angel and one a bad angel.
>
> And when he arrives home and finds the lamp burning, the table laid and the couch covered with a spread, the good angel exclaims, "May it be this way on the next Shabbat, too!" and the bad angel unwillingly responds, "Amen."
>
> But if not, then the bad angel exclaims, "May it be this way on the next Shabbat, too!" and the good angel unwillingly responds, "Amen."

The Lurianic extension of this Talmudic tradition involves greeting the angels and asking for their blessing. The following verses from Psalms also are recited: "God will command God's angels about you, to guard you in all your ways. May Adonai guard your going out and your coming in from now and for all time" (Psalms 91:11, 121:8).

Most early Reform prayer books omitted *Shalom Aleichem* because of its focus on angels. Over time, the popular melody by Israel Goldfarb (composed in 1918) made the text more familiar and acceptable in Reform circles, leading to its inclusion in *GOP*, and now *MT*, as a song rather than a ritual performance.

The Shabbat Evening Service and the Verses of the Day: *V'shamru*

The Shabbat evening service now continues with *Bar'chu* (C, pp. 146, 264; Sh, pp. 28, 146), introducing the recitation of the *Sh'ma* and the evening form of its surrounding blessings, including the special Shabbat conclusion of the last blessing, *Hashkiveinu* (see above, pp. 57–58).

After the last blessing following the *Sh'ma* and before the Shabbat evening recitation of the *T'filah,* the Shabbat theme is introduced by citing appropriate verses from Scripture. (This is done as well on the eve of the festivals and the High Holy Days, as we shall see below, pp. 176, and note 125 there.) Traditionally, Exodus 31:16–17, *V'shamru v'nei Yisrael et ha-Shabbat* ("The people of Israel shall keep Shabbat") is recited or chanted at this point. That is also the custom in *Mishkan T'filah* (C, pp. 162, 272; Sh, pp. 44, 154). But *MT* also provides a second option to be sung here, *Yism'chu v'malchut'cha shomrei Shabbat* ("Those who keep the Sabbath by calling it a delight will rejoice in Your realm"). In the Ashkenazic rite, this text appears in the *K'dushat HaYom* ("Sanctification of the Day") blessing of the morning *T'filah* without the first line, and fully in the same blessing of the *Musaf T'filah.* In the Sephardic rite, it also appears at our point in the Shabbat evening service. On that basis, it was inserted here in *Gates of Prayer*, and *MT* follows *GOP* in this regard. Prefacing the *T'filah* with either one of these texts nicely highlights what is special about Shabbat.

The Erev Shabbat *T'filah*

The text of the *T'filah* on Erev Shabbat (C, pp. 164–180, 273–285; Sh, pp. 46–62, 155–167) is identical with that on weekday evenings, with one crucial exception. While on weekdays the middle and longest section of the *T'filah* is a series of thirteen petitions, on Shabbat, the festivals, and the High Holy Days, these are replaced by a single benediction called *K'dushat HaYom*, "Sanctification of the Day " (C, pp. 172, 277–278; Sh, pp. 54, 159–160).[83] The reason for this substitution is twofold. First, it is deemed inappropriate to petition God at length on Shabbat and the festivals, when the day is meant for rest and celebration. This idea is nicely conveyed in the following rabbinic passage:

> We do not pray the [full] eighteen [benedictions] on Shabbat lest, if someone in the worshiper's family were ill, he would [be forced to] remember this when reciting [the *R'fuah* petition], "Healer of the sick among God's people Israel," and would thereby become distressed. But Shabbat was given to Israel only for holiness, enjoyment, and rest—and not to cause distress. Therefore, [on Shabbat] we pray the opening three benedictions and the closing three benedictions and [a benediction about Shabbat] rest in the middle. (*Midrash Tanchuma, Vayeira*, 1)

Second, the Jewish liturgical calendar is always reflected in the texts of the prayers for every particular day. Celebrating Shabbat in a liturgical context means special festive versions of regular daily texts or additions to them, as well as structural additions to the service. Changing the text of the *T'filah* on Shabbat is but one instance of this practice.[84]

The *K'dushat HaYom* benediction praises God for the gift of Shabbat rest and prays for divine acceptance of our rest as an act of observance of the covenant made between God and the Jewish people. The text of the benediction has an invariant core and a series of semi-poetic introductions that vary among the four traditional services held on Shabbat (evening, morning, *Musaf,* and afternoon). The invariant core is well known to generations of Reform Jews, because it was the sole portion of the benediction to be retained in the *Union Prayer Book.* It begins, *Eloheinu v'Elohei avoteinu* [today adding, *v'imoteinu*] *r'tzeih vim'nuchateinu,* "Our God and God of our ancestors, be pleased with our rest," and concludes with the *chatimah, Baruch atah Adonai, m'kadeish haShabbat,* "Praised to You, Adonai, who sanctifies the Sabbath" (C, pp. 172, 252, 277, 278, 329, 352, Sh, pp. 54, 159, 160, 211, 234).

On Erev Shabbat, the theme of the introductory paragraph is the Sabbath of Creation and God's cessation from the work of Creation on the seventh day (C, pp. 172, 277, Sh, pp. 54, 277). It includes the scriptural verses that end the first Creation story in Genesis (2:1–3; these same verses will be recited again when *Kiddush* is made over a cup of wine later in the service and in the home at the Erev Shabbat meal). Both *Gates of Prayer* and *Mishkan T'filah* give the full traditional text here. Earlier, the *Union Prayer Book* omitted the first paragraph—possibly for reasons of length, but surely also because of its highly mythic character, suggesting that the world was created in seven days. The *UPB* also deleted the Genesis verses from the beginning of the *Kiddush*—both in the synagogue and in the home—for the same reason. Some earlier Reform prayer books (notably, in America, those of Merzbacher and Wise) had retained the full traditional text here.

The Abbreviated *T'filah* for Erev Shabbat
Magein Avot V'Imahot: Shield of Our Ancestors

Traditionally, there is no reader's repetition of the *T'filah* in the evening service, in order to keep it brief. On Erev Shabbat, however, owing to the festive character of the day, a semi-exception was made to this leniency: an abbreviated reader's repetition of the Shabbat *T'filah* was recited. The *T'filah* on Shabbat is in any case shorter than that for weekdays (seven as opposed to nineteen benedictions), but the abbreviated version (sometimes called *Mei-ein Sheva*, "A Summary of the Seven") is shorter still. It is, in fact, an old poetic form of the Shabbat *T'filah* that, for the most part, elaborates the *chatimot* (concluding benedictory formulas) of each of the seven benedictions (C, p. 182; Sh, p. 182):

> *Magein avot bid'varo*
> [note: not *Magein Avraham*, the attested *chatimah*],
> *M'chayeih meitim b'maamaro.*
> *Ha-El hakadosh, she-ein kamohu.*
> Shield of our forefathers—through His word.
> Reviving the dead—through His utterance.[85]
> The holy God—who has no equal.

The next lines, representing the central *K'dushat HaYom* benediction, then elaborate on the theme of Shabbat:

> Who took joy in providing rest for Your people on Your holy Shabbat day.

The following lines then summarize the remaining three benedictions, and conclude with a peroration about the Sabbath:

> We will serve You reverently,
> acknowledging on each and every day forever, just who You are:
> the One to whom blessing goes.

An old (and correct) variant reading here, followed by *MT*, is *m'on hab'rachot*, "Source of blessings." Most (uncorrected) traditional prayer books read *mei-ein hab'rachot*, "substance of blessings."

> The One to whom thanksgiving is due,
> Source of peace, who recalls the time of Creation
> by sanctifying Shabbat, blessing the seventh day,
> and in holiness, granting rest to a people overflowing with joy.

This poetic version of the seven benedictions for Shabbat needs no further elaboration—but in the medieval rites, it is supplemented fore and aft by (1) the beginning of the *Avot* benediction (in order to begin with *Baruch atah Adonai*, with which all rabbinic liturgical blessings must commence)[86] and (2) a repetition of the main section of the standard *K'dushat HaYom* benediction ("Our God and God of our ancestors, be pleased with our rest"). These additions bring it more in line with a standard reader's repetition of the *T'filah*.

One of the earliest practical reforms of the synagogue service in early nineteenth-century Germany was the elimination of the twofold recitation of the *T'filah*; the repetition was deemed redundant and took up too much time. Generally, the individual silent *T'filah* was abandoned in favor of the more decorous public recitation by the service reader (or cantor), joined by the congregation for some responses. But the text of *Magein Avot* remains in many early German Reform prayer books as a passage to be chanted or sung in unison. In North America, the very first *Union Prayer Book* (1892, edited by Rabbi Isaac S. Moses prior to what became the "official" version of 1894–95) uses the abbreviated *Avot* introduction and the beginning of the poem (through "the holy God") to introduce the traditional *K'dushat HaYom* benediction, following the precedent of Rabbi Leo Merzbacher's 1855 prayer book for Temple Emanuel in New York. *Magein Avot* does not appear at all in the first two official editions of the *UPB* (1895 and 1918), but it was restored in the newly revised edition (1940), together with the first portion of the *Avot* benediction but without the "Be pleased with our rest" paragraph, as the sole version of the *T'filah* in the fourth Erev Shabbat service (pp. 56–57; the English translation is presented as a responsive reading). It also appears in the first (more traditional) service of *Gates of Prayer* (p. 141), but after the regular *T'filah* text, so it is not followed by what would be a repetition of the "Be pleased with our rest" paragraph. *Mishkan T'filah* follows the text of *GOP* but has rendered it gender-equal by including the Matriarchs together with the Patriarchs (*Magein avot v'imahot*). In neither *GOP* nor *MT* is a performance practice indicated, although the traditional practice of singing this after the regular *T'filah* text is certainly implied. *MT* also implicitly allows this two-page spread to be prayed as an alternative to the longer *T'filah* text on the previous pages.

The service for Erev Shabbat then concludes with *Aleinu* and Mourner's *Kaddish*, as it does on weekdays.

The Shabbat Morning Service

The service for Shabbat morning is simply an elaboration of the weekday morning service. It begins the same way, with the preliminary Morning Blessings and the Verses of Song, which prepare us for prayer. Additional psalms are recited on Shabbat, in particular Psalm 92, "A song for Shabbat," which was already recited at the beginning of the Shabbat evening service, as part of *Kabbalat Shabbat*. We expand here on our earlier examination of this psalm, since it is a highlight of the Shabbat morning service as well.

Psalm 92: A Song for Shabbat

We may ask what it is about the content of Psalm 92 (C, pp. 214, 302; Sh pp. 96, 184) that makes it particularly appropriate to recite on Shabbat—so much so that a biblical editor affixed to it the title "A song for Shabbat." A likely answer is that the psalm begins with the joyous musical praise of God (for voice and instruments) that celebrates God's handiwork:

> It is good to praise Adonai;
> to sing hymns to Your name, O Most High,
> to proclaim Your steadfast love at daybreak,
> Your faithfulness each night
> with a ten-stringed harp,
> with voice and lyre together.
> You have gladdened me by Your deeds, Adonai;
> I shout for joy at Your handiwork.
> How great are Your works, Adonai,
> how very subtle Your designs!

This is, in fact, the prime liturgical content of Shabbat—the day on which God's work of Creation is celebrated as complete and on which all creatures praise God's handiwork.

The rest of the psalm deals with God's moral governance of the world, which, according to the Psalmist, only a fool could fail to recognize—the wicked will be destroyed, while the righteous will "bloom like a date-palm," will "flourish in the courts of our God . . . attesting that Adonai is upright, my Rock, in whom there is no wrong."

The implicit connection between the psalm's two themes, God's Creation and God's governance of the world, is causal: *because* God is the author of Creation, the world remains under the watchful eye of a just divine providence. Note that the Psalmist (like us) is troubled by the fact that, at present, "the wicked sprout like grass and evildoers blossom" (Psalm 92:8). But it is the Psalmist's religious conviction that this situation is only temporary: in the future, evildoers will be punished and the righteous will flourish. *Mishkan T'filah* chooses to omit verses 8–12 (which had been retained in the *Union Prayer Book* and *Gates of Prayer*), where the Psalmist lashes out against his "watchful foes," evildoers, and God's enemies. The angry, resentful, and vengeful feelings expressed here are deemed inappropriate for contemporary Shabbat worship. But the remaining portions of the psalm well express the themes of Shabbat—joyous praise to the God of Creation. That is why there are so many musical settings of this popular psalm.

Nishmat Kol Chai: The Praise-Song of All Creation

The morning psalms, *P'sukei D'zimrah*, are framed by blessings fore and aft—as we noted before. The blessing preceding the psalms is *Baruch She-amar*; the blessing following them on Shabbat, the festivals, and the High Holy Days is *Nishmat Kol Chai* (C, pp. 219–223, 307–311, 446–450; Sh, pp. 101–105, 189–193; W/F, pp. 182–186). This is considerably more elaborate than the shorter blessing that follows the psalms on weekdays; it consists only of *Yishtabach*, which on Shabbat and holidays concludes *Nishmat Kol Chai* (C, pp. 223, 311, 450; Sh, pp. 105, 193; W/F, p. 186).

Nishmat Kol Chai, which climaxes the singing of psalms, is an extraordinary liturgical text. It is an extended, ecstatic hymn of praise and gratitude that enumerates at length God's praiseworthy attributes—God redeems and rescues, frees captives, and raises up all who are stooped under the weight of oppression or physical infirmity. At the same time, *Nishmat* protests at length that we humans really cannot adequately thank or praise God for all of the benefactions that we daily receive as part of the ultimate gift of life itself. In cascading poetic images, *Nishmat* argues that even if our mouths were filled with praise-songs as numerous as the drops of water in the ocean or as loud as the crash of its billowing waves, if our hands were spread out in gratitude as wide as eagles' pinions or our feet were as swift as deer to run after God, we could barely express the smallest fraction of our gratitude and wonder at God's daily gifts of blessing to us. Nonetheless, we must daily make the attempt to do so—because, as Rabbi Abraham Joshua Heschel so eloquently noted, we cannot fail to do otherwise upon experiencing the miracles of living. *Nishmat Kol Chai* thus links up thematically with the Morning Blessings recited at the beginning of daily worship and also with the *Hodaah* ("Gratitude") blessing in the *T'filah* that follows later in the service. It is an elegant and rapturous conclusion to *P'sukei D'zimrah.*

A full-length text of *Nishmat Kol Chai* appears in writing for the first time only in *Seder Rav Amram,* written sometime before 875 CE. But the three opening words, *Nishmat kol chai,* and much of the paragraph beginning *Ilu finu malei shirah kayam* ("Even if our mouths were full of song as the sea") are found in the Babylonian Talmud. *M. P'sachim* 10:7, dealing with the recitation of the *Hallel* psalms (113–118) at the seder meal, notes that the *Hallel* is concluded with the recitation of *Birkat HaShir,* "the Blessing over Song" (psalms). The Talmud (*B. P'sachim* 118a) seeks to clarify what specific wording is referred to as *Birkat HaShir.* Two rabbis propose two different formulations: Rav Judah says that this refers to *Y'hal'lucha* ("All Your works shall praise You"), while Rabbi Yochanan says that this refers to *Nishmat Kol Chai.* In post-Talmudic liturgy, *Y'hal'lucha* is the blessing used to conclude the recitation of *Hallel* in the synagogue on festival mornings (see below, p. 194), while *Nishmat Kol Chai* (our text) concludes the *Hallel* at the Passover seder as well as concluding *P'sukei D'zimrah* during Shabbat, festival, and High Holy Day morning services. A second Talmudic passage (*B. B'rachot* 59b), asks what blessing is to be recited for rainfall. Rav Judah says, "We give thanks to You for every single drop that You have caused to fall for us," and Rabbi Yochanan (again!) concludes, "Even if our mouths were full of song as the sea . . . we could never thank You adequately, Adonai, our God. . . . Praised are You, O God, to whom abundant thanks are due." So the imagery of numerous drops of water in the sea initially relates as well to the abundant drops of rainfall for which this text gives thanks.

The version in *Mishkan T'filah*, like that in *Gates of Prayer* before it, is somewhat abbreviated, since the original goes on at considerable length. (In the second Shabbat morning service of the *Union Prayer Book*, only the first paragraph appears, and only in English. The festival and High Holy Day morning services, on the other hand, include a Hebrew abbreviation, but it differs from that in *GOP*.) *Nishmat Kol Chai* concludes the preliminary portion of the Shabbat, festival, and High Holy Day morning services with a paean of praise to the God who creates and sustains life in the world and to whom abundant thanks are due.

As on weekday mornings, this is followed by *Bar'chu*, which introduces the recitation of the *Sh'ma* and the morning version of its benedictions. The traditional *Yotzeir Or* benediction is longer on Shabbat, because it also weaves the Shabbat theme into the theme of the blessing proper (the creation of light and of the luminaries). This was a fairly common practice in prayer texts from the Land of Israel, which are subject to creative reworkings and expansions. Most Reform prayer books give the same, shorter version of this blessing on both weekdays and Shabbat.[87] As on weekdays, the *T'filah* follows, here in its seven-blessing version for Shabbat, which omits the thirteen weekday petitionary prayers.

Changes in the Shabbat Morning *T'filah*

As mentioned previously, the central benediction in the Shabbat *T'filah* is called *K'dushat HaYom* and celebrates God's gift of Shabbat. Its invariant core ("Be pleased with our rest; sanctify us with Your mitzvot") is recited at all four Shabbat services, but the introductory paragraphs change. The introductory paragraph in the morning service begins with a short poem, *Yismach Mosheh b'mat'nat chelko* ("Moses rejoiced at the gift bestowed upon him"), which describes the giving of the Torah to Moses at Sinai, including the commandment to observe Shabbat. This is then spelled out through the citation of Exodus 31:16–17, *V'shamru v'nei Yisrael et ha-Shabbat* ("The people of Israel shall keep Shabbat"). The text continues by emphasizing that Shabbat was given as a special gift to the Jewish people—and to no one else. Therefore those who observe Shabbat and delight in it should also deserve to rejoice in the future fulfillment of God's kingdom in the messianic era (*Yism'chu v'malchut'cha shomrei Shabbat*).[88] This text leads directly into the invariant core *R'tzeih vim'nuchateinu*.

From this introduction, *Mishkan T'filah* retains *V'shamru* and *Yism'chu*, both of which have numerous musical settings that are popular for congregational singing. They are treated here as alternative selections (C, pp. 250, 328–329; Sh, pp. 132, 210–211). A note on performance practice: It is appropriate at this point in the *T'filah* to sing, chant, and/or recite both *V'shamru* or *Yism'chu* and *R'tzei vim'numchateinu*, rather than sufficing with one or the other of the first pair. As highlighted in the *Union Prayer Book* practice, it is the *latter* text that is the core of the benediction (and that includes its *chatimah*). Also, since *K'dushat HaYom* is the liturgical core of the *T'filah* and its distinctive textual element on Shabbat, it should always be recited or sung aloud rather than silently, thereby allowing worshipers to focus together on the unique part of the Shabbat liturgy.

The remainder of the Shabbat *T'filah* remains the same at all services and is identical to the weekday versions. Following the *T'filah* comes the Torah service, which is considerably more elaborate on Shabbat.

Seder K'riat HaTorah L'Shabbat
Reading the Torah on Shabbat

Seder Hotzaat HaTorah: Removing the Torah from the Ark

THE HIGH POINT of the Shabbat morning service each week is the public reading from the Torah scroll. This activity is, in fact, the oldest continuous element of Jewish public worship known to us; it is attested in texts and inscriptions from the Second Commonwealth period, both in the Land of Israel and in the Mediterranean Diaspora (particularly in Hellenistic Egypt). The precise details of public Torah reading, translation, and interpretation have differed from place to place and have changed over time.

In the traditional liturgy of Rabbinic Judaism, the public Torah reading is preceded by an elaborate, dramatic ceremony of removing the scroll from the ark while declaiming or singing thematically relevant verses from Scripture. The Torah traditionally is paraded through the congregation (called a *hakafah*, "encircling"), so that each person may symbolically receive or acknowledge it, through bowing or by touching the mantle of the scroll with one's tallit fringes.[89] At the end of this procession, the Torah scroll is returned to the reading desk on the bimah, where it is undressed and unwrapped for reading. Earlier Reform practice, in accord with nineteenth-century ideals of decorum, dispensed with the *hakafah* through the congregation and kept all activity, greatly simplified, on the bimah. More recent Reform practice has restored this practice as a way of physically engaging the congregation and of bringing Torah "out into the pews."

Most, but not all, of the texts that are recited or sung as the ark is opened and the Torah removed and processed through the congregation are biblical verses. There is variation among the regional medieval rites as to which, and how many, texts are recited and in what order. There is also "ritual" variation: Sephardim, for example, display the open scroll of the Torah portion to the congregation *before* it is read, rather than after (as is the Ashkenazic custom). In all rites, the ritual is more elaborate on

Shabbat mornings than on Monday and Thursday mornings and Shabbat afternoons, when the Torah is also read (the reading then is brief, limited to the beginning verses of the next week's Torah portion). North American Reform liturgy has generally been based on Ashkenazic practice but has sometimes incorporated texts from Sephardic practice (as we shall see below).

The Ashkenazic Shabbat morning Torah ritual begins with the singing of *Ein Kamocha* ("There is none like You"), a series of biblical verses (Psalm 86:8, Psalm 145:13, Exodus 15:18, and Psalm 29:11) as well as verse-fragments (from Psalms 10:16 and 93:1) that acknowledge God's sole sovereignty and power. These have routinely appeared in Reform prayer books, and *Mishkan T'filah* (C, p. 362; Sh, p. 244) is no exception in that regard.[90] This is followed by a rabbinic prayer for the restoration of Zion, beginning with the words *Av harachamim* ("Source of mercy"). This prayer was often omitted in Reform prayer books because of its topic, but it was restored in *Gates of Prayer*[91] and appears as well in *MT*.

Now the ark is opened. Before the open ark, Numbers 10:35 is recited, enacting what the narrative tells us that Moses would say when the Ark of the Covenant was about to move in front of the Israelites in their journey through the wilderness: "Arise, O God, and let your enemies be scattered!" This verse has consistently been omitted from Reform rites on account of its warlike and vengeful posture. It is followed by Isaiah 2:3, *Ki miTziyon* ("For from out of Zion"), and the rabbinic benediction *Baruch shenatan Torah* ("Blessed is the One who gave Torah"). The Isaiah verse was sometimes omitted from earlier Reform prayer books on account of its "localism/Zionism," but it was restored in *GOP*. *MT* inserts Psalm 24:9–10, *S'u sh'arim*, between *Ki miTziyon* (C, p. 364; Sh, p. 246) and *Baruch shenatan* (C, p. 366; Sh, p. 248). This placement generated some confusion when the prayer book was newly in use, since it interrupts a traditional textual and musical sequence, although the text itself is a familiar one. The singing or recitation of *S'u sh'arim* before the Torah is removed from the ark is an old Reform custom, found as early as the first Reform congregational prayer book (Hamburg, 1819). It derives from the Sephardic rite (as did many of the "deviant" practices and texts in the Hamburg Temple Prayer Book). Its liturgical use at this juncture in the Sephardic rite is based on a rabbinic interpretation that these words were recited by

Solomon when he brought the Ark of the Covenant into the Holy of Holies in the newly built Temple in Jerusalem (*Midrash on Psalms* 24:10). Notice again how many of the biblical texts recited when the ark is opened and the Torah is removed refer to the movement of the Ark of the Covenant and to the Temple in Jerusalem, from which God's word goes forth: this is how the liturgy would have us imagine what we are doing and how the past and the present are linked through ritual and myth.

Before the Torah is removed from the ark, many of the traditional prayer books include an Aramaic prayer from the Zohar, *B'rich sh'mei d'marei alma* ("Praised be the name of the Master of the universe"; *Zohar, Vayak'heil,* 206a); the *Zohar* deems this moment, when the ark is open and the Torah scrolls are visible, to be propitious for personal prayer. As a late, mystical addition to the liturgy, this prayer has not been included in most Reform prayer books (although it did appear in earlier drafts of *MT*).

The scroll is then removed from the ark, and the ark is closed. Holding the Torah scroll, the prayer leader faces the congregation and proclaims, *Sh'ma Yisrael!* (Deuteronomy 6:4). In Ashkenazic practice, this verse is then repeated by the congregation, responding to the prayer leader. The leader continues, beginning with the last word of the *Sh'ma* verse (*echad*), *Echad Eloheinu, gadol Adoneinu, kadosh sh'mo* ("Our God is One, Adonai is great, holy is God's Name"). In Ashkenazic practice, this affirmation too is repeated by the congregation. The leader then turns again toward the ark and, bowing, recites Psalm 34:4, *Gadlu l'Adonai iti* ("Exalt Adonai with me"). The congregation responds by singing or reciting I Chronicles 29:11, *L'cha Adonai* ("Yours, Adonai, is the greatness"), the praise ascribed there to David at the end of his reign, and Psalm 99:9, *Rom'mu Adonai Eloheinu* ("Exalt Adonai our God"), as the Torah scroll processes through the congregation. This liturgy is found in its entirety in *MT* (p. 366; Psalm 99:9, *Rom'mu,* omitted from many previous Reform liturgies, is given as the first "*hakafah* selection" at the top of p. 367).

Now the procession ends and the scroll is returned to the bimah, where it is undressed and unwrapped. After this dramatic congregational "close encounter" with the Torah scroll, as it is revealed once again, the Torah reading is about to begin.

The Left-Page Additional Texts

The opening of the ark, the removal of the Torah scroll, and the parading of the scroll through the congregation (*hakafah*) are moments of great liturgical drama, solemnity, and festivity. These actions are accompanied by the singing or recitation of (mostly) scriptural texts, often in a call-and-response pattern, by the reader and the congregation. We remarked above that there is a certain amount of variation even among traditional rites in the texts that are declaimed. That variety has existed in Reform prayer books as well, where a mixture of Ashkenazic, Sephardic, and additional textual selections have been used.

The additional, "left-page" texts that appear in *Mishkan T'filah* for the beginning of the Torah service (C, pp. 363, 365; Sh, pp. 245, 247) all derive from *Gates of Prayer* (1975). *GOP* offered five different options for the Torah-reading liturgies, the first being more traditional Ashkenazic—corresponding to the "right-page" text in *MT*—and the other four giving still other textual possibilities:

1. *Hak'heil et haam*, "Assemble the people" (Deuteronomy 31:12–13a; *MT*, top of C, p. 363; Sh, p. 245), is found at the beginning of *GOP*'s second Torah service (*GOP*, p. 425). This text is thematically appropriate, since it depicts God's instruction to Moses to gather the people every seven years during the festival of Sukkot for a public reading of "this Torah" in what amounts to a covenant renewal ceremony that is to take place all the time that the people inhabit the Land of Israel. (This ceremony is referred to in traditional shorthand as *hak'heil*, after the commandment's first word.) In mythic terms, this text is the earliest warrant for the public reading of Torah, so it nicely frames what the congregation is about to do. Rabbi Chaim Stern, in his commentary to this text in *Gates of Understanding* (p. 233), notes that "the use of this passage to introduce the Torah Service was an innovation of *Service of the Heart* [the 1967 British Liberal prayer book edited by Rabbis Chaim Stern and John D. Rayner that served as the model for *GOP*], p. 172."
2. *Ashrei adam matza chochmah*, "Happy is the one who finds wisdom" (Proverbs 3:13–15; *MT*, bottom of C, p. 363; Sh, p. 245),

is found at the beginning of *GOP*'s fourth Torah service (*GOP*, p. 437). The situational relevance of this text derives from the Rabbis' association of *chochmah*/wisdom in the Book of Proverbs (and in the biblical wisdom literature generally, which includes as well the Books of Job and Ecclesiastes) with Torah: for Rabbinic Judaism, Torah is the embodiment of divine wisdom.[92] Stern, in *Gates of Understanding* (p. 234) notes that these verses had been used at the conclusion of the Torah ritual in the British Liberal *Service of the Heart* (p. 195) and its predecessor, *Liberal Jewish Prayer Book* (1937 edition, edited by Israel I. Mattuck, p. 409).

3. *Lo yarei-u*, "They shall not hurt" (Isaiah 11:9) and *V'yashvu ish*, "And all shall sit" (Micah 4:4; *MT*, the top of C, p. 365), are found at the beginning of *GOP*'s third Torah service (p. 431). The situational thematic connection is to be found at the end of the Isaiah verse: in the messianic future there will be no more violence or warfare among humans because the earth will be filled with the knowledge of God. As before, this knowledge is associated with Torah. Stern, in *Gates of Understanding* (p. 233), notes that the usage of these verses in this context goes back to the *Union Prayer Book* (newly revised edition, 1940, p. 94), in the Torah service for Shabbat evening.
4. *V'chit'tu charvotam l'itim*, "They shall beat their swords into plowshares" (Isaiah 2:4; *MT*, bottom of C, p. 365; Sh, p. 247) is also found in *GOP*'s third Torah service (p. 435), when the Torah is returned to the ark, so that it serves as a "bookend" with *Lo yarei-u*. These two Isaiah texts had been associated in a popular musical setting by Cantor William Sharlin (incorporating a tune for *V'chit'tu* by Israeli composer Ezri Gabbai) for Reform services and camp settings prior to the publication of *GOP* (see *The Complete Shireinu*, p. 136.)
5. "In this scroll" (the blue-lined text that extends across C, pp. 364–365; Sh, pp. 246–247 in *MT*) derives from *GOP* (p. 437). It was written by Chaim Stern.

Additionally, *MT* gives four "*hakafah* selections" (C, p. 367; Sh, p. 249). These are biblical and rabbinic texts that can be sung when more material is needed beyond *L'cha Adonai* to cover the procession of the Torah scroll through the congregation and back to the bimah. Traditional liturgy in fact supplies more biblical text here for that purpose. The first *MT* selection, *Rom'mu* (Psalm 99:9), as noted, is part of traditional Ashkenazic liturgy at this point. Aside from their thematic relevance, the other selections appear here on account of their popular musical settings.

Torah Blessings

After the Torah scroll has been carried through the congregation, it is returned to the bimah, where its mantle and binder are removed, and it is prepared for reading. Traditionally, on Shabbat, seven people ascend (*olim*) to the bimah to recite the blessings over the Torah, before and after each section is read.[93] This honor is called an *aliyah* ("ascent, going up"). Traditionally, the first *aliyah* goes to a *kohein*, a member of the ancient priestly clan, and the second *aliyah* to a *Leivi*, a member of the tribe that assisted the priests in the Temple service. The remaining *aliyot* are given to any Israelite/Jew. (Traditionally, all of these people are men. The statuses of *kohein* and *Leivi* are inherited from father to son; daughters are designated as *bat Kohein* and *bat Leivi*, but no privileges are attached to these statuses.) The *kohein* is called up to the bimah with a festive formula that begins by invoking divine protection on all who trust in God and inviting the congregation to praise God: *Hakol havu godel l'Eloheinu ut'nu chavod laTorah*, "Let all declare the greatness of our God and give honor to the Torah." The invocation ends with the repetition of *Baruch shenatan Torah*, to which the congregation responds, "And you who cling to Adonai your God are all alive today" (Deuteronomy 4:4).

In the nineteenth century, the Reform Movement eliminated the privileges of the priests and Levites as remnants of the Temple cult—the restoration of which was no longer hoped for—and called up to the Torah all (male) Jews without distinction. The length of the Torah portion read each week was shortened considerably: only excerpts from the weekly portion were read. Consequently, there was no longer a need for seven *aliyot* on Shabbat. In North America, the custom of calling people up to the Torah was gradually abandoned in many Reform congregations in the late nineteenth and early twentieth centuries, as a way of instituting decorum and eliminating "clutter" and "traffic" from the service. The Torah blessings were recited by the rabbi, who also read from the scroll. This is the practice that is taken for granted in all three editions of the *Union Prayer Book* (1894–95, 1918–22, 1940–45). Over the past decades (since the 1970s), more of the traditional customs surrounding the reading of the Torah have been revived in Reform worship—the *hakafah*, or procession with the Torah scroll both before and after the reading; the *aliyot* (though not always the full seven on Shabbat; seven *aliyot* do not work well with an abbreviated Torah reading if they appear to take more time and focus than the reading itself!); and, since the 1990s, the prayers for healing (*Mi Shebeirach*) that follow upon the reading from the scroll.

Mishkan T'filah (p. 368) gives the address to the congregation, *Havu godel l'Eloheinu*, before the *aliyah* is called up. In *Gates of Prayer* and the *Union Prayer Book*, this sentence appeared before the Torah was removed from the ark; no *aliyot* were indicated in these prayer books. *MT* then suggests that "one who makes an *aliyah* might offer: *Adonai imachem* (May God be with you!)," to which the "congregation responds: *Y'varech'cha Adonai* (May God bless you!)" This suggested exchange of blessings is new to North American Reform liturgy; it is a Sephardic custom.

The blessings recited before and after the Torah is read are the same in the traditional and Reform prayer books. Before the Torah is read, the person reciting the blessing first invites the congregation to praise God: *Bar'chu et Adonai ham'vorach* ("Bless Adonai who is blessed"), to which the congregation responds, *Baruch Adonai ham'vorach l'olam va-ed* ("Blessed are You, Adonai, who is blessed now and forever"). The response is then repeated softly by the reader, to indicate that he or she includes him- or herself in the addressed congregation as well. (Classical Reform practice generally omitted the congregational response; both the invocation and the response were recited by the reader.) This, of course, is the same invocation-and-response that begins public worship morning and evening. It appears in both of these contexts in the Mishnah and the Talmud of the Land of Israel (*Y. B'rachot* 7:3).

The Torah blessings praise God for having given the Torah to Israel, thereby "implanting within us eternal life." The text of the blessing before the Torah reading first appears in the Babylonian Talmud, *B'rachot* 11b.

There it is given as one of three alternative formulas to be recited before private Torah study each morning. (The other two, *laasok b'divrei torah,* "who has commanded us to engage with words of Torah," and *v'haarev na,* "let the words of Torah be sweet in our mouths," now appear in the introductory portion of the morning service; see *MT*, C, p. 42, 204, 296–297, 430; Sh, pp. 86, 178–179; W/F, pp. 42, 166; all three appear together in the traditional Preliminary Morning Service). The blessing recited after the reading of the Torah is first found in Tractate *Sof'rim,* which deals with the writing of Torah scrolls, *t'fillin,* and mezuzot; it also contains our earliest account of the rabbinic Torah-reading liturgy and derives from the Land of Israel around the eighth century CE.

In the nineteenth century, many Reform congregations eliminated the traditional chanting of the Torah as too "oriental" (i.e., "non-Western," or foreign), incompatible with Western (Protestant) aesthetics and worship styles. Instead, the Torah was simply read in Hebrew and in the vernacular. The last several decades (since the 1970s) have seen a significant return to the custom of chanting the Torah in Reform synagogues. Similarly, the custom of bar mitzvah at the age of thirteen was replaced in the nineteenth century by the practice of confirmation at the age of sixteen or seventeen, following the parallel custom in Protestant Christianity, and on the theory that thirteen-year-olds were still too immature in Western society to accept upon themselves the adult obligations and mature understanding of the Jewish faith. The custom of bar and bat mitzvah, too, has had a resurgence in North American Reform congregations over the past forty or so years. While the return to more traditional customs in the North American Reform Movement is often (and not incorrectly) seen as a phenomenon initiated in the late 1960s and early 1970s, responding to the breakup of the "melting pot" theory of American culture in the wake of the cultural upheavals of that era and the resurgence of ethnic pride among minorities (and Jewish ethnic pride after the Six-Day War), it actually has its roots as early as the 1920s and 1930s, with the influx into Reform congregations of the children of Eastern European Jewish immigrants, who sought a more tangibly and familiarly Jewish worship experience.

Blessings for Those Called to the Torah

In the traditional liturgy, it is customary on Shabbat to offer a blessing for each of those who have received an *aliyah laTorah* (those who have been called to the Torah to recite a blessing over it). This blessing takes the form *Mi shebeirach avoteinu . . . hu y'vareich* ("May the One who blessed our forefathers . . . bless . . ."). The Israeli liturgical scholar Joseph Heinemann, in his book on the rhetorical forms of rabbinic prayer, noted that all private blessings and those blessings that are not part of the mandatory liturgy (the *Sh'ma* and the *T'filah*) avoid using the four-letter name of God (which is euphemistically pronounced *Adonai*) and instead use a circumlocution like *Baruch she-amar v'hayah haolam* ("Praised be the One who spoke and the world came into being") or *Mi shebeirach avoteinu* ("May the One who blessed our forefathers") or *Mi she-asah nisim laavoteinu* ("May the One who performed miracles for our forefathers").[94] This form of blessing is also used at this point in the traditional service on behalf of a sick person and, on the occasion of naming a newborn daughter, on behalf of the recovery of the new mother.[95] Also at this point in the service, one who has recently recovered from an illness or come safely through a dangerous experience recites publicly *Birkat HaGomeil*, the blessing thanking God for having showered one with kindness by saving one's life. The congregation responds with the wish that God may forever bestow kindness upon this person.

For many years, the North American Reform Movement eliminated these blessings from its prayer book, together with the *aliyot laTorah*, because they were deemed to detract from the decorum of the service (too much traffic to and from the bimah, which removed the focus from the Torah reading itself and also prolonged the service). In recent years, the movement has acknowledged liturgically the benefit both of more community participation in the service and of publicly recognizing moments of passage in the life and health of its members. So *Mishkan T'filah* provides an inclusive form of the blessing for those who have come up to the Torah, for those who are in need of healing (as well as the text of the Debbie Friedman setting), and for those who have survived a life-challenging situation. In the last case, the traditional blessing has been modified from "who bestows favors on the undeserving and has shown *me* every kindness" to "who has bestowed every goodness upon *us*." The traditional phrase about being undeserving is deleted, since it seems a bit too self-deprecating, while the first-person singular referent is changed to a first-person plural, whereby the person reciting the benediction includes him- or herself in the community. The congregational response is also altered to the plural.

It should be noted that the left side of the two-page spread in *MT* (pp. 108–109, 370–371, 510–511; Sh, pp. 252–253; W/F, pp. 108–109, 246–247) is not providing alternatives to the right side, but additional occasional blessings that are recited while the Torah is on the reading desk. The normal order would be: *Mi Shebeirach* for *aliyah*, prayers for healing, and *Birkat HaGomeil* (although if this is recited by one of the *aliyot*, it would be recited before the healing prayers). After these blessings, those who will be raising (*hagbahah*) and rolling and wrapping (*g'lilah*) the Torah scroll are called up to the bimah. When three columns of the raised scroll are displayed to the congregation, the congregation responds, *V'zot haTorah*, "This is the Torah which Moses placed before the people of Israel, God's word through the hand of Moses." The first phrase of this text comes from Deuteronomy 4:44, and the second from Numbers 9:23. The second phrase has been controversial for much of the history of the Reform Movement, since traditionally it is understood to mean that the Torah text as we now have it was dictated verbatim by God to Moses—a claim of literal inspiration that has been rejected by most modern understandings of the Torah. So this text was deleted from most of the earlier Reform prayer books. It reappears as an option in *Gates of Prayer*. Here is an instance in which popular custom trumps theology, since most Eastern European Jews entering the Reform Movement were familiar with the custom of singing this text during *hagbahah*; the text returns with the custom of lifting the scroll and displaying it to the congregation, irrespective of its precise meaning and theological implications.

Haftarah Reading and Its Blessings

The Hebrew word *haftarah* means "dismissal" or "discharging (of an obligation)." In the context of the public reading from Scripture, the term means "conclusion," as it is used in the idiom *maftirin b'navi*, "We conclude with [a reading from] a prophet" (*M. M'gilah* 4, multiple times).[96] It is specifically the messianic promises of divine redemption found in the words of the Literary, or "Latter," Prophets (*N'vi'im Acharonim*) that would be read out loud after the Torah reading in the early rabbinic synagogue in order to conclude with a "word of consolation."[97] Similar words and scriptural citations from the Prophets would conclude the public exposition of Scripture (*d'rashah*) as well.[98] Subsequently, readings from the prophetic literature also came to include selections from the Books of Joshua, Judges, Samuel, and Kings (the so-called Former Prophets, *N'vi'im Rishonim*). In the annual cycle of Torah readings that is used today, each weekly *parashah* is accompanied by a specific reading from one of the books of Prophets, determined on the basis of some thematic association (however loosely construed) with the Torah reading itself. There is some variation in haftarah readings among the several traditional rites. Many early Reform prayer books abandoned entirely the reading of haftarot on Shabbat during the year, likely both out of a desire to shorten the service and because the thematic associations between the traditional haftarot and the traditional Torah readings tended to reflect a premodern rabbinic mind-set and were not always deemed to be sufficiently uplifting to moderns. Haftarot were in all cases retained on the High Holy Days. In North America, weekly haftarot appear (or are listed) in most Reform prayer books. Because of the shortening of the weekly Torah readings, multiple options generally have been listed in these prayer books for both Torah and haftarah readings. Suggestions for haftarot often include psalms and readings from other parts of Writings as well as from Prophets. Since the 1981 publication of Rabbi W. Gunther Plaut's Torah commentary, which includes haftarot (and particularly its second, more synagogue use-oriented edition, published in 2005), the selection of weekly haftarot in North American Reform congregations has tended to follow the passages given in this volume, most of which are traditional (with some abbreviation).[99]

The haftarah reading, just like the Torah reading that it follows, is framed fore and aft with rabbinic blessings. The blessing before the reading emphasizes the truth of the prophetic words about to be read. (In Ashkenazic practice, it is chanted using the same melodic patterns by which the prophetic text itself will be read.) Traditionally, the haftarah is followed by a series of four blessings. The first praises "the faithful God" who keeps God's promises, specifically the prophetic assurances that the people Israel in the future will be redeemed and restored to their land and polity. The second, specifying this theme, urges God to have compassion for Zion and return her children to her midst. The third requests that God speedily send us Elijah the prophet and the messianic heir of King David, who will restore the Jewish kingdom. The final blessing gives thanks to God for the Torah and for the Sabbath (or festival) day; it is a shorter variant of the *K'dushat HaYom* benediction in the *T'filah* and concludes the series.

North American Reform prayer books generally have shortened the blessings after the haftarah, omitting entirely the explicitly messianic second and third benedictions, while shortening the first benediction (omitting its last half, including the *chatimah, HaEl hane-eman b'chol d'varav,* "God who is faithful regarding all His words/promises") and sometimes shortening the final benediction as well (generally, as in the *Union Prayer Book,* by omitting only a word or two). It is noteworthy that *Gates of Prayer* gives the full traditional text as an alternative version (pp. 421–422) to the abbreviated one that is based on the *UPB,* but restores the full text of the final benediction. *Mishkan T'filah* (C, p. 372; Sh, p. 254) provides only the abbreviated version from *GOP*. Its left-page alternative (C, p. 372; Sh, p. 255) is an English responsive reading written by Rabbis Harvey J. Fields and Chaim Stern (*GOP,* pp. 182–183) that emphasizes themes of social justice from the prophetic literature.

Seder Hachnasat HaTorah: Returning the Torah to the Ark

Just as the Torah reading was preceded by an elaborate ceremony removing the Torah scroll from the ark and parading it through the congregation, accompanied by the chanting of thematically appropriate texts from Scripture, so (traditionally) is the Torah scroll's return to the ark accompanied by another ceremonial *hakafah* through the congregation and chanting of scriptural texts. While many Reform congregations in recent years have restored the *hakafah* through the congregation that precedes the reading of the Torah, most still omit the *hakafah* after the Torah is read. The text that traditionally accompanies this *hakafah* on Shabbat morning is Psalm 29 (which is also chanted as part of *Kabbalat Shabbat,* where it appears in *MT,* C, pp. 136–137; Sh, pp. 18–19). This psalm, depicting the power of God in a thunderstorm, is associated by the Rabbis with the giving of the Torah on Mount Sinai, which took place amid thunder and lightning; that is why it is recited when the Torah is paraded through the congregation on Shabbat (according to one rabbinic tradition, the giving of the Torah on Mount Sinai took place on Shabbat; see above, p. 116).

The other scriptural text that introduces the *hakafah* is Psalm 148:13–14. *Y'hal'lu et shem Adonai, ki nisgav sh'mo l'vado* ("Let us praise the Name of Adonai, for God's Name alone is exalted!") is the prayer leader's invitation to the congregation to join in the praise of God. The congregation joins in with the psalm's continuation, *Hodo al eretz v'shamayim* ("God's majesty is above the earth and heaven"), as the Torah procession begins.

As the Torah is returned to the ark (C, pp. 110, 374, 514; Sh, p. 256; W/F, pp. 110, 250), the verses Proverbs 4:2 (*Ki lekach tov natati lachem*, "For I have given you good instruction"), Proverbs 3:18 (*Eitz chayim hi*, "It is a tree of life"), Proverbs 3:17 (*D'racheha darchei no-am*, "Its ways are ways of pleasantness"), and Lamentations 5:21 (*Hashiveinu Adonai eilecha v'nashuvah*, "Return us to You, Adonai, and we will return") are recited, and the ark is closed. It is worth noting that three of these four final verses are from Proverbs. In its original context, Proverbs 4:2 refers to the teaching of a father to his son, while Proverbs 3:17–18 refers to wisdom, *chochmah*. Because Proverbs 4:2 uses the word *torah* ("instruction"), the Rabbis understood this verse to refer specifically to *the* Torah, *divine* instruction, which God gives out like parents to their children. And because wisdom was understood to come from God and, for the Rabbis, to be revealed specifically in the Torah, these verses too were applied to Torah. The last verse, from Lamentations, asks God to take back the people of Israel and to restore their fortunes; in its original setting, the plea was both religious and political. For this reason, it was omitted from many earlier Reform prayer books (including the *Union Prayer Book*), but restored in *Gates of Prayer* (followed by *Mishkan T'filah*), since it can be construed solely in a religious and spiritual sense.

In traditional liturgy, the verses that accompany the returning of the Torah to the ark begin with Numbers 10:36 ("When the Ark rested, Moses would say") and Psalm 132:8–10 ("May your priests be clothed in righteousness"), followed by Proverbs 4:2, and so on. The Numbers verse forms a frame with Numbers 10:35 ("When the Ark ventured forth, Moses would say"), which is recited at the beginning of the traditional Torah service. Both of these texts have been omitted in many Reform prayer books, because of their warlike associations. Similarly, the Psalms text has been omitted from most Reform prayer books because of its associations with the Temple cult and its personnel. They continue to be omitted in *MT*.

As a left-page alternative text, *MT* gives Psalm 19:8–10, *Torat Adonai t'mimah* ("God's Torah is perfect"). The use of this text in the Torah service, while not traditional, has a venerable Reform pedigree; it goes back to the first published liturgies of the Berlin Reform circle (*Die Deutsche Synagogue*, 1817), the prayer books of the radical Berlin Reformgemeinde (1845–48), and Rabbi David Einhorn's *Olat Tamid* (1856–58), where it was recited in German; it appears in Hebrew and English in the first *UPB* (1892, then 1894–95). The second left-page alternative text is a creative reading on the meaning of Torah by Rabbis John D. Rayner and Chaim Stern, based on rabbinic teachings (from *GOP*, p. 441; the original, by Rayner, appears in the British Liberal *Service of the Heart*, 1967, pp. 257–258; the specific rabbinic texts alluded to are listed by Stern in *Gates of Understanding*, p. 261, note 1122).

The Torah service in its entirety thus reenacts the Jewish people's encounter with God at Sinai, through the revelation, proclamation, and teaching of Torah, and its continuation and affirmation in the words of the prophets and sages.

Prayers for the Community

It is customary to offer prayers for the community—for the congregation, the country and its government, and (now) for the State of Israel—while the Torah scroll is still out. On the Shabbat preceding Rosh Chodesh, the first day of the new month, *Birkat HaChodesh*, the blessing over the new month, is also recited at this point in the service. *Mishkan T'filah* gives contemporary versions of these prayers, as well as blessings and prayers that may be recited by the parents of a bar or bat mitzvah or for a couple who receive an *aliyah* on the Shabbat before their wedding at an *Aufruf* ("summoning," "calling up") (C, pp. 376–381; Sh, pp. 258–263). While these appear in *MT* *after* the Torah is returned to the ark, they in fact should be recited *before* this takes place—and this is where they appear in a traditional prayer book.[100] Also given here is *T'filat Haderech*, the prayer recited by an individual before setting out on a journey. In traditional prayer books, this is found in the back of the book among the private, individual prayers. *MT* records it here as an option for public, communal acknowledgment of the journey about to be taken by a member or members of the congregation.

The traditional liturgy gives three prayers at this point in the service—two in Aramaic, both beginning with the phrase *Y'kum purkan min sh'maya* ("May salvation arise from heaven"), and one in Hebrew, beginning *Mi shebeirach avoteinu* ("May the One who blessed our forefathers"). The latter two prayers are both for the welfare of the community and those who support its religious, educational, and charitable activities. The former is for teachers of Torah and for the yeshivot in the Land of Israel and Babylonia (a very old prayer!). The contemporary equivalent in *MT* is an English prayer written by Rabbi Elyse D. Frishman (top of C, p. 376; Sh, p. 258), which nicely encapsulates the values we wish our congregations to embody. The *chatimah*, or concluding benedictory formula, is that of the *Avodah* benediction (for the acceptance of our worship) in the *T'filah*, according to the old rite of the Land of Israel as found in texts from the Cairo Genizah and used in many Reform prayer books.

Following prayers for the community, the traditional liturgy gives a prayer for the government, *Hanotein t'shuah lam'lachim* ("May He who gives victory to kings"). Too often in history, Jewish communities have been at the mercy of local or imperial rulers; this medieval prayer invokes blessing on those rulers, that they might be well disposed to their Jewish subjects. The modern equivalent in most Reform prayer books has been the vernacular prayer for our country and its government, as we find in *MT* (C, p. 376; Sh, p. 258).[101] Here we invoke those civic qualities to which we aspire for our country, its citizens, and its government—particularly social justice, as proclaimed in the verses from Isaiah 58 at the outset of the prayer.

The prayer for the welfare of the State of Israel, recited after the prayer for our country, was written in September 1948 by the chief rabbis of the State of Israel at that time, Isaac Halevi Herzog and Ben Zion Uziel, and edited by the noted writer Shmuel Yosef Agnon.[102] *MT* gives an abbreviated version of this prayer, following the model of the North American Conservative movement's *Siddur Sim Shalom* and using its concluding sentence (p. 149 there). It is noteworthy that *MT* is the first CCAR prayer book to include this prayer; it does not appear in either version of *Gates of Prayer*.

More prayers for the community are given in a second two-page spread in *MT* (C, pp. 378–379, 260–261). The first of these, *T'filat Haderech*, the prayer to be recited upon setting forth on a journey, traditionally is considered to be a private, rather than a communal, prayer. In the traditional siddur, it is given at the back of the book among the prayers and blessings that are recited by the individual on various occasions, as we have already noted.[103] This prayer, too, has a Talmudic origin (*B. B'rachot* 29b): Elijah instructs Rav Judah that a person should always take counsel with the Creator before setting forth on a journey.[104] This is interpreted to mean that a person should recite a prayer for divine protection before going forth. The prayer given in the Babylonian Talmud reads as follows:

> May it be Your will, Adonai my God, to lead me forth safely and direct my steps safely and uphold me in safety, and deliver me from the hand of every enemy and ambush along the way, and send a blessing on the works of my hands, and cause me to find grace, kindness, and mercy in Your eyes and in the eyes of all who behold me. Praised be You, Adonai, who hearkens to prayer.

It is then objected that a person should always associate oneself with the community; thus, one's prayer should be uttered in the first-person plural ("to lead *us* forth safely and direct *our* steps safely"). It is, indeed, in the first-person plural form (but slightly more elaborated) that this prayer is taken up into the medieval prayer rites—and perhaps partly for this reason that *MT* gives this prayer for offering in a public, communal context. (That choice also provides an opportunity for one going on a journey to let this be known to the congregation.)

The wording in *MT* is changed somewhat from the traditional text; there is less emphasis in *MT*'s version on the dangers that might befall the traveler on the way. The *chatimah* (final benedictory formula) that summarizes the theme of the prayer is also changed. The traditional *chatimah* is [*Baruch atah Adonai*] *shomei-a t'filah*, affirming that God hearkens to prayer, while *MT*'s chatimah is *shomeir Yisrael laad* (as in the weekday version of the evening *Hashkiveinu* prayer), asserting that God forever protects the people Israel.

MT (C, p. 379; Sh, p. 261) gives the prayer for the new month, traditionally called *Birkat HaChodesh*, the blessing of the new month. This is recited on the Shabbat before Rosh Chodesh and announces to the congregation the day on which the new month will begin. (In *MT*, it is also recited on Rosh Chodesh itself when that day falls on a Shabbat.) The traditional text has four parts: (1) a prayer that the new month may bring blessings, spelled out at some length; (2) a prayer that the new month may bring redemption to the people of Israel; (3) the announcement of the day on which the new month begins; (4) a prayer that the new month may bring renewed well-being, gladness, and redemption to the entire people of Israel.[105] *MT* omits the second and fourth parts and abbreviates somewhat the first and third. *GOP* (p. 453) had already restored the Hebrew text of the blessing for the new month to North American Reform liturgy (it had been included in an English version in all editions of the *Union Prayer Book*) and, after giving the same somewhat abbreviated version of the first paragraph, actually gives a fuller text of the rest, including the second and fourth parts that *MT* omits.

The next two-page spread (C, pp. 380–381; Sh, pp. 262–263), which concludes *MT*'s section of prayers for the community, contains more prayers for special occasions, specifically for the parents of a bar or bat mitzvah and for honoring those who are about to be married (an *Aufruf*, in German: for those who are "called up" to the Torah before their wedding). These are all creative texts in English. It is worth noting that the prayer at the top of the left-hand page (C, p. 381; Sh, p. 263) is Rabbi Lawrence Kushner's adaptation of a Talmudic blessing (*B. Berachot* 17a). In its original context, this blessing is offered by Rabbis on behalf of their teacher when they are departing from his study house (*beit midrash*). The Talmudic version reads as follows:

> May you see your needs provided for in your lifetime,
> and may your final destiny be for the world to come
> and your hope for many generations.
> May your heart contemplate understanding,
> Your mouth speak wisdom,

And your tongue sing songs of praise.
May your eyelids look straight before you,
Your eyes be enlightened with the light of Torah,
And your face shine like the bright heavens.
May your lips utter [words of] wisdom,
Your innards rejoice in uprightness,
And your footsteps run to hear the words of the Ancient of Days.

Once the Torah scroll has been returned to the ark, the Shabbat morning service concludes with *Aleinu* and Mourner's *Kaddish*.

Shabbat Afternoon Service
Atah Echad: "You Are One"

THE SHABBAT AFTERNOON service (*Minchah*[106]) consists of three elements: (1) a recitation of the *T'filah*, which is the core of every worship service, and (2) a brief Torah reading, both of which are preceded by (3) a recitation of *Ashrei* (Psalm 145, preceded by the two "*Ashrei*" verses, Psalms 84:5 and 144:15).

As noted earlier, there is a Talmudic dictum (*B. B'rachot* 4b) that enjoins the recitation of *Ashrei* three times a day.[107] Liturgical tradition fixes those three times as here at the beginning of the afternoon service and twice in the morning service—once toward the beginning as part of *P'sukei D'zimrah* (the recitation of psalms before *Bar'chu*), and once toward the end after the *T'filah* and *Tachanun* (the supplicatory weekday prayers omitted from most Reform prayer books); on Monday, Thursday, and Shabbat mornings; when the Torah is read, this second morning *Ashrei* follows the Torah service.

In a traditional afternoon service, *Ashrei* is followed by a series of biblical verses and texts beginning with Isaiah 59:20–21 (*Uva l'Tzion go-eil*, "A redeemer will come to Zion") that sound the theme of messianic redemption. This series of texts is also called *K'dushah D'sidra* (the recitation of the *K'dushah* in conjunction with the *sidra*, the Torah reading), since it includes yet another recitation of the *K'dushah* (including an interpretive translation of the verses into Aramaic) and usually follows the Torah reading in the traditional daily morning service. This material generally has been omitted from Reform prayer books, for reasons both of redundancy and length and of theme. Traditionally, the Shabbat afternoon Torah reading follows directly at this point, preceding the *T'filah*. *Mishkan T'filah* gives the *T'filah* first, followed by the Torah reading, presumably because this is the order to which most Reform Jews are accustomed from morning services

While the main weekly Torah reading is, of course, on Shabbat mornings, the Torah is also read on Shabbat afternoons and on Monday and

Thursday mornings. What is read on these latter three occasions is the first section of the portion that will be read in its entirety the following Shabbat morning—so the Shabbat afternoon Torah reading is from the *next* week's portion. Traditionally, three people are called up to the Torah to recite the blessings.[108] The traditional liturgy for removing the Torah from the ark and returning it to the ark is less elaborate than on Shabbat mornings; it is identical with that for weekdays. Because *MT* gives only one liturgy for reading the Torah on Shabbat and places it after the afternoon service (C, p. 362ff.; Sh, p. 244ff.), the impression is created that this liturgy is to be used for the Shabbat afternoon service as well. More appropriate to this service, however, is the weekday Torah-reading liturgy (C, p. 104ff.; W/F, p. 104ff.).

The *T'filah* for Shabbat afternoon is identical to that for the other Shabbat services. The only point of textual difference among the three Shabbat services, as we have remarked above, is in the *K'dushat HaYom* ("Sanctification of the Day") benediction that is unique and central to the Shabbat *T'filah*. This benediction has an invariant core: *Kad'sheinu b'mitzvotecha*, "Sanctify us with Your mitzvot." What varies among the three services is the poetic introduction to this core. In the afternoon service, the introduction is a poem, *Atah echad v'shimcha echad*, "You are *One*, and Your name is *one*, and there is none like Your people Israel, a people *unique* on earth" (C, p. 352, Sh, p. 234; the italicized words are the same in Hebrew: *echad*, which forms the poetic spine of the text). The theme of this passage is the special relationship between Israel and God that is marked out by their observance of Shabbat rest—"a rest of peace and serenity, tranquility and security, a perfect rest which You so desire. . . . This sacred rest links them to You, and through their rest they sanctify Your name." It is these poetic textual differences, each of them embellishing the invariant core of the blessing, that give each of the *T'filot* for Shabbat its special feeling or atmosphere.

Havdalah
Distinguishing between the Sacred and the Ordinary

JUST AS SHABBAT begins with a ritual of sanctification enacted over a cup of wine (*Kiddush*) that moves us from the ordinary time of the workday week to the sacred time of Shabbat rest, so it ends with a ritual of separation enacted over a cup of wine (*Havdalah*) that transitions back from the sacred time of Shabbat to the ordinary time of the workday week. Both of these rituals are, in fact, doubled in traditional liturgy—both form a part of the *T'filah* on Friday and Saturday evenings, respectively, and then are recited (with varied wording) over a cup of wine at the conclusion of the evening service in the synagogue and again at home. In this way, there can be no question that everyone has acknowledged both the beginning and the end of Shabbat through their enacted behavior.

At the beginning of Shabbat, the *K'dushat HaYom / Kiddush HaYom* blessing ("Be pleased with our rest") forms the centerpiece of the evening *T'filah* and is repeated in varied form during all of the Shabbat services in place of the weekday *T'filah* petitions. At the end of Shabbat, we return to the weekday form of the *T'filah* and include a *Havdalah* insertion (*Atah chonantanu*) in the first of the weekday petitions, the prayer for knowledge and discernment (*Binah*). It reads as follows:

> You have graced us with the knowledge of Your Torah
> and have taught us to perform the statutes of Your will.
> You have distinguished, O Eternal our God,
> between sacred and ordinary,
> between light and darkness,
> between Israel and the nations,
> between the seventh day and the six days of work.
> Our Father, our King, may the days approaching us bring peace;
> may we be free from all sin,
> cleansed from all iniquity,
> holding fast to our reverence for You.

I cite this text in full because most Reform Jews have never seen it; it does not appear in most Reform prayer books nor does it appear in *Mishkan T'filah*, since most Reform congregations do not hold evening services at the end of Shabbat (other than *Havdalah* bar/bat mitzvah services, which use the afternoon liturgy).

What most Reform Jews *are* familiar with, though, is the repetition of this ritual over a cup of wine, together with blessings over spices and the lights of fire that are recited at the conclusion of the Saturday evening synagogue service and at home. This is the more dramatic and experiential enactment of the end of Shabbat. This ritual, too, was only gradually reclaimed by the North American Reform Movement in the years following the Second World War, initially (so it seems) at Saturday evening youth group events. This is the ritual that appears in *MT* (C, pp. 610–617; Sh, pp. 306–313), appropriately, in the section of "Blessings for the Home and Synagogue."

The ritual begins with the singing or recitation of a series of verses, mostly from the psalms, that deal with the theme of God's protection and blessing and anticipate the future redemption, concerns that were—and are—on people's minds contemplating the uncertainties of the week about to commence:

> Behold, the God who gives me triumph! I am confident, unafraid.
> For Adonai is my strength and might, and has been my
> deliverance . . . [Isaiah 12:2–3].
> The Jews enjoyed light and gladness, happiness and honor
> [Esther 8:16].
> So may it be with us!

The surrounding of liturgical action with biblical verses is an ancient Jewish custom. The recitation of biblical texts invokes God's power and attention, since the texts were deemed to derive from God. This set goes back to the early Middle Ages and varies considerably in extent and specific verses from rite to rite.

The core ritual comprises a series of four blessings, all recited over a cup of wine. That is why, although the wine blessing is recited first, the wine is not actually drunk until after the last of the blessings has been recited. (The same logic applies, for example, to the *Kiddush* at the beginning of

Shabbat and to the Seven Wedding Blessings, also recited over a cup of wine; the wine is drunk only after all the blessings have been recited.) The wine celebrates the sweetness and joy of living.

The blessing over spices, which follows, hints at the early locus of this ceremony: after the third meal on Shabbat. Spices (including lighting incense) were used literally to "clear the air" at the end of a meal, to fumigate the room. Over time, the sweet smell of the spices acquired other, more homiletical meanings—such as acting as smelling salts to revive us at the departure, at the end of Shabbat, of our additional "Shabbat soul" (*n'shamah y'teirah*) in traditional lore.

The third blessing, over the lights of fire, is the practically important one. The fresh kindling of a flame, over which it is recited, signifies and embodies the resumption of the week's activities. It is customary to use the light by observing the flickering shadows of your fingers on your palms as you hold them up to the flame, thus personally acknowledging the beginning of the workweek.

Finally, the fourth and longest blessing is the *Havdalah* benediction proper, which marks out the distinctions that God made in creating the world and that we are to enact in our daily lives, "between the holy and ordinary, between light and dark, between Israel and the nations, between the seventh day and the six days of work." (*Gates of Prayer*, which restored this ritual to the North American Reform prayer book, nonetheless omitted "between Israel and the nations," as intimating a sense of Jewish exclusiveness or superiority.)

The ritual concludes with the singing or recitation of a medieval hymn that begins with the words of the final blessing, *Hamavdil bein kodesh l'chol / chatoteinu hu yimchol*, "May the One who distinguishes between the holy and the ordinary / pardon our sins." *MT* gives only the first verse of this hymn, since this is what is most frequently sung. *GOP* gives four verses; the full hymn has nine verses. The blessing/greeting for the end of Shabbat, *Shavua tov* ("A good week"), is not part of this hymn, but is sung as a refrain in the most familiar Ashkenazic folk melody. Finally, another hymn is sung that greets the prophet Elijah, who in Jewish lore will return to herald the time of the divine redemption. Since Shabbat, in Jewish tradition, is deemed to be a foretaste of the redeemed world, there is no need for Elijah to come on Shabbat; but as Shabbat ends and the new workday week begins, our ancestors looked forward once again to the speedy coming of Elijah, the harbinger of redemption, and we are reminded, too, of the sacred tasks that lie before us.

Just as we greet the arrival of Shabbat with song each week, so do we mark its departure, carrying forward into the new week some of its special glow and feeling as we look forward to a world redeemed.

Festivals and Seasons

Introduction to the Festivals

THE THIRD and final set of worship services in *Mishkan T'filah*, after those for weekdays and Shabbat, is for the three seasonal festivals of the Jewish year—Pesach, Shavuot, and Sukkot. In Hebrew, these are called the *Shalosh R'galim*, the Three Pilgrimage Festivals (literally "three times, occasions," as at Exodus 23:14—*shalosh r'galim tachog li bashanah*, "Three times a year you shall hold a festival for Me"). At these seasons, it was customary for Israelites to make a pilgrimage to Jerusalem to attend the festivities and rituals at the Temple.

The seasonal festivals mark out crucial transition points in the agricultural year, which is tied to the cycles of the sun. The spring equinox marks the end of the rainy season in the Land of Israel, as well as the beginning of the barley harvest and the birthing of new calves and kids in the herds and flocks (hence the connection of Pesach with the firstborn and with the offering of the omer, the first new sheaf of barley, as well as with the clearing out of the old grain that has leavened or mildewed during the rainy season). The barley harvest season lasts seven weeks (*shivah shavuot*). At the end of this period, the Festival of Shavuot ("Weeks"; also called *Atzeret*, "Conclusion") marks the end of the barley harvest and the beginning of the wheat harvest, as well as that for other produce of the season (*bikurim*, "first fruits"; the festival is also referred to as *Chag HaBikurim*, or *Chag HaKatzir bikurei maasecha*, "the Feast of the Harvest, of the first fruits of your work"—Exodus 23:16).

The autumnal equinox marks the time of ingathering of the summer crops (*Chag HaAsif*, "the Feast of Ingathering at the end of the [agricultural] year, when you gather in the results of your work from the field"—Exodus 23:16), as well as the beginning of the rainy season in the Land of Israel. The name Sukkot ("Booths") for this festival likely has to do with the fact that harvesters stayed out in the fields day and night during this period, in order to work with the crops, and erected booths there in which to eat and sleep, so as not to lose any work time.

The process of "historicization" (or "mythicization") of these three agricultural festivals already begins in the Torah, where the distinctive seasonal elements of Pesach (firstborn, clearing out the leaven) are associated with the story of the Israelite redemption from Egyptian slavery, and the harvest booths of Sukkot are associated with the story of the wilderness wanderings ("in order that future generations may know that I made the Israelite people live in booths when I brought them out of the land of Egypt"—Leviticus 23:42–43). For Shavuot, this process appears to be postbiblical, since the association of Shavuot with the giving of the Torah on Sinai is nowhere mentioned in the Bible itself. It appears explicitly in *Seder Olam Rabbah* and in the Babylonian Talmud (*Shabbat* 86b ff.).

Rabbinic liturgy takes for granted all of these associations, both mythical and agricultural. Thus the traditional Torah reading for Shavuot is Exodus 19–20, the giving of the Torah at Sinai and the Ten Commandments; the reading for the first day of Pesach is the story of the last plague on Egypt, the killing of the firstborn sons at midnight and the redemption of the Israelite firstborn, and for the seventh day, the crossing of the Sea of Reeds (assumed by the Rabbis to have taken place on that day) and the Song at the Sea.[109] The seasonal prayer for rain is first recited at the end of Sukkot, on Sh'mini Atzeret, and the prayer for dew on the first day of Pesach. The Scroll of Song of Songs is read during Pesach (either on the Shabbat that falls during Pesach or on the first day), since it depicts love in bloom at the springtide of the year in the Land of Israel; the Scroll of Ruth is read on Shavuot, because its crucial incidents take place during the time of the barley harvest in the Land of Israel; and the Scroll of Kohelet (Ecclesiastes) is read on Sukkot, with its autumnal mood and stress on the fragility of life, like the fragility of the harvest booth as a *dirat arai* ("temporary dwelling").[110]

The rabbinic festival calendar is broadly identical to that of Leviticus 23 and Numbers 28–29 but has also been subtly reconceived. Pesach falls on the first full moon of the springtime, the fifteenth of the month. In the calendar of the Torah, that is the month of Aviv, the first month of the year. The rabbinic calendar, on the other hand, has been influenced by the Israelite exile to Babylonia—the names of the months are Babylonian (here, Nisan instead of Aviv), and the year begins at the autumnal equinox instead of the vernal one, as was the case with the old Babylonian calendar (thus "the first day of the seventh month" of Leviticus 23:24 becomes the rabbinic Rosh HaShanah, the New Year; the biblical observances of the first and tenth day of the seventh month, by the way, are preparatory to the ingathering of the harvest on Sukkot—this is one long ritual sequence).

Otherwise, the order of festivals remains the same. The seventh, or final, day of Pesach is also observed as a festival. Shavuot falls on the sixth of Sivan, fifty days after the first day of Pesach. Sukkot falls on the full moon of the rabbinic first month, Tishrei, which is the biblical seventh month, and lasts for seven days. The eighth day is also observed as a festival, Atzeret (called by the Rabbis, Sh'mini Atzeret, "the eighth-day festival").

What is totally new in the rabbinic calendar (and thoroughly rabbinic in its Torah-centered ethos) is Simchat Torah, the day of "Rejoicing in the Torah," which marks the (now annual) conclusion and recommencement of the synagogue cycle of Torah readings.[111] The custom is post-Talmudic and is associated with the diasporic "second day" of Sh'mini Atzeret in early Ashkenazic liturgical-halachic literature.[112] Reform congregations that, since the nineteenth century, have not observed the diasporic second day of the festivals, as well as congregations in Israel, celebrate Simchat Torah on Sh'mini Atzeret (on Reform calendars this appears as Sh'mini Atzeret–Simchat Torah).

Structurally speaking, rabbinic liturgy treats the Three Pilgrimage Festivals together as a group, but also finds ways to delineate and specify each of them.

The Jewish Calendar—and Reform Options

In order to understand and appreciate more fully the logic and significance of the festivals in Jewish tradition, we need to consider further the Jewish calendar and the cycle of the Jewish year. The calendar in use today is a rabbinic elaboration of the biblical calendar. That calendar is lunisolar. While the months are determined by the cycles of the moon (and particularly by the appearance of the new moon), the year is determined by the cycle of the sun.[113] Specifically, Pesach must fall out each year in the spring, so the year is intercalated (that is, extra days are added) before the month of Nisan, in which Pesach occurs.[114]

The lunar month—astronomically speaking, the period between one conjunction of the moon with the sun (during which the moon is not visible) and the next—is 29 days plus a remainder (12 hours, 44 minutes, and 3½ seconds). Since only full days are counted in the calendar, this means that some months in the Jewish year will have 30 days (Nisan, Sivan, Av, Tishrei, Sh'vat, Adar I), while the rest will have 29 (Iyar, Tammuz, Elul, Tevet, Adar II). The months of Cheshvan and Kislev can vary in this regard from year to year.

Because the orbit of the earth around the sun is elliptical rather than circular, the exact length of the solar year is 365 days plus a remainder (48 minutes and 46 seconds). Since the solar year is about 11 days longer than the lunar year, an additional month (Adar II) is added in each of seven out of the nineteen years that constitute the lunar cycle. While some of the mathematical principles and calculations involved in the periodic intercalation of the calendar were already worked out by the Rabbis of the Talmud, the full regularization of the Jewish calendar, as we know it today, did not take place until the tenth century.[115]

As we noted above, the festivals of the Jewish year are all agricultural in origin; they are tied to the phases of the sun. The vernal equinox[116] marks the beginning of spring. In the Land of Israel, this is the end of the rainy season and the period of the wheat and barley harvests, as well as the birthing season for flocks and herds. The spring festival cycle begins with Pesach, at the full moon of the spring month (fifteenth of Nisan). Agriculturally speaking, Pesach celebrates the new grain crop (hence the requirement to remove anything leavened—fermented—in order to begin the year with new, unsullied grain produce) as well as the new life among domesticated animals. The first sheaf (omer) of the grain and the first-born of the flocks and herds are offered up to God, who owns the land and governs its fertility, as an act of gratitude and in order to ensure future fertility. Wheat matures approximately seven weeks later than barley, so seven weeks are counted before bringing in the wheat harvest and other first fruits of the crops, as well as marking the end of the barley harvest (Shavuot).

The autumnal equinox[117] marks the beginning of autumn. In the Land of Israel, this is the beginning of the rainy season and the time of harvest for late summer crops. The Festival of Sukkot, which begins at the full moon of the biblical seventh month (rabbinic first month) is the time of ingathering, when the rains are eagerly anticipated and fervently prayed for. Booths are put up in the fields so that the harvesters may stay out with the crops. The priestly festival calendars of Leviticus 23 and Numbers 28–29 also mark out the first and tenth days of the (biblical) seventh month for ritual attention. The first day of the month is the time for blowing loud blasts (*t'ruot*), presumably to call God's attention to the plight of the Israelite people, whose lives and livelihoods depend at this time of year on adequate rainfall and an abundant harvest. The tenth day of the month is when the sanctuary must be purged of all impurities—and the people purified from their sins that defile the land and the sanctuary—in advance of the harvest ingathering and the onset of the rains.

The winter solstice is marked by the lighting of lights during Chanukah. The summer solstice is no longer marked on the Jewish festival calendar (although Ezekiel 8:14 refers disparagingly to the women's rite of weeping for Tammuz, the Babylonian fertility god, as vegetation died in the intense midsummer heat). Instead, fasts connected with the destruction of the Temple (seventeenth of Tammuz, ninth of Av) are observed.

The major seasonal festivals of spring (Pesach) and fall (Sukkot) each last a week, with an eighth-day concluding festival (called by the Rabbis Shemini Atzeret) at the end of Sukkot. Chanukah, too, lasts eight days (it is modeled in this regard after Sukkot). Shavuot, on the other hand, is observed for a single day, as are Rosh HaShanah and Yom Kippur. In the Babylonian Diaspora, certainly by the time of the Talmud, it became customary to add a day to the observance of all of the biblical festivals (except, of course, for the fast of Yom Kippur, so as not to cause undue physical distress). The reason for this two-day observance was that the beginning of each festival was set in the Land of Israel and proclaimed by the rabbinical courts in the land. It could take as long as a second day for the proclamation to be received in Babylonia—so a second day was observed as a precautionary measure (one of the two days observed was certainly the festival day). By the time the calendar came to be set according to foolproof mathematical calculations rather than fallible empirical astronomical observation, the second-day observance (*yom tov sheini shel galuyot*) had become a long-standing and hallowed custom in Babylonia (and in the Mediterranean Diaspora under its influence)—and thus the custom was retained. In the Land of Israel only a single festival day was observed, and that remains customary today in the State of Israel.

The custom of observing two days of Rosh HaShanah has a different rationale that obtains even in the Land of Israel: namely, doubt as to when the new moon of Tishrei actually occurs—particularly when this was dependent on the testimony of eyewitnesses. The theoretical possibility of observing two days of Rosh HaShanah for this reason is raised in the Mishnah (*M. Rosh HaShanah* 4:4),[118] but the list of festival Torah readings given at *M. Me'gilah* 3:5 and *T. M'gilah* 3:6 suggests that, in fact, the Mishnaic custom was to observe only a single day of Rosh HaShanah (no reading is listed in either the Mishnah or *Tosefta* for a second day of Rosh HaShanah). The present custom of observing two days of Rosh HaShanah in the Land of Israel as well dates from the twelfth century, when Jews from Provence settled there and instituted the custom.

In the modern Reform Movement, the question of whether it was necessary or desirable to observe the second day of the festivals—since their rationale was perceived to be artificial and outdated—was taken up in Germany in the 1840s.[119] As early as 1846, the Reform rabbis in the German states assembled in conference in Breslau declared that the Diaspora second-day observances of the festivals "have lost their meaning for our time. Congregations are therefore fully justified in abolishing the second-day holidays if they are inclined to do so" (cited in *CCAR Yearbook* 1 [1890], p. 96). North American Reform congregations routinely opted not to observe the second festival day. The second day of Rosh HaShanah, on the other hand, was observed in most German Reform congregations and in some North American Reform congregations as well. But it was not observed in the *Union Prayer Book* (vol. 2) of 1894 or its significant predecessors (Rabbi Leo Merzbacher's prayer book [1855] for Temple Emanuel in New York, Rabbi David Einhorn's *Olat Tamid* [1858]) or in Rabbi Isaac Mayer Wise's *Minhag America* (vol. 2; 1866). On the other hand, *Gates of Repentance* (1978) provided two sets of services for Rosh HaShanah, allowing for the possibility of a second-day observance, and the multiple options in the two-page spreads of *Mishhan HaNefesh* (2015) allow for the same possibility.

The decision of virtually all Reform congregations not to observe the diasporan second day of the festivals (including the eighth day of Pesach and Simchat Torah as the second day of Sh'mini Atzeret)[120] leads to some interesting complications for the weekly cycle of Torah readings when the traditional eighth day of Pesach or the second day of Shavuot fall on a Shabbat. Traditional congregations on these days read special Torah portions for these festivals. Reform congregations, on the other hand, resume the regular Torah-reading cycle of the year (usually, but not always, *Parashat Sh'mini* after Pesach and *Parashat Naso* after Shavuot). In this, they concur with all congregations in the Land of Israel. If the decision is made to simply conform the weekly Torah reading schedule at this point to the schedule used in Israel, it will diverge from the diasporan reading schedule for anywhere between six and fifteen weeks, depending on the length and type of the year.[121] Some North American congregations have chosen to follow this custom, in symbolic identification with the Jewish community in Israel. But it can potentially cause confusion closer to home. In order to preserve relative uniformity within local communities and to avoid this kind of confusion, the CCAR Responsa Committee has consistently recommended other practices over the past forty years, particularly to split the first *parashah* after the holiday into two halves and to distribute them over two weeks; during the second week, the reading is then back in sync with the diasporan Torah-reading cycle and the rest of the local community. (Most recently, this practice has been endorsed for the forthcoming app Reform Luach.) Other possibilities include repeating the festival reading from the previous day or reading from Deuteronomy 14:22–16:17 (the reading for the extra festival day) on the first Shabbat and then resuming the regular cycle on the second.[122]

A similar decision needs to be made by Reform congregations regarding the observance of Rosh Chodesh during those months that have thirty days. Traditionally in these circumstances, both the thirtieth day of the month and the first day of the next month are observed as Rosh Chodesh, since there is doubt as to when the actual new month begins. Some Reform congregations decide to observe only a single day of Rosh Chodesh, namely the first day of the new month (so that, ironically, it is the traditional second day that is observed). This has additional liturgical consequences with regard to the Shabbat haftarah that might be read on the day before Rosh Chodesh (*Machar Chodesh,* I Samuel 20:18–42) or on the day of Rosh Chodesh itself when it falls on Shabbat (Isaiah 66:1–13,

23): if the thirtieth day of the month is not observed as Rosh Chodesh, then, if it falls out on Shabbat, one would read *Machar Chodesh* instead of the reading for Shabbat Rosh Chodesh. If the thirtieth day of the month falls on a Sunday, one would not read *Machar Chodesh*. (Some Reform congregations choose not to read either of these haftarot in any case, but simply read the regular weekly haftarah.) Any of these decisions can be validly grounded. As we consider these issues, we should not wonder that calendar has so often been a source and a marker of sectarian/social divisions in Jewish history.

The Festival Liturgy

An Overview

As we mentioned above, rabbinic liturgy treats the Three Pilgrimage Festivals as a single entity, with a uniform liturgical structure; the services are essentially modifications and elaborations of those held on Shabbat. Added to the Shabbat structure on all three festivals in the morning service is the recitation of *Hallel*, Psalms 113–118, immediately following the *T'filah*. These psalms had been chanted by the Levites in the Temple on festival days, according to *M. Tamid* 7:5.

The specification and individuation of each of the festivals—Pesach, Shavuot, and Sukkot—are accomplished by slight verbal variations in the central *K'dushat HaYom* ("Sanctification of the Day") benediction in the *T'filah*; by special Torah, haftarah, and scroll readings for each day that are themed for the occasion; and by special rituals that are unique to each day (the prayer for dew on the first day of Pesach, the prayer for rain on Sh'mini Atzeret, the blessing over the *lulav* and the processions with it around the synagogue while intoning the *Hoshanot* prayers that ask for salvation through rainfall on Sukkot, the processions with the Torah [*hakafot*] and elaborate rituals for calling up those who will offer Torah blessings on Simchat Torah). Additionally, in the traditional liturgy there is an abundance of *piyutim* (hymns, poetry) that deal with the special themes of each day.

Our liturgy today is a direct descendant of the Babylonian rite that has its roots in the Babylonian Talmud and was elaborated and disseminated by the post-Talmudic rabbinic authorities there (*geonim*, "eminences"). These authorities wanted to create textual forms and structures that could be learned without too much difficulty by far-flung Jewish communities. That is why they kept the basic texts the same for all three festivals and built in only slight verbal variations for each. An alternative to this practice is visible in those prayer books of the old rite of the Land of Israel that have been preserved in fragmentary form in the Cairo Genizah. Here, there are much more elaborate verbal expansions that particularize each of the three festivals, just as there are (for example) Shabbat versions of standard *K'riat Sh'ma* and *T'filah* blessings that weave together the theme of Shabbat with the specific theme of each blessing.

Reform liturgy historically excised many of the *piyutim* that gave a specific flavor to each of the holidays. (Some of these *piyutim* are also no longer recited in many traditional synagogues.) Additionally, Reform congregations often excised or heavily abbreviated some of the particular rituals for each of the festivals (prayers for rain and dew, *Hoshanot* and *hakafot* processions, waving the *lulav*); many, but not all, of these rituals are being reclaimed and refashioned by Reform congregations today. On the other hand, Reform liturgy particularized each of the festivals with newly created English readings and prayers (mostly introductory) that interpreted the meaning of each festival in both a historical and contemporary vein.

In the next sections, we will look at those aspects of the liturgy that are unique to the festivals. It is therefore important at the outset to lay out the structure of the various festival services as elaborations of the more familiar parts of Shabbat services:

Festival Evening Service

1. *Sh'ma* and Its Blessings (no textual changes)
2. *T'filah*: seven blessings, as on Shabbat (the only textual changes are in the central *K'dushat HaYom* blessing, detailed below)
3. Counting the Omer (between the second day of Pesach and Shavuot)
4. Closing prayers: *Aleinu*, *Kaddish*

Festival Morning Service

1. Morning Blessings (identical to Shabbat and weekdays)
2. *P'sukei D'Zimrah* psalms, framed by blessings (identical to Shabbat; psalms identical to weekdays)
3. *Sh'ma* and Its Blessings (identical to weekdays)
4. *T'filah*: seven blessings, as on Shabbat (the only textual changes are in the central *K'dushat HaYom* blessing)
5. *Hallel* psalms: unique to festivals; preceded during Sukkot by *lulav* blessing

6. Reading of the special scroll for each of the festivals (the custom is to do this on the first day; traditionally it is usually done at this point on the intermediate Shabbat during the festival [Pesach or Sukkot] but is always done on the last day of Pesach and on Shemini Atzeret if those days fall on Shabbat)
7. Torah and haftarah reading
8. *Yizkor* memorial prayers: on the last day of each of the festivals (historically, eighth day of Pesach, second day of Shavuot, Sh'mini Atzeret; for Reform, seventh day of Pesach, the one day of Shavuot, Sh'mini Atzeret–Simchat Torah)
9. On the first day of Pesach and on Sh'mini Atzeret: traditionally the prayers for rain and dew are incorporated into the *Musaf T'filah* at this point; during Sukkot, *Hoshanot* are recited in a procession with the *lulav* at the end of *Musaf*
10. Closing prayers: *Aleinu, Kaddish.*

In the coming sections, we will elaborate on each of these changes. Even more than the textual changes, it is the specific melodies for the festivals that make their liturgy distinctive.

Festival Evening Service
Opening Readings

The traditional evening and morning services for the festivals begin with no special fanfare; the evening service begins with *Bar'chu,* and the morning service begins with the usual *Birchot HaShachar* blessings and prayers. Reform prayer books, on the other hand, from the nineteenth century onward, have taken the opportunity at the very outset of the services to frame them with special occasional meditations/readings/prayers in the vernacular that serve to highlight the significance of the festivals generally and of each one in particular, as well as to recast their religious meanings in contemporary terms. This practice, following Rabbi David Einhorn in particular, was "codified" for North American Reform Jews in the *Union Prayer Book* (1895), which began each service with an appropriate psalm text to be sung and a generic reading for all three festivals (the specific readings for each of them followed a few pages later). The 1940 *UPB* began both the evening and morning services with a specific reading for each festival (somewhat longer in the evening than in the morning). *Gates of Prayer* (1975) combined these practices, beginning each service with a generic prayer (evening) or psalm (morning), then immediately offering a series of special readings to choose from for each festival. *Mishkan T'filah,* hewing to its two-page-spread format, offers in both the evening and the morning services only a single, brief meditation/prayer for each festival, so that all of the materials may fit onto a single spread (all of the readings are different in the evening and morning services).

Each of the introductory readings in the evening service captures an essential theme of its festival, while indicating its contemporary relevance and moral force. Thus the reading for the first day of Pesach focuses on the kinds of slavery that persist today and the recognition that freedom still remains a goal to be achieved. The reading for the seventh day of Pesach focuses on our singing of the Song at the Sea as an act that acknowledges contemporary experiences of redemption. The reading for

Shavuot compares the coming of summer with the vision of Torah: the one a promise of harvest fulfilled, the other a promise of goodness fulfilled. The reading for Sukkot sees the fall harvest and the fragile shelter of the sukkah as opportunities to share our bounty with those in need. The reading for Sh'mini Atzeret–Simchat Torah is a prayer and an exhortation for the internalization by each of us of Torah's life-affirming wisdom.

In the evening service for the festivals in *Mishkan T'filah*, only the introductory reading for Shavuot had been composed for a previous Reform prayer book. It was written by Rabbi Chaim Stern for *GOP* (p. 466), the first two verses of a poetic meditation there. The Pesach meditation on slavery and freedom, appropriately, comes from Leonard Fein, the founder of both Mazon: A Jewish Response to Hunger and *Moment* magazine. The meditation for the seventh day of Pesach was written by Rabbis Bernard Mehlman and Lawrence Hoffman, two members of the Siddur Publishing Team. The meditation for Sukkot is by Rabbis Richard Levy and Elyse D. Frishman, and that for Simchat Torah is by poet Daniel Siegel.[123]

Kabbalat Panim for Festivals
An Overview

The festival evening service in *Mishkan T'filah*, like the Shabbat evening service, begins with *Kabbalat Panim*—Welcoming. For the festivals, this rubric includes the blessings over the festival lights and the festival *Kiddush* over a cup of wine (or grape juice). Traditionally, these blessings are recited in the home. Candles are lit, as on Shabbat, before the festival begins, and *Kiddush* is recited over wine at the beginning of the evening meal (which is eaten after returning from the evening service in the synagogue). The North American Reform Movement, by 1940, had moved both additionally into the synagogue. The rationale for this move was to ensure that congregants who might not perform these rituals at home were exposed to them in the synagogue (just as the traditional rationale for reciting *Kiddush* over wine in the synagogue on Shabbat evenings was to make sure that everyone had the opportunity to fulfill this mitzvah).

The form of both blessings on the festivals corresponds to their form on Shabbat. Festival lights are kindled with the words *l'hadlik ner shel Yom Tov* ("to kindle the light of this festival"). When the festival falls on Shabbat, the words are *l'hadlik ner shel Shabbat v'shel Yom Tov*; the more common occurrence (Shabbat) takes precedence. The wording of the festival *Kiddush* includes some of the same phrases as on Shabbat (notably, *Ki vanu vacharta v'otanu kidashta mikol haamim*, "For You have chosen us from all the peoples and consecrated us to Your service"), but otherwise its wording is distinctive to the festivals (just as the wording of the Shabbat *Kiddush* focuses on the theme of Shabbat). Here, the theme is that God's singling out of the people Israel from among all other peoples is manifest particularly in the divine gift of the festival calendar itself. The festivals of the Jewish year are themselves signs of God's love. In addition to their generic treatment, each festival is epitomized in a specific phrase: Pesach is *Chag HaMatzot, z'man cheiruteinu* ("the Feast of Unleavened Bread, the season of our liberation/freedom"); Shavuot is *z'man matan*

Torateinu ("the season of our receiving Torah"); Sukkot and Sh'mini Atzeret are *z'man simchateinu* ("the season of our rejoicing"). The *chatimah,* or concluding blessing formula, in the festival *Kiddush* is *m'kadeish Yisrael v'haz'manim,* "who sanctifies Israel and the festivals"—Israel is mentioned first, because it is only on account of God's singling out Israel that we have been given the sacred festivals. The traditional Ashkenazic melody for chanting the festival *Kiddush* is different from that for Shabbat.

A further blessing recited at the conclusion of the festival *Kiddush* is the so-called *Birkat HaZ'man,* the blessing expressing gratitude upon reaching a special occasion, also called *Shehecheyanu. Mishkan T'filah* records this a second time after the candle blessing, following a late medieval usage.

Verses of the Season

The traditional evening service liturgy on Shabbat and the festivals is, for the most part, verbally identical to the weekday liturgy until one arrives at the end of the *K'riat Sh'ma* rubric. *Hashkiveinu*, the final blessing after the *Sh'ma* in the evening, concludes on both Shabbat and the festivals with a more elaborate *chatimah* (summary blessing formula): instead of the weekday *shomeir amo Yisrael laad*, "Eternal Guardian of Israel," we praise God as *haporeis sukat shalom aleinu v'al kol amo Yisrael v'al Yerushalayim*, "whose shelter of peace is spread over us, over all Your people Israel, and over Jerusalem"—an allusion to the messianic hope of restoration that is anticipated in the peaceful experience of both Shabbat and the festivals.

Before reciting the *Chatzi Kaddish* (not included at this point in *Mishkan T'filah*), which marks off this section of the service from the *T'filah* that follows, we chant or recite special scriptural verses that give voice to a major theme or idea of the special occasion: *V'shamru* (Exodus 31:16–17) on Shabbat, which reminds us of the covenant of rest from work on the seventh day, when Israel emulates God's rest from the act of Creation;[124] and *Vay'dabeir Moshe* (Leviticus 23:44), the conclusion of the laws of festival observances in Leviticus, as the special verse for each of the three festivals. This verse relates how Moses proclaimed to Israel the appointed times ordained by God.[125] All of these verses generally are chanted or sung.

The Festival *T'filah*

The festival *T'filah* is structurally similar to that on Shabbat. Here, too, the daily petitionary blessings are replaced by a single blessing, *K'dushat HaYom*, that deals with the special sanctity of the holy day, in this case, the particular festival. The invariant core of this blessing (*kad'sheinu b'mitzvotecha*, "sanctify us / make us holy with Your mitzvot") is well known to most Reform Jews from its use on Shabbat as well. The first three and the last three blessings of the *T'filah* are recited as on Shabbat and weekdays. The reason for the deletion of the weekday petitions on the festivals is the same as on Shabbat: these are occasions for rest and enjoyment, not for worrying about one's daily needs.

The wording of the festival *K'dushat HaYom* blessing is generic for all festivals (as well as, with some modifications, for Rosh HaShanah and Yom Kippur; all but the last paragraph of the blessing is different from that on Shabbat). The blessing begins, *Atah v'chartanu mikol haamim*, "You have chosen us from among all peoples" (C, p. 478; W/F, p. 214). The theme of this first paragraph is that the people Israel's observance of the divinely ordained festivals and festival calendar is a sign of God's special love for them. According to tradition, only to the Jewish people did God reveal the cosmic calendar, according to which the world was created and whose seasons are observed by Israel in their proper times. That is also why the *chatimah* (concluding benedictory formula) of this blessing is *m'kadeish Yisrael v'haz'manim*, "who sanctifies the House of *Israel* and the festivals" (C, p. 482; W/F, p. 218)—the divine election of Israel precedes, and is made manifest in, their observance of the divinely ordained sacred occasions. The first paragraph, then, praises God for the gift of the sacred seasons as a whole, but also epitomizes the character of each individual festival on which this blessing is recited: Pesach (*Chag HaMatzot*, "the Holiday of Unleavened Bread") is characterized as the "season of our freedom/ liberation"; Shavuot, as the "season of our receiving Torah"; and Sukkot and Sh'mini Atzeret (the eighth-day festival), as the "season of our rejoicing."

The second paragraph of the benediction, *Yaaleh v'yavo* ("Be mindful of Your people, Israel"; literally "May [the mindfulness of Your people Israel] ascend and come [before You]"; C, p. 480; W/F, p. 216), is a petition for God's attentiveness on the festival day—a request for divine blessing and compassion (so there *is*, in fact, a supplicatory prayer that is deemed appropriate and necessary on the festivals![126]). This paragraph is also recited during *chol hamo-eid*, the intermediate days of the festival, both on weekdays and Shabbat; it is inserted then into the *Avodah* benediction (see below, pp. 207–209, on the seasonal insertions into the weekday *T'filah*).

The third, and final, paragraph of the benediction begins with the words *V'hasi-einu . . . et birkat moadecha*, "Bestow upon us the blessing of Your holy festivals" (C, p. 482; W/F, p. 218) and continues with the invariant core of this blessing, which is recited on Shabbat, the festivals, and the High Holy Days: *kad'sheinu b'mitzvotecha*, "sanctify us / make us holy with Your commandments." The conclusion of this paragraph, which transitions into the *chatimah*, again takes up the theme of the specific occasion on which the blessing is being recited; so here, on the festivals, it reads, "Let Your holy festivals remain our heritage, and let us celebrate them with joy, so that all Israel, hallowing Your name, may have cause to rejoice." When the festival day falls on a Shabbat, the characteristic phrases for Shabbat ("love and favor") are also added here.

We should note that some of the left-page readings for the festival *T'filah* are parts of the traditional liturgy that would be recited during the morning service only:

1. The left-page selections for the *G'vurot* (C, p. 473; W/F, p. 209) are abbreviations of the extended traditional prayers for rain and dew that are recited in the *Musaf* (additional) services on the first day of Pesach (the prayer for dew) and on Sh'mini Atzeret (the prayer for rain). These conform to the agricultural calendar of the Land of Israel and had been deleted from many earlier Reform prayer books for that reason. They are inserted into the first sentence of the *G'vurot* benediction in the *T'filah*, which praises God's power over life and death.[127] The insertion for dew is first recited each year during the *Musaf* service on the first day of Pesach and is made more elaborate by the inclusion

of liturgical poems (*piyutim*) that deal with the blessings of dew. The prayer at the top of the left-hand page is an abbreviated English adaptation of one of those poems.[128] Similarly, the prayer at the bottom of that page is an adaptation of one of the traditional "rain" poems for Sh'mini Atzeret, when the insertion for rain is first recited.[129] On both occasions, the prayers conclude with the plea that the rain or dew descend "for blessing and not for curse"—in the right amount, not too much or too little.

2. Similarly, the prayer on the left-hand page for the third paragraph of the *K'dushat HaYom* (C, p. 483; W/F, p. 219) is a *piyut* that is recited in the Sephardic rite as part of the traditional prayer for dew on the first day of Pesach. The version here is based on Chaim Stern's translation in *Gates of Prayer*, pp. 493–494.

Several other elements of the festival evening services need to be mentioned here:

1. Between the second day of Pesach and Shavuot, the Omer is counted in the evening service after the *T'filah* and before *Aleinu* (C, p. 570; W/F, p. 306). This is discussed in the next section below.
2. On Simchat Torah, the Torah is read *both* in the evening and in the morning service (this is the *only* time in the traditional liturgy that the Torah is ever read in an evening service). In the evening service, this immediately follows the *T'filah*; in the morning service, it follows the *Hallel* psalms. The liturgy for the Torah service on Simchat Torah is extended and festive. It includes seven *hakafot*, processions around the congregation or around the bimah, with all of the Torah scrolls. This, too, will be discussed below at greater length. We should point out here that, traditionally, the full Torah reading for Simchat Torah is done only in the morning; the evening reading is just from the beginning of *V'zot Hab'rachah*.

Counting the Omer

Traditionally, most of the special liturgical rituals (such as reading from Scripture; reciting *Hallel* psalms on the festivals and Rosh Chodesh; handling the *lulav* on Sukkot; and blowing the shofar on Rosh HaShanah), as well as those mitzvot fulfilled in the synagogue on special occasions (such as *b'rit milah*), take place in the morning.[130] In part, this is because people tend to be more attentive earlier in the day; this is why the morning service is the main service every day, while the evening service traditionally was purposely kept brief so that people could get home before dark, eat their evening meal, and go to bed. (Remember that these liturgical practices and preferences were instituted long before the electrification of both homes and public places!) So, too, the Rabbis of the Talmud thought that these important activities should take place in broad daylight—when everyone can see them—rather than in darkness or by artificial light. The one significant exception to this rule is the counting of the Omer during the seven weeks between the second day of Pesach and Shavuot; this always takes place as soon as the new day begins—in the evening service, right after the *T'filah* (in the traditional liturgy, after the *Kaddish Shaleim* ["Full *Kaddish*"] with which the *T'filah* concludes).[131] Let's back up now and discuss this custom, its origin, and its import.

Shavuot, the time of the wheat harvest in the Land of Israel, is the only agricultural festival whose calendrical date is not fixed in the Torah. (It is also the only agricultural festival that does not begin at the full moon.) Instead, in the manner of a farmer's almanac, it is calculated according to a rule of thumb: the wheat harvest comes seven full weeks after the start of the barley harvest, which begins during Pesach and concludes seven weeks later. So the Israelites are commanded to count seven complete weeks from the day when they bring to the priest their offering to God of the first sheaf (*omer*) of the barley harvest (Leviticus 23:9–21).[132]

After the destruction of the Second Temple in 70 CE, the *omer*, or offering of the first sheaf of the barley harvest, could no longer be brought to the priest and offered to God on the altar. But the counting of the seven complete weeks that began on the second day of Pesach and continued until the arrival of Shavuot on the fiftieth day (= Pentecost, in Greek; "fiftieth [day]") was, of course, mandated by the Torah and continued as part of rabbinic synagogue ritual. This came to be known as the "counting of the Omer" (*S'firat HaOmer*; even though the term *omer* originally refers to the offered sheaf, not to the counting).

The forty-nine-day period during which the Omer is counted is often called the *s'firah* period. The post-Talmudic Babylonian authority Natronai Gaon (eighth century CE) proclaims this as a period of mourning, basing this ruling on a Talmudic tradition (*B. Y'vamot* 62b) that students of Rabbi Akiva all died during this period, on one account from a fatal plague. Some modern historians have speculated as to whether this Talmudic tradition conceals the memorialization of a difficult period during the Bar Kochba rebellion against Rome in 135 CE. At all events, rabbinic tradition forbids weddings, shaving/haircutting, and the playing of musical instruments during this period, with the exception of Lag BaOmer, the thirty-third day (*lamed* = 30 + *gimel* = 3, in rabbinic enumeration) of the Omer counting. While kabbalistic interpretation in sixteenth-century Safed under the influence of Isaac Luria maintained these restrictions, it also began to view the *s'firah* period as one of intense self-purification and spiritual preparation to receive the Torah on Shavuot. (The all-night *Tikkun Leil Shavuot* on the eve of Shavuot is one of their ritual innovations.)[133]

The act of counting the Omer takes place after the *T'filah* during the evening service. The congregation stands and recites a blessing (*v'tzivanu al s'firat haomer*, "commanding us to count the Omer"), then proceeds to count: *Hayom x yamim laomer*, "Today is the x day of the Omer." This is followed by a brief prayer that the Temple be restored. The kabbalistic followers of Isaac Luria in sixteenth-century Safed added a *kavanah* at the outset before the blessing, announcing one's intention to fulfill the mitzvah, as well as the recitation of Psalm 67 and two prayers at the end, requesting that the worshiper be cleansed of impurity during this forty-nine-day period of purification. One way that Jews traditionally "beautified the commandment" (*hidur mitzvah*) of counting the Omer was to make specially illustrated Omer calendars and Omer counters.

Most North American Reform prayer books eliminated this ritual entirely, as connected with the Temple worship and with Talmudic and kabbalistic penitential practices. In recent years, it has been re-embraced by many Reform congregations and is reclaimed in its basic form, without most of the kabbalistic elaborations, in *Mishkan T'filah* (C, p. 570; W/F, p. 306), particularly as a way of spiritual preparation for receiving the Torah on Shavuot.

Festival Morning Service
Opening Readings

THE TRADITIONAL festival morning service (*Shacharit*) begins identically to the daily and Shabbat morning services: with the preliminary morning benedictions (*Birchot HaShachar*) followed by the recitation of various psalms (*P'sukei D'zimrah*), framed fore and aft by benedictions (*Baruch She-amar* before and *Nishmat Kol Chai* afterward; the latter is the more extended and poetic version of the closing benediction used on Shabbat). With regard to text, there is nothing distinctive in the traditional festival morning service until one arrives at the *T'filah*,[134] and specifically the central *K'dushat HaYom* ("Sanctification of the Day") blessing (see above, pp. 125–126). In the Ashkenazic rite, the only way one knows, before arriving at the *T'filah*, that this is a *festival* service is through its musical performance. The end of *Nishmat Kol Chai*, the benediction that concludes *P'sukei D'zimrah*, is chanted according to a mode that is reserved for the festivals and is associated specifically with the blessings that surround the *Sh'ma*, which immediately follow upon this text and the *Chatzi Kaddish* and *Bar'chu* that follow.

Reform prayer books, on the other hand—particularly those in North America—have often begun the festival morning service with introductory readings in the vernacular that articulate either the general themes of the festivals or those of the specific festival being observed, or perhaps both—as a way of framing the service that follows and of focusing one's thoughts (*kavanah*) at the outset. This is how the festival morning service begins in the newly revised *Union Prayer Book*, *Gates of Prayer*, and *Mishkan T'filah*.

The service in *Mishkan T'filah* begins with a two-page spread that offers brief *kavanot* for each of the festivals (C, pp. 412–413; W/F, pp. 148–149). The *kavanah* for the first day of Pesach plays with the Chasidic revoicing of *Mitzrayim* (Egypt) as *meitzarim*, "straits" or "narrow places," framing the Exodus from Egypt in personal and psychological terms as going out from our own "narrow spaces."

The seventh day of Pesach traditionally is celebrated as the day when Israel crossed the Sea to freedom; the *kavanah* given for this day is Exodus 15:20–21, emphasizing the singing and dancing of the Israelite women, led by Miriam the prophetess.

The *kavanah* for Shavuot, written by Rabbi Bernard H. Mehlman, draws on a midrashic interpretation of Exodus 19:18),[135] comparing the Torah, which was given amidst fire, to fire—by the light of which we warm ourselves.

The Sukkot *kavanah*, written by Rabbi Elyse D. Frishman, is also based on a midrashic tradition[136] that compares the four species that we are to take up on Sukkot (myrtle, palm, willow, citron) to four parts of the human body through which we are to worship God in our daily acts.

Finally, the *kavanah* for Atzeret–Simchat Torah, also written by Rabbi Mehlman, celebrates the value of Torah and Torah study, whose teachings are "eternal and inexhaustible," just as the cycle of Torah reading constantly renews itself and never ends.

Each of these *kavanot* helps us to think about the significance of each of the festivals, and to enter the festival worship service with these thoughts in our hearts.

Psalm 100

As noted above, the preliminary portions of the festival morning service—the *Birchot HaShachar* (Morning Blessings) and *P'sukei D'zimrah* ("Verses of Song," i.e., psalms and other psalm-like scriptural texts)—are identical, textually, with those same sections in the Shabbat morning service.[137] The textual changes for the festivals in fact only begin in the *T'filah* (although the musical changes begin at the end of *P'sukei D'zimrah*, as we have noted).

Mishkan T'filah, however, gives Psalm 100 specifically for festival mornings at the beginning of the *P'sukei D'zimrah* psalms (C, p. 440; W/F, p. 176). This is an innovation taken over from *Gates of Prayer* (p. 507, where it is given for a festival morning that falls on a weekday), and ultimately from the British Liberal *Service of the Heart* (1967), which Rabbi Chaim Stern also co-edited, together with Rabbi John D. Rayner. *GOP* additionally gives this as a psalm for recitation on Shabbat, at the beginning of Morning Service II (p. 318). In *Gates of Understanding* (p. 222),

Stern makes the following remarks about these choices: "Traditionally recited in the morning service on weekdays only. It appears in many ancient rites, but not in the oldest (e.g., *Seder Rav Amram*). It was associated, in Temple times, with thank offerings (cf. Lev. 7:12). It was the practice at times during the Middle Ages to recite this psalm on Sabbaths and festivals and, following *Service of the Heart*, we offer it for the Sabbath [as well as for the festivals]."

Several of the psalm's themes actually can be related to the festivals. In verse 1, the congregation is enjoined to shout joyfully to God and to worship with gladness. Joy and gladness are, of course, emotions encouraged on the festivals. In verse 4, the congregation is further enjoined to enter God's gates and courts (i.e., the gates and courts of the Temple) with thanksgiving and praise. This, too, is appropriate to the practice of Temple pilgrimage during the festivals. The psalm concludes with a variant of the festival *Hallel* refrain, "Praise Adonai, for God is good, God's steadfast love is eternal." All of this makes this psalm appropriate for performance on the festivals, and there are several musical settings that capture its spirit of jubilant celebration.

Festival Morning *T'filah*

Insertions for Rain and Dew

PESACH MARKS the end of the rainy season in the Land of Israel; Sh'mini Atzeret, at the end of Sukkot, marks its beginning. The traditional liturgy always maintained a tangible link between the Jewish people and the land by marking out the transition between these seasons in the festival *T'filah*, specifically in the second benediction, *G'vurot* ("Divine Powers"), which praises God as Master of life and death, causing the revivifying rains to fall in the winter (*mashiv haruach umorid hagashem*) and the dew to "fall" in the summer (*morid hatal*). The first day of Pesach marks the official beginning of the season of dew, just as Sh'mini Atzeret marks the official beginning of the season of rain.

Many North American Reform prayer books, wary of maintaining the nationalistic connection with the Land of Israel, or of suggesting that Jews yearned to return there, eliminated altogether the seasonal insertions in the second *T'filah* benediction and heavily curtailed the prayers for rain and dew on Pesach and Sh'mini Atzeret (moving them, of course, to the morning service, since *Musaf* was eliminated). All that remained of these in the newly revised *Union Prayer Book* were the phrases *Livrachah v'lo liklalah / Lasova v'lo l'razon / L'chayim v'lo lamavet*, "For blessing and not for curse / For satiety and not for famine / For life and not for death" (p. 265).[138] In the traditional liturgy, these phrases refer to the quality and quantity of moisture sought for the land—just enough to thrive, not too little, not too much. Here in the *UPB*, they are preceded by the generic request "Let rain and dew descend upon the fields of our land" (while *which* land that might be is left ambiguous). This itself is preceded by a spiritualization of the image of rainfall—"Let Thy doctrine descend as the rain, Thy word distil as the dew" (drawing on the imagery of Deuteronomy 32:2)—since the scientific understanding of the natural world subscribed to by most Reformers understood that petitionary prayer would not alter meteorological conditions.

Gates of Prayer retains a portion of the Spanish-Portuguese Sephardic poetic prayer for dew as an introductory reading for the first day of Pesach (pp. 493–495), as well as the *Livrachah* verses as a supplement to the *G'vurot* benediction (p. 517), with an English introductory prayer (p. 516) that recasts some of the themes from the *UPB*. *Mishkan T'filah* gives this material (C, p. 473; W/F, p. 209) as a left-page alternative or supplement to the regular *G'vurot* benediction on the facing right page (C, p. 472; W/F, p. 208). *MT* appropriately gives separate readings for the first day of Pesach and for Sh'mini Atzeret. The Pesach reading (also indicated there for Shavuot and Sukkot, going beyond the traditional usage) is a contemporary adaptation of the Sephardic "dew" poem *B'tal'lei Orah* ("With dewdrops of light and blessing . . .") that also appears in *GOP* on p. 495.[139] The prayer for Sh'mini Atzeret is a contemporary adaptation of the Byzantine-era "rain" poem written in the Land of Israel by Eleazar Kallir, *Z'chor Av* ("Remember the Patriarch [i.e., Abraham] who poured out his heart to you like water").

It is possible to use *both* the right- and left-page texts here in order to approximate the style of the traditional liturgical insertions: Begin on the right page, down to *rav l'hoshia*; then move to the left page, reading the top prayer for the first day of Pesach and the bottom prayer for Sh'mini Atzeret–Simchat Torah, including *Livrachah* on each occasion, then resuming on the right page with the appropriate insert, and finishing the blessing.

Blessings over the *Lulav* and Sukkot Customs

On each of the seven days of Sukkot, the *lulav* and *etrog* are "taken up," that is, grasped and waved (*n'tilat lulav*), during the morning service after the *T'filah* and directly before the recitation of *Hallel*. As with the performance of all mitzvot, this action is preceded by a blessing, which appears in *Mishkan T'filah* toward the back of the book (C, p. 571; W/F, p. 307).

Leviticus 23:40 states that "on the first day [of Sukkot] you shall take the product of the *hadar* trees [*p'ri eitz hadar*], branches of palm trees, boughs of leafy trees, and willows of the brook, and you shall rejoice before your God seven days." The Rabbis, following the practice of late Second Temple Judaism, interpret the difficult expression *p'ri eitz hadar* as referring to the fruit of the citron tree, the *etrog*. This, then, is held together with palm, willow, and myrtle branches (the latter being "boughs of leafy trees")—the three latter bound together as the *lulav*. Together these are referred to as the *arbaah minim*, the "four species."

Traditionally, the four species are brought to the synagogue and used there during the morning service each day of Sukkot (except for Shabbat, when it is prohibited to carry an item from one domain to another). The blessing over the *lulav* is recited daily between the *T'filah* and *Hallel*. (Because most Reform congregations in North America do not conduct daily services during Sukkot, Reform Jews will encounter this custom only on the first day of Sukkot.)

On the first day, this blessing is recited, standing, together with *Shehecheyanu* (known in Talmudic literature as *Birkat HaZ'man*, the blessing to be recited on festive occasions). The act of "taking up" the *lulav* involves grasping and lifting up the *lulav* and *etrog* together. The *etrog* is first held upside down. This is done so that the blessing over the *lulav* may precede the physical act of "taking" it. Once the blessing has been recited, the *etrog* is turned around, with the *pitom* facing up, and the *lulav* is shaken six times: in the direction of the four winds, then up and down. This constitutes the act of "taking," or making use of the four species once the blessing has been recited (since blessings over mitzvot require the performance of those activities immediately afterward).[140] *MT* prefaces the *lulav* blessings with relevant biblical verses (Psalm 28:9 and Deuteronomy 16:14), which also may be sung.

Hallel is then recited, while still standing and holding the *etrog* and *lulav*. During the chanting of the last *Hallel* psalm (Psalm 118), the *lulav* will be shaken again in the six directions during each of the first four verses (the ones with the refrain *Ki l'olam chasdo*). The *lulav* is also shaken during the *Ana Adonai* verse, and once more during the very last verse.

One further use of the *lulav* and *etrog* is made in a traditional service, but not in most Reform ones: the *hakafah* (procession) around the congregation (or around the Torah reading desk if it is in the middle of the congregation) with *lulav* and *etrog* during the chanting of the *Hoshanot* hymns during the additional (*Musaf*) service. *Hoshanot* (which feature the congregational refrain *Hoshanah*, a contraction of *Hoshiah na*, "Save us!" from Psalm 118)[141] are essentially prayers for rain at the beginning of the rainy season in the Land of Israel (*M. Rosh HaShanah* 1:2 holds that the world is judged on Sukkot with respect to rainfall). Most Reform prayer books have omitted these prayers, early on partly because of the connection to the Land of Israel, but mostly because of discomfort with what was perceived to be a kind of sympathetic magic: ritual activity intended to induce rainfall. There is more sympathy to the ritual today if it is viewed in more symbolic, rather than instrumental, terms.

Hallel
Festival Psalms of Praise

Hallel ("praise") is what the Rabbis call Psalms 113–118, which are sung or recited in the synagogue on all festivals (including intermediate days), as well as on Rosh Chodesh (the first day of each month), on all eight days of Chanukah, and, in recent years, on Yom HaAtzma-ut, Israel Independence Day.[142] *Hallel* is also recited on the eve of Pesach during the seder.[143] According to early rabbinic tradition (*M. P'sachim* 5:7), the Levites chanted these *Hallel* psalms in the Temple courtyard while the Passover lambs were being slaughtered; they are also associated with the waving of the *lulav* during Sukkot (*M. Sukkah* 3:9). In the synagogue, *Hallel* is recited immediately following the *T'filah* and before the Torah reading (or the reading from the festival *m'gilah*, which precedes the Torah reading).

The thematic connections between this particular set of psalms and the festivals, beyond their appropriate tone of praise and thanksgiving, are several:

1. Psalm 114 dramatizes God's power during the Exodus from Egypt—how the sea split and the hills skipped like rams.
2. Psalm 115 invokes God's blessing on the Houses of Israel and Aaron—appropriate to large gatherings of people in the Temple during the Pilgrimage Festivals.
3. Psalm 116 concludes with the speaker's determination to pay his vows to God in the presence of all the people in the courts of God's House (the Temple) in Jerusalem—again appropriate to the festival gathering.
4. Psalm 118 concludes with the command to "bind the festal offering to the horns of the altar with cords," an obvious festival reference; invokes God's blessing from the Temple: "May the one who enters be blessed in the name of Adonai; we bless you from the House of Adonai"; and beseeches God's deliverance,

> one of the themes of the festival prayers: *Ana Adonai hoshiah na / Ana Adonai hatzlichah na*, "O Adonai, deliver us! O Adonai, let us prosper!"[144]

Like all extended biblical texts that are performed liturgically, the *Hallel* psalms are surrounded by blessings, fore and aft. The blessing before *Hallel* (C, pp. 558, 560; W/F. pp. 294, 296) is phrased as a *birkat mitzvah*, a blessing recited before performing a commandment (*asher kid'shanu b'mitzvotav v'tzivanu*, "who hallows us with mitzvot, commanding us"); here, *likro et haHallel*, "to recite Hymns of Praise." The concluding blessing, *Y'hal'lucha*, expresses the wish that God may be praised forever by all creatures and concludes with the *chatimah, Baruch atah Adonai, Melech m'hulal batishbachot*, "Praise to You, Adonai, Sovereign, praised in song."

The first *Hallel* psalm, 113 (C, p. 561; W/F, p. 297), begins appropriately with the exhortation *Hal'luyah!* ("Praise God!") and then elaborates: let all servants of God praise God; may God's name (God's reputation, qualities/attributes) be praised eternally on account of God's mighty acts. While enthroned above the heavens, God is still mindful of everything on earth, including the plight of the poor and the needy, who will be exalted, and the barren woman, who will bear children. The psalm closes as it began: *Hal'luyah!*

Psalm 114 (C, p. 562; W/F, p. 298), as noted above, praises God in an exultant tone for having delivered Israel from Egypt. In the Torah, God's redemption from Egypt of the Israelite people is the ultimate proof and experience of the divine power to save—it is constantly invoked as the paradigm, and assurance, for future salvation. Here, it is God's power over nature in the service of redeeming the people of Israel—splitting the sea, convulsing the hills—that is ecstatically depicted.

The "middle" two of the six *Hallel* psalms, 115 and 116, sometimes get "shorter shrift" than their neighbors on either side. The reason for this is that during the last six days of Pesach and on Rosh Chodesh they are traditionally abbreviated: the first eleven verses of each of these psalms are not recited.[145] The full psalms are recited only during Sukkot (all days), Chanukah (all days, on the model of Sukkot), the first day of Pesach, and Shavuot.[146] A later rationale for this difference is that the Torah does not prescribe special distinctive sacrifices for each day of Pesach after the first, while it does so for Sukkot (see Numbers 28:24 vs. 29:17-38). The custom of reciting *Hallel* on Rosh Chodesh is Babylonian (*B. Arachin* 10b) and was observed only locally there; so a full *Hallel* was not ordained when the custom spread.

In Psalm 115 (excerpted: C, p. 563; W/F, p. 299), the Psalmist asks God to vindicate Israel in the sight of all the nations by publicly demonstrating divine attentiveness to the needs of the Israelite people through responding to them, whereas other "gods" are incapable of doing anything, since they are nothing but images fashioned by humans. The second part of the psalm spells out the blessings of fertility and fecundity that God will bestow on the Israelite people and the House of Aaron, their priestly ministers.

Psalm 116 (excerpted: C, p. 564; W/F, p. 300) begins with the same idea, but now addressing the fate of the individual: God responds to the pleas of people in need and saves them from death. The Psalmist here speaks rhetorically in the first person of his own experience. In gratitude for his salvation, he vows to bring a thank-offering to God's Temple in Jerusalem, where the sacrificial animal will be bound with cords to the corners of the altar, and the Psalmist will fulfill his vow in the sight of the entire community.

Both of these psalms, fittingly, end with the word *Hal'luyah*, an exhortation for all to bear witness by praising God.

The final two *Hallel* psalms, 117 (C, p. 565; W/F, p. 301) and 118 (C, pp. 565–68; W/F, pp. 301–304), also serve as the "short form" of the *Hallel* ("*Hallel* I") in both *Gates of Prayer* and *Mishkan T'filah* (C, pp. 558–59; W/F, pp. 294–95). Psalm 117 in fact is the shortest psalm in the entire Psalter. It is two verses long, but powerful precisely in its directness:

> Praise Adonai, all you nations;
> extol God, all you peoples,
> for great is God's steadfast love toward us;
> Adonai's faithfulness endures forever.
> Hallelujah!

For those who have just experienced the trustworthiness of divine protection, what more is there to say?

The lengthier Psalm 118, on the other hand, is one of the highlights of the *Hallel* and so well known that it has long been performed in Reform liturgy as emblematic of the whole. The first part of this psalm is what is called a litany, a call-and-response: the leader exhorts various groups among the people to praise God, and the congregation responds with the recurring line *ki l'olam chasdo*, "for/indeed God's steadfast love is eternal." There are many beloved musical settings of this text. Traditionally among Ashkenazic communities, it is sung to a different characteristic melody for each of the three festivals. (During Sukkot, the *lulav* is waved to the four winds and up and down during each of the first four verses, as well as at *Ana Adonai hoshia na*—v. 25—and at the very end, which recapitulates the beginning.)

The psalm's second section is vastly different in tone and voice: we now hear the testimony of an individual who has called upon God in personal distress and was answered, being set free. This voice acclaims God's protection in the face of his enemies: "I shall not die but live / and proclaim the works of Adonai." The Psalmist now approaches the gates of the Temple, preparing to enter them to thank God:

> Open the gates of righteousness for me
> that I may enter them and praise Adonai.
> This is the gateway to Adonai—
> the righteous shall enter through it.

All of the verses that follow are traditionally intoned by the prayer leader and then repeated by the congregation. The Psalmist again expresses thanks for his wondrous salvation:

> I praise You, for You answered me,
> and have became my deliverance.
> The stone that the builders rejected has become the
> chief cornerstone.
> This is Adonai's doing; it is marvelous in our sight.
> This is the day that Adonai has made—
> let us exult and rejoice on it.

In rabbinic culture, this last verse is associated with the festivals, those days ordained by God for rejoicing.

What follows is a dramatic dialogue between the assembled congregation and the priests in the Temple. The congregation asks God for salvation and the blessing of prosperity (another characteristic theme of, and liturgical action on, the festivals):

> O Adonai, deliver us!
> O Adonai, let us prosper!

The priests respond by blessing the people on behalf of God:

> May the one who enters be blessed in the name of Adonai;
> we bless you from the House of Adonai.

Next, reference is made to the sacrificial offerings on the festivals:

> Adonai is God;
> God has given us light;
> bind the festal offering to the horns [the four raised corners]
> of the altar with cords.

Finally, the psalm concludes with a recapitulation of its first theme of thanksgiving:

> You are my God and I will praise You;
> You are my God and I will extol You.
> Praise Adonai, for God is good,
> God's steadfast love is eternal.

On this exultant note, *Hallel* comes to an end. *Hallel* is one of the musical highlights of the festival liturgy; there are many melodies for each of the *Hallel* psalms.

The concluding blessing after the *Hallel* (C, p. 569; W/F, p. 305) is a version of what is known generically as *Birkat HaShir*, "the Blessing over Song," recited after all extended liturgical performances of psalms. There are three verbal forms of this blessing in the medieval rites: (1) *Y'hal'lucha*, which concludes the *Hallel*, is the briefest. Somewhat longer is (2) *Yishtabach*, which concludes *P'sukei D'zimrah*, the daily psalms in the weekday morning service. The longest form is (3) *Nishmat Kol Chai*, the lengthy praise of God that concludes *P'sukei D'zimrah* in the Shabbat and festival morning service and that incorporates the weekday *Yishtabach* as its final paragraph. All three of these texts conclude with the same *chatimah*, thereby establishing their functional identity. Jewish liturgical tradition nonetheless prefers to vary the wording of the body of the blessing on each separate occasion.

The Three *M'gilot* for the Festivals

THE PUBLIC READING and interpretation of Scripture is the oldest religious activity attested to have taken place in ancient synagogues—older even than public prayer (certainly in the Land of Israel).[147] The Rabbis mandated Torah readings four times a week—Shabbat mornings and afternoons, and Monday and Thursday mornings—as well as on the festivals and the intermediate days of the festivals (*chol hamo-eid*), the High Holy Days, Chanukah, Purim, Rosh Chodesh, and fast days. Prophetic readings of comfort that promised divine deliverance concluded these Torah readings on Shabbat and festival mornings. Psalms also were regularly recited as part of the rabbinic prayer service. Thus large portions of the books of *N'vi-im* (Prophets) and *K'tuvim* (Writings), as well as the entire Torah, came to be read publicly in the synagogue.

Five other books among the Writings also came to be included in public worship: these are known collectively as the *Chameish M'gilot* (the Five Scrolls). The earliest of these to be used liturgically is the one we all refer to as *the M'gilah*, namely the Scroll of Esther, read on Purim. This custom is already attested in the Mishnah, where an entire tractate (fittingly named "*M'gilah*") is devoted to the topic. The custom of reading the Scroll of Lamentations (*Eichah*) on Tishah B'Av (the ninth day of the Hebrew month of Av), the traditional anniversary of the destruction of both Temples, is attested in the Byzantine-era (fifth century?) midrashic anthology *P'sikta D'Rav Kahana* from the Land of Israel. Additionally, a special scroll is read on each of the three festivals: the Song of Songs (*Shir HaShirim*[148]) on Pesach, Ruth on Shavuot, and Ecclesiastes (*Kohelet*[149]) on Sukkot.

The midrashic association of the Song of Songs with Pesach (and Shavuot) is quite old: the book itself is understood in early rabbinic literature as a figurative depiction of the deep love between God (identified as the book's male persona) and Israel (identified as the book's female persona). Many of the book's images of intimacy are understood as referring to moments in the early history of Israel's relationship with God. Thus, the redemption from Egypt (and particularly the salvation at the

Sea of Reeds) is understood to be the moment of betrothal between God and Israel, while the covenant at Sinai is deemed to be the moment of marriage.[150] Additionally, the book abounds in nature images of the Land of Israel in the spring.

The Book of Ruth is associated with Shavuot because its story takes place at the time of the barley harvest in the Land of Israel and, later, because Ruth, who chooses to become a Jew, is likened to the Israelites at Sinai, who choose on Shavuot to enter into God's covenant. Their physical preparation there to receive the covenant, through purification, is likened to that required of converts to Judaism.[151] The liturgical reading of Song of Songs on Pesach and of Ruth on Shavuot is first attested in *Sof'rim* (14:3; ed. Higger—14:1), an eighth-century(?) tractate mostly from the Land of Israel that deals with the laws for copying Torah scrolls, as well as *t'fillin* and mezuzah parchments. The text also discusses public Torah readings and their liturgical accompaniments.

The association of Ecclesiastes with Sukkot is later, first attested in medieval Ashkenaz (Franco-Germany).[152] There is no obvious thematic or homiletical reason for this association, as there is for that of the other two scrolls with their festivals.[153] (One might associate the autumnal mood of Ecclesiastes with the approach of winter in northern climes and view its weary wisdom as a sober contrast to the festival's rejoicing—but all of this is after the fact.)

There have always been a variety of customs as to precisely when during the festival the appropriate scroll is read. Song of Songs and Ecclesiastes are generally read during the morning service of the Shabbat that falls during the festival (Shabbat Chol HaMo-eid) but are sometimes read on the last day of the festival (the seventh day of Pesach, Sh'mini Atzeret). Ruth is read in traditional diasporic communities on the second day of Shavuot. The reading of the festival scroll takes place after the recitation of *Hallel* and before the reading of the Torah. There are also communities and rites that have read the scrolls in the afternoon service. The Ashkenazic rite uses a special musical mode (called *Shir HaShirim* trope) for the chanting of the three festival scrolls.[154]

Festival Additions to the Torah Service

THE LITURGY surrounding the reading of the Torah is mostly composed of a selection of thematically relevant biblical verses in praise of God's rulership and divine instruction (which is the root meaning of the word *torah*). This liturgy is more elaborate on Shabbat morning than on weekdays and just slightly more elaborate on festival mornings than on Shabbat. As might be expected, it is most elaborate on Simchat Torah.

The basic liturgy for taking out the Torah scroll and returning it to the ark on the three festivals (C, pp. 494–498, 510–519; W/F, pp. 230–234, 246–255) is identical to that for Shabbat morning: *Ein Kamocha*, a series of psalm verses extolling God's majesty; followed by *Av HaRachamim*, a rabbinic petition for the restoration of Zion; followed by *Ki miTziyon* (Isaiah 2:3), acknowledging that divine instruction comes forth from Zion; and the rabbinic blessing *Baruch shenatan Torah*, "Blessed is God who in holiness gave the Torah to the people Israel."

On the festivals (as well as on the High Holy Days), this is followed by a threefold repetition of Exodus 34:6–7, *Adonai Adonai, El rachum v'chanun* (C, p. 496; W/F, p. 232):

> Adonai, Adonai, a God compassionate and gracious,
> slow to anger, abounding in kindness, and faithfulness,
> extending kindness to the thousandth generation,
> forgiving iniquity, transgression and sin, and granting pardon.

These verses have an interesting history of interpretation and liturgical use. In their biblical context, they are the climax of God's self-revelation to Moses after having forgiven the sin of the Golden Calf. Moses has asked to see God as a sign of divine favor; God refuses this request (since no human can see God and live) but consents to show Moses a portion of the Divine Presence after passing by, so that Moses can "see" only what trails behind God. Jewish tradition understands that God thereby revealed to Moses the divine attributes that were proclaimed in Moses's hearing.[155] Indeed, the Rabbis understood that God here gave to Moses a liturgical formula that can be used in the future to invoke divine pardon and forgiveness whenever Israel sins, just as happened in the story of the Golden Calf:

> *Adonai passed by before him and proclaimed* (Exodus 34:6). Rabbi Yochanan said: Were it not written in Scripture, it would be impossible for us to say such a thing; this verse teaches that the Holy One drew God's robe round God like a service leader [*sh'liach tzibur*] and showed Moses the order of prayer. He said to him: Whenever Israel sins, let them carry out this service before Me, and I will forgive them. (*B. Rosh HaShanah* 17b)

It is on the basis of this understanding that these verses came to be used as a liturgical invocation of God's mercy during the penitential season, specifically in the *s'lichot* liturgies of Yom Kippur. Much later, the kabbalists who followed the teachings of Isaac Luria (Safed, sixteenth century) instituted the recitation of these verses during the month of Elul to prepare for the coming Days of Awe. They also instituted their threefold recitation before the open ark on Rosh HaShanah and Yom Kippur, prior to removing the Torah from the ark for reading. Finally, they transferred this custom to the festivals as well, seeing these occasions as further propitious times for penitence and seeking forgiveness.

No doubt because of the emotional and musical associations with this custom and because of the theological appropriateness of the content, these verses have appeared in most Reform prayer books for both the festivals and the High Holy Days—although they have not always been recited three times (since a certain magical efficacy clings to that mode of performance).

The rest of the texts sung or recited when removing the Torah from the ark and when returning it to the ark are the same as on Shabbat mornings. As left-page readings, *Mishkan T'filah* gives thematically relevant biblical texts for each of the festivals and then appropriate songs to accompany the *hakafah* with the Torah on the festivals.

Seder K'riat HaTorah on Simchat Torah

THE SERVICE for reading the Torah on Simchat Torah is the most elaborate and festive of the entire liturgical year. This is the occasion on which we affirm the ultimate value of Torah and its never-ending study: upon concluding the reading of *D'varim* (Deuteronomy), we immediately recommence the reading of *B'reishit* (Genesis), so that "the circle will be unbroken."[156] Indeed, in symbolic terms, this may be seen as an affirmation of the eternity of the Torah and of the Jewish people who devote themselves to its study, as well as of the perpetual renewal, generation after generation, of life itself.

Traditionally, Simchat Torah also has come to be the only liturgical occasion on which the Torah is read in the evening as well as in the morning. The main reading, of course, is in the morning, but in order to add festivity to the evening service, the custom of removing the Torah from the ark and parading it through the congregation seven times (*hakafot*, "circumambulations"), accompanied by dancing, was included as well in the evening service. Since, according to halachah, the Torah may only be removed from the ark in the context of a public service if it is going to be read,[157] a short section from the beginning of the *parashah* is read in the evening, while the full *parashah* will be read in the morning.

Removing the Torah from the ark is always preceded and accompanied by the chanting or recitation of thematically relevant verses from Scripture—more on Shabbat and the festivals than on weekdays. On Simchat Torah (both evening and morning), this series of scriptural verses is expanded even further to encompass fourteen verses (in the traditional Ashkenazic ritual). The first of these verses is Deuteronomy 4:35, *Atah horeita ladaat*, "You have been shown, that you may know, that Adonai alone is our God; there is none else." Traditionally these verses are chanted by the prayer leader, with the congregation repeating each one aloud, back and forth. Both the 1940 edition of the *Union Prayer Book* (pp. 258–259)[158] and *Gates of Prayer* (pp. 538–539) included a selection of these verses. *Mishkan T'filah* (C, p. 495; W/F, p. 231), because of a formatting decision that the appropriate left-hand page would include brief texts for *all* festivals, includes only the first of these verses for Simchat Torah.

The seven *hakafot* of the Torah around the congregation are then accompanied by the singing of a liturgical poem (*piyut*), *Ana Adonai hoshia na* ("O Adonai, please deliver us!"). Thematically, this text is another *Hoshanah* poem, similar to those that are traditionally recited during the seven days of Sukkot when the congregation marches in a circle around the sanctuary, each person carrying a *lulav* and *etrog*, in emulation of the Sukkot processions around the altar that would take place in the Temple courtyard before its destruction (see *M. Sukkot* 4:5). Because these processions were associated with rain-making rituals and prayers for rain in a quasi-magical sense, they have always been omitted from Reform prayer books. Only this one, recited on Simchat Torah to accompany the procession of Torah scrolls, remains. The full *piyut* is given in the 1940 edition of the *UPB* (pp. 260–261), in *GOP* (pp. 540–541), and in *MT* (C, pp. 500–504; W/F, pp. 236–240, right sides). *MT* omits from the refrain the phrase *Ana Adonai* ("Please, O Adonai!"), avoiding the penitential rhetoric of groveling before God. *MT* also provides additional songs for *hakafot* on the three left-hand pages (pp. 501, 503, 505; W/F, pp. 237, 239, 241).

Once the processions and dancing with the Torah have ended, the Torah is read. In the morning, this is accompanied by further ritual elaborations. It is customary in many traditional communities for everyone in the congregation to receive an *aliyah* on Simchat Torah. Sometimes this is accomplished by breaking up into groups around each of the congregation's Torah scrolls and reading the first part of the *parashah* multiple times in each group so that everyone can have a chance to recite the Torah blessings. In Reform congregations, sometimes different groups of people will take an *aliyah* together, or the entire congregation will take an *aliyah* at the same time.

Two special *aliyot* that end and recommence the annual reading of the whole Torah are reserved as special congregational honors. The person who makes the blessing over the conclusion of the Torah reading is called *chatan Torah* ("the bridegroom of the Torah"; *MT* proposes *kalat Torah*, "the bride of Torah" as the feminine equivalent). The person who makes the blessing over the recommencement of the Torah is called *chatan B'reishit* ("the bridegroom of Genesis"; *MT* again provides the feminine equivalent, *kalat B'reishit*). Special elaborate poetic formulas are used to call up these two people to the Torah. Each of these ends with a threefold summons to the *aliyah*: *Amod! Amod! Amod!* ("Arise! Arise! Arise to bless over the Torah!"). *MT* provides abbreviated versions of these poems (C, pp. 506, 508; W/F, pp. 242, 244), both restored here for the first time to the North American Reform prayer book, and adds as well a feminine version of the summons to the *aliyah*: *Imdi! Imdi! Imdi!* The end of Deuteronomy and the beginning of Genesis are read from two separate scrolls, so as not to tax the congregation by having to roll a single scroll from end to beginning.[159]

The rituals for reading the haftarah (which is the beginning of the Book of Joshua, resuming the narrative where Deuteronomy left off) and for returning the Torah scrolls to the ark are the same as on Shabbat and other festivals, although the concluding blessing after the haftarah on the festivals differs in small verbal details from the familiar Shabbat version. These differences align with the festival version of the *K'dushat HaYom* benediction in the *T'filah.* The relevant festival is mentioned by name, and the festivals are characterized together as having been given *l'sasson ul'simchah,* "For gladness and joy." The *chatimah,* or conclusion, of the benediction, is identical with that of the *K'dushat HaYom* benediction: *m'kadeish Yisrael v'haz'manim,* "for sanctifying Israel and the festivals."

Yizkor Memorial Prayers

On the last day of each of the *Shalosh R'galim* (in Reform congregations, on the seventh day of Pesach, the single day of Shavuot, and Sh'mini Atzeret–Simchat Torah) and on Yom Kippur, *Yizkor* memorial prayers are recited for our deceased relatives as well as for the martyrs of the Jewish people (in our own day, particularly for those who died in the Holocaust). This is an old custom, going back to the time of the Crusades in the Rhineland (eleventh to twelfth centuries).

The aftermath of those massacres gave rise to a series of ritualized memorials—initially of communal martyrs on the anniversary of the slaughter (around the time of Shavuot), including children mourning lost parents and parents mourning lost children. The use of the *Kaddish* as a memorial prayer recited on behalf of one's deceased parents originated in this milieu, as did the customs of observing the anniversary (*yahrzeit*) of a parent's death and kindling a memorial candle. The *Yizkor* prayers, beginning with the words *Yizkor Elohim nishmat*, "May God remember the soul of," were first formulated then.[160] Eventually this ritual was regularized on Yom Kippur and spread beyond the Rhineland to other Jewish communities. The recitation of *Yizkor* prayers also on the last days of the festivals apparently originated in Central Europe following the massacres of Jews in the German lands during the Black Death of the fourteenth century but became more common in Eastern Europe in the seventeenth century, with the popularization of Lurianic Kabbalah by mystics who stressed the penitential aspect of the festivals. The prayer *El Malei Rachamim*, a central element of the memorial service, originated in seventeenth-century Ukraine at the time of the Chmielnicki massacres. It implores God to bind up in the bond of everlasting life the soul of the deceased.

These core memorial prayers in the Ashkenazic rite are recited, together with several psalm texts, after the reading of the haftarah, before the Torah is returned to the ark. The devising of a separate and extended *Yizkor* "service" is modern, the creation of nineteenth-century Reform Judaism, particularly in America. To extend the memorial rite beyond the basic traditional prayers, various other thematically relevant psalms and original vernacular readings and meditations were added. This is the structure and content of the *Yizkor* service in all modern prayer books.

The *Yizkor* service (C, pp. 574–583; W/F, pp. 310–319) begins with *Adonai, mah adam* ("Adonai, what are we?"), a series of biblical verses, mostly from psalms, that deal with the fragility of human life and conclude with the confident assurance that "Adonai, You redeem the soul of Your servants, and none who trust in You shall be desolate." *Mishkan T'filah* continues with Psalm 23, a statement of confidence in God that is well loved in the Western world, and Psalm 121, another well-known expression of confidence that "the Guardian of Israel neither slumbers nor sleeps." These are followed by Psalm 16:8–11, *Shiviti Adonai l'negdi tamid*, "I am ever mindful of Adonai's presence; God is at my right hand; I shall never be shaken. . . . For You will not abandon me to Sheol." All of these psalms are frequently recited at funerals as well.

Following these psalm texts are the *Yizkor* prayers proper, for deceased loved ones and for the martyrs of the Jewish people. These prayers are very brief; all begin with the formula *Yizkor Elohim*, "May God remember." The primary custom was to memorialize deceased parents, so the traditional formulations are for one's father and mother (*Yizkor Elohim nishmat avi mori / imi morati*, "May God remember the soul of my father, my teacher / my mother, my teacher"). Noteworthy is the fact that one's parents are also memorialized as one's teachers—since teachers, teaching, studying, and learning are so highly prized in Jewish tradition, and our parents are our first teachers. At this point in the prayer, the name of one's father or mother is inserted, and then the prayer continues:

> . . . who has gone to his/her eternal home—and for this I pledge to give charity on his/her behalf, that his/her soul may be bound up in the bond of everlasting life together with the souls of Abraham, Isaac, and Jacob, Sarah, Rebecca, Rachel, Leah, and all the other righteous men and women in the Garden of Eden,[161] and let us say, Amen.

Prominent in the medieval theology of memorializing is that living children can help to redeem/release the souls of their deceased parents from purgation by contributing charity on their behalf and by reciting *Kaddish* and other memorial prayers such as Yizkor in their memory. This theology has been rejected by most modern Jewish movements, and the text of the Yizkor prayers has been revised accordingly. The formulation in *Mishkan T'filah* goes back to the 1940–45 newly revised *UPB* (earlier versions of the *UPB* dispensed with the Hebrew text here). It continues from the point after the insertion of the departed's name as follows:

> . . . who has gone to his/her eternal home. May his/her soul be bound up in the bond of everlasting life and may his/her rest be honorable. *Your presence is perfect joy; delights are ever in Your right hand* (Psalm 16:11).

This formulation, of course, is less specific in its theological claims than the traditional one.

Many traditional prayer books include *Yizkor* formulations for deceased spouses as well as deceased parents. *Gates of Prayer* (followed by *MT*) provides a generalized *Yizkor* formulation remembering "the souls of all of my dear ones," so that all deceased relatives and friends may be included in the memorial prayers. This is followed, as in the traditional liturgy, by a *Yizkor* prayer memorializing the martyrs of the Jewish people. The differences between the traditional and the Reform formulations of this prayer correspond exactly to the differences already discussed in the personal *Yizkor* prayers.

The *Yizkor* prayers are followed by *El Malei Rachamim.* While the former generally are recited silently (certainly the personal prayers), the latter is usually chanted in mournful and heartrending tones. This prayer originated in Eastern Europe in the aftermath of the wholesale slaughter of large numbers of Jews by marauding Cossacks under the leadership of Bogdan Chmelnicki in the Ukraine (mid-seventeenth century). This prayer beseeches God to "grant fitting rest on [or 'under'] the wings of the *Shechinah,* in the lofty heights of the sacred and pure whose brightness shines like the very glow of heaven" to the souls of those who have gone to their eternal home. "Source of mercy: Forever enfold them in the embrace of Your wings; secure their souls in eternity. Adonai: They are Yours. They will rest in peace." The traditional version of this text also prays that God do this "for the sake of the charity that I pledge to give on their behalf."

Here, too, there are personalized versions of the prayer, which allow the insertion of the names of the deceased (as at a funeral), and communal versions, which mourn the martyrs of the Jewish people.

El Maleh Rachamim is a more extensive text than the *Yizkor* formula, and both overlap somewhat thematically. The offering of both prayers—one private, the other very public—at memorial services adds to the gravity and emotional pull of those services. There is no significant thematic or structural difference between the memorial services that are held at the end of each of the three festivals and on Yom Kippur. The latter, in Reform prayer books, is generally longer (on account of the greater solemnity of Yom Kippur)—but the lengthening is accomplished solely by the addition of more psalms and English readings. Mourner's *Kaddish* is not recited at this point, because it will be said at the end of the entire service.

The several original meditations and poems that *MT* gives as left-page readings have also become very popular in recent decades on account of their power to move us: Rabbi Alvin Fine's poem "Birth Is a Beginning"; Zelda [Mishkovsky]'s poem *L'chol Ish Yeish Shem*, "Each of Us Has a Name"; Leah Goldberg's poem *Mibeit Imi*, "From My Mother's House"; and "We Remember Them," by Rabbis Sylvan Kamens and Jack Riemer. New to *MT* is Menahem Rosensaft's poem "I Used to Be Part of You." Each of these poems adds depth and meaning to the memorial moments.

Seasonal Inserts in the Weekday Liturgy

How do the seasonal rhythms of the Jewish year find their expression in the daily liturgy? The answer to this question, devised mostly by the Rabbis of Babylonia in the period of the Talmud and immediately thereafter, is the inclusion of seasonal "inserts" into the regular texts of the daily prayers. It is clear that this method (as opposed to composing entirely different prayer texts for special seasons, as was sometimes done in the Land of Israel, according to the testimony of some fragmentary prayer books in the Cairo Genizah) was chosen for its relative simplicity and efficiency. In the days before printed prayer books, it was easier for those who were not liturgical virtuosi to make brief insertions into the regular prayers—fewer changes that needed to be remembered!

Virtually all of these seasonal inserts appear in the *T'filah*, the liturgy's core petitionary prayer series. Working through the daily *T'filah*, blessing by blessing, we find the following inserts:

1. *Avot V'Imahot*: During the Ten Days of Repentance between Rosh HaShanah and Yom Kippur (and also on those two days), *Zochreinu l'chayim* ("Remember us for life"), a brief poetic prayer that God remember us for life, is inserted before the transition phrase that leads to the *chatimah* (the concluding blessing formula). The word *chayim* appears at the end of each of the four lines of this poem. The first word, *zochreinu*, repeats the first verb of the previous line (*v'zocheir chasdei avot v'imahot*, "remembers the love of our mothers and fathers").
2. *G'vurot*: During this same period, *Mi chamocha Av harachamim* ("Who is like You, Compassionate God?") is inserted before the transition phrase to the *chatimah*. This, too, is a brief poem (both lines end with the word *rachamim*; the opening words, *mi chamocha*, repeat the beginning of the previous line).

   Between the end of Sukkot (Sh'mini Atzeret) and the beginning of Pesach, corresponding to the rainy season in the Land of Israel, the description of God as *mashiv haruach umorid hagashem* ("who causes the wind to shift and rain to fall") is inserted into the first phrase of this blessing. Between the first day of Pesach and the end of Sukkot, the dry season in the Land of Israel, the Sephardic rite inserts *morid hatal* ("who rains dew upon us"); the Ashkenazic rite lacks this latter insert. Because of the large number of Sephardim in the State of Israel, most Israeli prayer books (including the Progressive ones) now include this phrase, and that is why it appears in *Mishkan T'filah*. (As noted above, many earlier North American Reform prayer books did away with these last two seasonal inserts because they were tied to the agricultural calendar of the Land of Israel and not to local weather conditions.)

3. *K'dushat HaShem*: During the Ten Days of Repentance, the *chatimah* is changed from *HaEl hakadosh* ("the holy God") to *HaMelech hakadosh* ("the holy Sovereign"), in keeping with the theme of God's Sovereignty during this season.
4. There is a special insert for fast days (*Aneinu*, "Answer us!") in the traditional liturgy between the sixth and seventh blessings of the *T'filah* that does not appear in most Reform liturgies, including *MT*. Other traditional insertions that do not appear here are the insert of the prayer for dew in the *Birkat HaShanim* during the dry season and the change of *chatimah* in the *Mishpat* blessing, from "who loves righteousness and justice" to "the Sovereign who judges" during the Ten Days of Repentance.
5. *Avodah*: A portion of the special *K'dushat HaYom* blessing for the festivals, *Yaaleh v'yavo*, is inserted into the *Avodah* blessing before the transition to the *chatimah* on *chol hamo-eid* (the intermediate days of the festivals) and on Rosh Chodesh (the first day of each month). This is a prayer that God may remember us for blessing all the days of the festival. It is likely the association of the festivals with pilgrimage to the Temple in Jerusalem that accounts for the insertion of this prayer into the *Avodah* blessing, which prays (traditionally) for the restoration of the Temple worship in Jerusalem. (See more on this below in the next chapter.)

6. *Hodaah*: During the Ten Days of Repentance, the phrase "Inscribe all the children of Your covenant for a good life" is inserted before the transition to the *chatimah*.

   During the eight days of Chanukah and on Purim, a lengthy narrative insert, *Al HaNisim* ("For the Miracles"), is included at this point. It thanks God for the miraculous delivery of the Jewish people at the time of the Maccabees and at the time of Mordecai and Esther, respectively. (These texts are found toward the back of *MT*: C, pp. 556, 557; W/F, pp. 292, 293.)

   It has become customary in many liberal congregations to include a specially composed version of *Al HaNisim* in the *Hodaah* blessing for Yom HaAtzma-ut (C, p. 555; W/F, p. 291). *MT* also provides a special insert in this blessing for Yom HaShoah (C, p. 554; W/F, p. 290).
7. *Shalom*: During the Ten Days of Repentance, *B'sefer chayim*, a prayer for life, peace/well-being, and ample sustenance in the year ahead, is inserted before the transition to the *chatimah* of this blessing. The *chatimah* itself changes during this period, from *ham'vareich et amo Yisrael bashalom* ("who blesses Your people Israel with peace," the Babylonian wording) to *oseih hashalom* ("who makes peace," the wording from the Land of Israel).[162]

The only other periodic insert into the weekday service is *Hallel* (Psalms 113–118), which is recited during the intermediate days of the festivals, on Rosh Chodesh, and (now) on Yom HaAtzma-ut. Traditionally only the so-called Half *Hallel* (omitting the first eleven verses in both Psalms 115 and 116) are recited on these days, as explained above (pp. 191–92). The fuller version of *Hallel* ("*Hallel* II," C, pp. 560–569; W/F, pp. 296–305) in *MT* already omits these verses, and thus corresponds to the traditional "Half *Hallel*."

MT includes additionally in the Torah service a blessing for the new month to be recited on Rosh Chodesh (C, p. 519; W/F, p. 255). This is a version of the text that is recited traditionally at this point in the service on the Shabbat *before* the new month begins.

The *T'filah* Occasional Insert in the *Avodah* Benediction

Yaaleh V'Yavo: For God's Attentiveness during Festivals

Two festivals during the Jewish liturgical year, Sukkot and Pesach, extend over the period of a week. The first and last days are full festivals, on which work traditionally is prohibited. When these days fall on Shabbat, the version of the *K'dushat HaYom* benediction ("Sanctification of the Day") recited in the *T'filah* is that for festivals (beginning with the words *Atah v'chartanu,* "You have chosen us," C, pp. 478–482; W/F, pp. 214–218). But when Shabbat falls during the intermediate days of the festival (*chol hamo-eid*, literally "the regular/non-holy days of the festival," on which work is permitted), and also when Rosh Chodesh (the first day of the new month, which is treated as a "half holiday" like *chol hamo-eid*), falls on a Shabbat, the version of the *K'dushat HaYom* benediction recited is that for a regular Shabbat. The half holiday nonetheless is acknowledged liturgically by inserting one paragraph of the festival *K'dushat HaYom* benediction—the one beginning with the words *Yaaleh v'yavo*—into the regular *Avodah* benediction (C, p. 92; W/F, p. 92). (This same insertion is made during *all* of the intermediate days of the festivals, including weekdays; it is also made when Rosh Chodesh falls on a weekday. That is the reason the insert is added to one of the benedictions that is recited daily and not just on Shabbat.)

Yaaleh v'yavo is a petition for divine attentiveness during the festivals: may God take providential note of the needs of Israel at these crucial turning points in the year and shower blessing (in the form of rain or dew) upon the land and the people Israel. The traditional version of the prayer, longer than that in most Reform prayer books, also asks for the hastening of the messianic redemption, when Israel will be restored to its land and the Temple will be rebuilt (this theme, of course, is omitted in the various Reform versions, as—for stylistic reasons—are the multiple synonymous verbs at the beginning of the prayer). It is likely because of the thematic connection with the Temple worship and its restoration that *Yaaleh v'yavo* is inserted on half holidays specifically into the daily *Avodah* benediction, which also deals with this theme.

An interesting historical note is that fragments of festival prayers have been discovered among the (pre-rabbinic) Dead Sea Scrolls from Qumran. (The fragmentary liturgical manuscripts from Qumran, by the way, are the only surviving evidence of regular communal prayers recited by *any* group in the Land of Israel during the Second Temple period.) These festival prayers are petitionary in nature and begin with the words *Zachor Adonai ki*, "Remember/take note, Adonai, that." Here, too, an appeal is made for divine providential attention during the festival days.

We conclude with one stylistic observation about the form of the *Yaaleh v'yavo* prayer found in *Mishkan T'filah*, following *Gates of Prayer*. The prayer concludes with a threefold invocation of blessing: "[On this festival day—]Remember us for well-being. / Visit us with blessing. / Help us to a fuller life." The word "Amen," which appears at the end of each of these three invocations, is not, in fact, a part of the prayer, but is a "spontaneous" congregational response (the word literally means "In truth, this is so"). Because most Reform Jews do not "know" to do this (i.e., have not been socialized into this custom), Chaim Stern (in *GOP*) decided to include the word three times in the text of the prayer to "cue" the proper response—but did not indicate visually in the text through either explicit directions, spacing, or typeface that this is a *congregational* response.

For the record, "Amen" in traditional Jewish liturgical praxis is always an active *response* to hearing *someone else's* blessing; it is a relational utterance. It is never said by the person who recites the blessing itself; that would be like saying "yes" to yourself—it is redundant (or schizophrenic). Only in Christian liturgical practice—where the Hebrew word was taken over into Greek and then Latin texts without a full understanding of its contextually appropriate use and meaning—did it become customary to conclude one's own blessing or prayer with "Amen."

Marking the Historic Events of Our Times

In Observance of Yom HaShoah, Yom HaZikaron, and Yom HaAtzma-ut

THE WORLD-HISTORICAL events that have befallen the Jewish people worldwide during the twentieth century—both tragic and uplifting—have also been marked out in ritual and liturgical observances created and regularized over the past forty to fifty years. All of them find a place in *Mishkan T'filah* (C, pp. 521–555; W/F, pp. 257–291).

Yom HaShoah

The catastrophic destruction of the vast bulk of European Jewry between 1933 and 1945, which the names "Holocaust" and "Shoah" (Hebrew, "destruction") symbolically evoke but hardly do justice to in terms of the horrific cost in human life and suffering, has been commemorated as Yom HaShoah v'HaG'vurah ("Holocaust and Heroism Remembrance Day") since the early 1950s every spring on the twenty-seventh of Nisan (which generally falls sometime during April). The day of the commemoration, set by the Israeli government in 1953, initially was proposed to fall on the fourteenth of Nisan, the date of the Warsaw Ghetto uprising, but since this took place the day before Pesach, the commemoration was moved back to the week following Pesach.[163] (Some Orthodox groups felt that the tragedy should instead be subsumed into the rites of Tishah B'Av, the traditional day of mourning for all of the historical catastrophes experienced by the Jewish people, beginning with the destruction of the two Temples.) The dual focus on destruction and resistance was crucial to Israeli civic culture in the 1950s: it was simply too painful (and, for some, too shameful) to commemorate Jewish slaughter without also celebrating those pockets of armed Jewish resistance to the slaughter that took place as well, which served as models for Israeli resistance to armed aggression and terrorism. In North America, public annual commemoration of the Holocaust was sporadic in the 1950s and early 1960s, and usually did not take place in the synagogue. Several events in the 1960s, both cultural and historical, served at a distance of fifteen to twenty years from the events to give voice and form to public Jewish discourse on the Holocaust: the publication in 1960 of English translations of two works written originally in French, Elie Wiesel's searing memoir *Night*, and André Schwartz-Bart's moving novel *The Last of the Just*, followed the next year by the trial in Jerusalem of Adolf Eichmann, who oversaw the deportation and extermination of Europe's Jews, brought the Holocaust again into the public forum in a dramatic fashion, as did the perceived threat to Israel's existence in May 1967 when Egypt embargoed all Israel-bound shipping in the Suez Canal. The lightning victory of Israel's defense forces in the next month's Six-Day War gave some narrative form and closure to American Jews' traumatic memories and fears. The years immediately following the Six-Day War were the period during which Holocaust education and Holocaust commemoration in the synagogue began to take root.

Gates of Prayer was the first CCAR prayer book to include a service for Yom HaShoah (indeed, it was the first North American Reform prayer book to be edited and published after the end of the Second World War). That text (pp. 573–589) was constructed as a regular weekday service that could be used for both Yom HaShoah and Tishah B'Av—its English meditations and texts focused on Yom HaShoah, while its *T'filah* texts included the traditional insertions for Tishah B'Av (the adapted petitions *Aneinu* and *Nacheim*, on pp. 584 and 585).

For *Mishkan T'filah*, the decision was made to produce a freestanding ceremony for Yom HaShoah (C, pp. 521–33; W/F, pp. 257–269; as well as ones for Yom HaZikaron and Yom HaAtzma-ut, as we shall see), rather than a service. This allows for flexibility in the use and context of the observance. By the late 1990s, it had become customary in many North American Yom HaShoah observances to structure the ceremony, and the texts, around the lighting of six memorial candles, one for each of the roughly six million Jews murdered in the Holocaust. That format is followed in *MT* as well. Among the texts that appear are some poems and songs that have become strongly associated with Yom HaShoah over the past decades: *Ashrei Hagafrur* ("Blessed is the match"); *Ani Maamin*

("I believe with perfect faith"); the Partizaner Lied ("Song of the Partisans"), *Zog Nit Keynmol* ("You must not say that you now walk the final way"); and Abraham Shlonsky's poem "An Oath."

Ashrei Hagafrur (C, p. 522; W/F, p. 258) is by Hannah Senesh, the Hungarian-Palestinian (i.e., pre-state) poet. Upon her emigration to Palestine, Senesh joined a kibbutz, trained as a Haganah fighter, and parachuted back into Yugoslavia to help save Hungarian Jews from the Nazis. She was captured, tortured, and executed. *Ashrei Hagafrur* is the last poem that she wrote, while she was already behind enemy lines in Yugoslavia. The poem (and its several musical settings) has been used in Holocaust commemorations worldwide for many years. Senesh is also the author of *Yeish Kochavim* ("There are stars"), which appears in *MT* as one of the memorial readings before the Mourner's *Kaddish* (C, p. 595; W/F, p. 331), and *Halichah l'Kaysariah* ("A Walk to Caesarea"), better known by its first line, *Eli Eli shelo yigameir l'olam* ("O God, my God, I pray that these things never end"), which appears in *MT* (C, p. 653; W/F, p. 389) in the selection of songs and hymns at the back of the book. (Its familiar musical setting is by Israeli composer David Zahavi.)

Ani Maamin (C, p. 531; W/F, p. 267) is a song that, according to Jewish lore from the period, was sung by many Jews in the concentration camps. Its message is one of continued hope and faith in the coming of the Messiah, even when current reality is bleak. The text is a version of one of Maimonides's Thirteen Principles of Faith. These appear originally in his commentary to the Mishnah, *Sanhedrin* 10:1. The particular version used here is found in the traditional Ashkenazic siddur at the end of the daily morning service. There all of Maimonides's principles are phrased as a creedal statement: "I believe with perfect faith in/that. . . ." The belief in the coming of the Messiah is the twelfth of Maimonides's thirteen principles. The melody has been attributed to Azriel David Fastag, a Modzitzer Chasid.[164]

The Partizaner Lied (C, p. 531; W/F, p. 267) was written by Hirsch Glick, a young Jewish inmate of the Vilna Ghetto who had been inspired by news of the April 1943 armed Jewish uprising in the Warsaw Ghetto. Set to preexisting music (a 1937 Soviet Russian song, "The Terek Cossacks' Marching Song," by brothers Daniel and Dmitri Pockrass), it became an anthem of various Jewish resistance groups from 1943 onward.[165]

Abraham Shlonsky's poem *Neder* ("An Oath"; C, p. 525; W/F, p. 261) has appeared in the context of Holocaust remembrance in CCAR publications since *A Passover Haggadah* (1974; p. 46), edited by Rabbi Herbert Bronstein; *MT* reproduces Rabbi Bronstein's translation. Shlonsky (1900–1973) was a prominent poet, author, and essayist in pre-state Palestine and Israel. His poem *Neder* was written specifically to commemorate the victims of the Holocaust. The text is on display at Yad Vashem, the Holocaust Memorial in Jerusalem, and has regularly been used in Israel and elsewhere at Yom HaShoah commemorations. Rabbi Bronstein noted, in 1974, that the poem "is recited at many *s'darim* as a regular practice, in the land of Israel."

These songs and poems are supplemented by newly gathered materials excerpted from testimonies of Holocaust survivors. Noteworthy is a passage (C, p. 529; W/F, p. 265) from the writings of Regina Jonas, the first woman to be ordained a rabbi (in 1935). Deported to Terezin in 1942, Rabbi Jonas continued her rabbinical work in the camp until she was deported to Auschwitz in 1944 and murdered there.

The ceremony concludes with the chanting of *El Malei Rachamim* in a textual version that specifically invokes the memory of the six million martyrs of our people, and the recitation of Mourner's *Kaddish*. The left page (C, p. 533; W/F, p. 269) of the two-page *Kaddish* spread gives a special version of this prayer that intersperses the traditional words with the names of the concentration and death camps. This is attributed in the prayer book to Elie Wiesel, but an earlier version appears in André Schwartz-Bart's Holocaust novel *The Last of the Just* (French original: *Le dernier des justes*), which was first published in 1959.

Yom HaZikaron: Israeli Memorial Day

The day before Yom HaAtzma-ut (Israel Independence Day) has been observed since 1951 as Yom HaZikaron, the memorial day for Israel's fallen soldiers and all victims of the wars and terrorist incidents both before and since the founding of the state. (The full official name of the day is Yom HaZikaron L'chalalei Maarachot Yisrael Ul'nifge-ei Pe'ulot Ha-eivah, "Memorial Day for the Fallen Soldiers of Israel and Victims of Terrorism.") *Mishkan T'filah* is the first North American Reform prayer book to include a ceremony for Yom HaZikaron (C, pp. 534–537; W/F,

p. 270–273). That ceremony is relatively brief, but powerful. In addition to Israeli poet Natan Alterman's poem *Magash Hakesef* ("The Silver Platter"), which has frequently been read at Yom HaZikaron ceremonies in Israel and abroad, it includes the prayer for peace of an Israeli teenager, Shlomit Grossberg (age thirteen at the time this prayer was written). The ceremony concludes with the chanting of *El Malei Rachamim*, in a version specifically for Yom HaZikaron that mentions "those among our people who bravely gave their lives for the redemption" of the Land of Israel.

Yom HaAtzma-ut: Israel Independence Day

The North American Reform Movement was the first to include a special full service for Yom HaAtzma-ut in one of its prayer books, when *Gates of Prayer* was published in 1975. For *Mishkan T'filah*, an entirely new and freestanding observance has been created (C, pp. 538–553; W/F, pp. 274–289), not as a service (i.e., it does not incorporate regular prayers like the *T'filah*). The initial drafting of this ceremony was assigned to two rabbis who have worked extensively in the Israeli Movement for Progressive Judaism, Karyn Kedar and Kinneret Shiryon.

The ceremony is built around the lighting of seven lamps or candles. Since the seven-branched menorah of the Jerusalem Temple appears on the seal of the State of Israel, as well as prominently as a sculpture in front of its Knesset building in Jerusalem, such a seven-branched menorah is recommended for use in this ceremony. The text is built around seven thematic excerpts from Israel's Declaration of Independence (for the miracle of rebirth, for the beauty of the land, for the ingathering of the exiles, for a just society, for the renewal of Jewish learning and language, for hope and peace, for the courage of Israel's people), each of which is read before the kindling of one of the seven lights. Thematically relevant selections from biblical and rabbinic literature follow the kindling of each light. The left-hand side of each two-page spread gives brief meditations by prominent Jewish thinkers and creative writers as well as several Israeli songs. The ceremony then concludes with the official prayer for the State of Israel and the singing of *HaTikvah*, the Israeli national anthem.

Blessings for the Home and Synagogue

JUDAISM is a religion of the home as much as it is a religion of the synagogue. The family is the primal social unit. Jewish piety is as much personal as it is communal. For all of these reasons, *Mishkan T'filah*'s final section (C, pp. 602–617; Sh, pp. 298–313; W/F, pp. 338–353) is devoted to the home and, in particular, to blessings and rituals around the family table at meals.

Dinner on Erev Shabbat traditionally is a time to acknowledge the contribution of our spouse and to bless our children. *Eishet Chayil* ("A woman of valor;" Proverbs 31) is the text customarily recited in praise of one's wife. In affirming gender equality, *MT* also provides a comparable scriptural text, Psalm 112, to be recited in praise of one's husband (both texts are given on C, p. 602; Sh, p. 298, W/F, p. 338). Following this are the traditional blessings bestowed by parents on their children. For girls, the traditional role models are the Matriarchs—Sarah, Rebecca, Rachel, and Leah—all of whom God blessed. For boys, the traditional role models are Joseph's sons—Ephraim and Manasseh—whom Jacob blessed on his deathbed with the words, "By you shall Israel invoke blessings, saying: God make you like Ephraim and Manasseh" (Genesis 48:20). The latter part of this verse is quoted in the traditional blessing. The substance of the blessing, for both sons and daughters, is the Priestly Blessing of Numbers 6:24–26, "May God bless you and keep you. . . ."

Since the texts of the *Kiddush* for the eve of Shabbat (C, pp. 122–123, Sh, pp. 4–5) and the festivals (C, p. 386; W/F, p. 122) are already given earlier in the prayer book at the points where they would be recited or chanted in the synagogue, they are not repeated here in the section of blessings for the home. Instead, we are given only the texts of the *Kiddush* to be recited or chanted on Shabbat (C, p. 604, Sh, pp. 300–301) and festival (C, p. 605; W/F, p. 340) mornings at the lunchtime meal. The Shabbat morning *Kiddush* (C, p. 604; Sh, pp. 300–301) traditionally called *Kiddusha Rabbah*—the Great or the Long *Kiddush*, even though it is short!—is introduced by the singing of *V'shamru* (Exodus 31:16–17), one of several articulations of the Shabbat commandment in the Book of Exodus. This is followed by the verse *Al kein beirach Adonai et Yom HaShabbat vay'kadsheihu*, "Therefore God blessed the day of Shabbat and hallowed it" (Exodus 20:11), which concludes the Shabbat verses in the Ten Commandments. Finally, the blessing over wine is chanted. On the festivals (C, p. 605; W/F, p. 340), the paradigmatic scriptural texts that precede the wine blessing are Leviticus 23:4 and 23:44, in which Moses proclaims God's festivals to the Israelite people.

Following the wine blessing, *MT* gives the blessing over bread (*HaMotzi* C, p. 606; Sh, p. 302; W/F, p. 342), always recited at the beginning of a meal (that is why a piece of bread is traditionally eaten at the outset of every meal, since a meal was defined by the eating of bread), and *Birkat HaMazon* (C, pp. 606–609; Sh, pp. 302–305; W/F, pp. 342–345), the series of blessings recited at the end of every meal acknowledging the divine gift of food. On Shabbat, this begins with the singing of Psalm 126, "When Adonai restores the fortunes of Zion . . . those go forth weeping . . . shall come back with songs of joy."

Birkat HaMazon is made up of four blessings: for the gift of food (*hazan et hakol*), for the gift of the Land of Israel and its bounty (*al haaretz v'al hamazon*), for the rebuilding of Jerusalem (*boneh Y'rushalayim*), and for God's benevolence (*hatov v'hameitiv*; see *B. B'rachot* 46a–b). This is followed by a series of petitions, all beginning with the invocation *Harachaman* ("The Merciful One! May God . . ."), concluding with a prayer for peace found also at the end of the *Kaddish*, *Oseh shalom bimromav* ("May the Source of peace grant peace"), and followed by a series of biblical verses. *MT* gives a shorter form of the series of blessings, abbreviating the second and third while eliminating the fourth. It also abbreviates the series of *Harachaman* petitions and the verses of Scripture that follow. (By contrast, *Gates of the House* [1977], pp. 6–16, gives a fuller, though not complete, text.)

When three or more people eat together, it is customary for *Birkat HaMazon* to be recited together out loud and for one of the party to invite the other two to recite the blessings with him (this already in *M. B'rachot* 7:1ff.). This invitation (*zimmun*) traditionally begins with the words *Rabbotai n'vareich* ("My masters, let us bless!"). It has also become customary to use a non-hierarchical form of invitation, *Chaverai n'vareich* ("My friends/colleagues, let us bless!"). *MT* uses the latter form, but is gender inclusive: *Chaverim vachaveirot n'vareich* ("Male friends and female friends, let us bless!").

Finally, *MT* concludes this section with the ritual of *Havdalah* ("separation," "distinction") for the end of Shabbat (C, pp. 610–617; Sh, pp. 306–313; W/F, pp. 346–353). The ritual is the same whether it is being performed in the synagogue at the end of the evening prayer or at home. It has already been discussed above (pp. 155–58), in the context of the evening service at the end of Shabbat.

Songs and Hymns

FINALLY, a word is in order about the selection of song and hymn texts that are given at the back of *Mishkan T'filah*. In keeping with its ideals of inclusivity, *MT* is the very first North American Reform prayer book to have included on its Siddur Editorial Committee not only rabbis (members of the Central Conference of American Rabbis) but also cantors, representing the American Conference of Cantors, and one lay member, representing the congregations of the Union for Reform Judaism. The selection of song and hymn texts was made by a committee of cantors under the leadership of Cantors Jeffrey Klepper and Roslyn Barak, members of the Siddur Editorial Committee.

The collection is quite extensive and broad in its scope. It includes standard liturgical hymns and texts that are routinely sung during services,[166] of course, as well as songs and hymns for Shabbat and the festivals, but it also includes Israeli songs that have become quasi-liturgical in North American synagogues, as well as more recent songs with texts for meditation and healing (in both English and Hebrew) that reflect more contemporary concerns and trends. It also includes the national anthems of the United States, Canada, and Israel, as well as several U.S. anthems, among them "God Bless America" by Irving Berlin (born Israel Beilin).

Musical settings (some more contemporary) for many of the texts may be found in the eight volumes published to date (2003–16) of the *Shabbat Anthology*, a project of Transcontinental Music Publications, which is a division of the American Conference of Cantors.

FOR FURTHER READING

On Jewish Liturgy and the History of Jewish Worship

Elbogen, Ismar. *Jewish Liturgy: A Comprehensive History.* Translated by Raymond P. Scheindlin. Philadelphia: Jewish Publication Society, 1993. (This is the encyclopedic treatment of the topic, and very dense.)

Hoffman, Lawrence A. *The Art of Public Prayer: Not for Clergy Only.* 2nd ed. Woodstock, VT: Jewish Lights, 1988.

———. *Beyond the Text: A Holistic Approach to Liturgy.* Bloomington: Indiana University Press, 1987.

———, ed. *My People's Prayer Book: Traditional Prayers, Modern Commentaries.* 10 vols. Woodstock, VT: Jewish Lights, 1997–2007.

Reif, Stefan. *Judaism and Hebrew Prayer: New Perspectives on Jewish Liturgical History.* Cambridge: Cambridge University Press, 1993.

On Reform Jewish Worship in Europe

Meyer, Michael A. *Response to Modernity: A History of the Reform Movement in Judaism.* New York and Oxford: Oxford University Press, 1988.

Petuchowski, Jakob J. *Prayerbook Reform in Europe: The Liturgy of European Liberal and Reform Judaism.* New York: World Union for Progressive Judaism, 1968.

Plaut, W. Gunther. *The Rise of Reform: A Sourcebook of its European Origins.* New York: World Union for Progressive Judaism, 1963; reprint: Philadelphia, Jewish Publication Society, 2015.

On Reform Jewish Worship in the United States

Ellenson, David. "Reform Judaism in Nineteenth Century America: The Evidence of the Prayerbooks." In Ellenson, *Between Tradition and Culture: The Dialectics of Modern Jewish Religion and Identity*, 179–96. Atlanta: Scholars Press, 1994.

———. "Reform Judaism in Twentieth Century America: The Evidence of the *Union Prayerbook* and *Gates of Prayer*." In Ellenson, *Between*

Tradition and Culture: The Dialectics of Modern Jewish Religion and Identity, 197–207. Atlanta: Scholars Press, 1994.

Friedland, Eric L. "The Historical and Theological Development of the Non-Orthodox Prayerbooks in the United States." PhD diss., Brandeis University, Waltham, MA, 1967.

——. *Were Our Mouths Filled with Song: Studies in Liberal Jewish Liturgy*. Cincinnati: HUC Press, 1997.

Hoffman, Lawrence A., ed. *Gates of Understanding: A Companion Volume to "Shaarei Tefillah: Gates of Prayer."* New York: CCAR Press, 1977.

Kaplan, Dana Evan, ed. *Platforms and Prayerbooks: Theological and Liturgical Perspectives on Reform Judaism*. Lanham, MD: Rowman & Littlefield, 2002.

Meyer, *Response to Modernity: A History of the Reform Movement in Judaism*. New York and Oxford: Oxford University Press, 1988.

Meyer, Michael A. and W. Gunther Plaut. *The Reform Judaism Reader: North American Documents*. New York, UAHC Press, 2000.

Plaut, W. Gunther. *The Growth of Reform Judaism: American and European Sources to 1948*. New York: World Union for Progressive Judaism, 1965; reprint: Jewish Publication Society, 2015.

On the Morning Blessings

Ellenson, David H. "Modern Liturgies." In *My People's Prayer Book: Traditional Prayers, Modern Commentaries*, vol. 5, *Birkhot Hashachar (Morning Blessings)*, ed. Lawrence A. Hoffman. Woodstock, VT: Jewish Lights, 2001.

Frankel, Ellen. "A Woman's Voice." In *My People's Prayer Book: Traditional Prayers, Modern Commentaries*, vol. 5, *Birkhot Hashachar (Morning Blessings)*, ed. Lawrence A. Hoffman. Woodstock, VT: Jewish Lights, 2001.

Jacobson, B. S. *The Weekday Siddur: An Exposition and Analysis of Its Structure, Contents, Language and Ideas*. Tel Aviv: Sinai, 1973, 40–41, 44–50.

Kahn, Yoel H. "On Gentiles, Slaves, and Women: The Blessings 'Who Did Not Make Me'; A. Historical Survey." In *My People's Prayer Book: Traditional Prayers, Modern Commentaries*, vol. 5, *Birkhot Hashachar*

(Morning Blessings), ed. Lawrence A. Hoffman, 17–27. Woodstock, VT: Jewish Lights, 2001.

Landes, Daniel. "On Gentiles, Slaves, and Women: The Blessings 'Who Did Not Make Me'; B. Halakhic Analysis." In *My People's Prayer Book: Traditional Prayers, Modern Commentaries*, vol. 5, *Birkhot Hashachar (Morning Blessings)*, ed. Lawrence A. Hoffman, 28-34. Woodstock, VT: Jewish Lights, 2001.

Marx, Dalia Sara. "The Morning Ritual (*Birkhot Hashahar*) in the Talmud: The Reconstitution of One's Body and Personal Identity through the Blessings." *Hebrew Union College Annual* 77 (2006): 103–130.

Petuchowski, Jakob J. "Modern Misunderstandings of an Ancient Benediction." In *Studies in Modern Theology and Prayer*, 183–191. Philadelphia: Jewish Publication Socety, 1998.

On *Aleinu* and Its Medieval Censorship

Langer, Ruth. "The Censorship of Aleinu in Ashkenaz and Its Aftermath." In *The Experience of Jewish Liturgy: Studies Dedicated to Menahem Schmelzer*, ed. Debra Reed Blank, 147–166. Leiden and Boston: Brill, 2011.

On the Mourner's *Kaddish*

Marcus, Ivan G. *The Jewish Life Cycle: Rites of Passage from Biblical to Modern Times*, 221–244. Seattle: University of Washington Press, 2004.

Shyovitz, David I. "'You Have Saved Me from the Judgment of Gehenna': The Origins of the Mourner's Kaddish in Medieval Ashkenaz." *AJS Review* 39, no. 1 (April 2015): 49–73.

On *Kabbalat Shabbat*

Green, Arthur. "Some Aspects of Qabbalat Shabbat." In *Sabbath: Idea, History, Reality*, ed. Gerald Blidstein, 95–118. Beersheva: Ben-Gurion University of the Negev Press, 2004.

Hoffman, Lawrence A. "Welcoming the Shabbat: The Power of Metaphor." *Liturgy* 8, no. 1 (1989): 17–23.

On the Torah Service

Langer, Ruth. "Celebrating the Presence of the Torah: The History and Meaning of Reading Torah." In *My People's Prayer Book: Traditional*

Prayers, Modern Commentaries, vol. 4, *Seder K'riat HaTorah (The Torah Service)*, ed. Lawrence A. Hoffman, 19–27. Woodstock, VT: Jewish Lights, 2000.

——. "From Study of Scripture to a Reenactment of Sinai: The Emergence of the Synagogue Torah Service." *Worship* 72, no. 1 (January 1998): 43–66.

On the Prayer for the Government

Sarna, Jonathan D. "Jewish Prayers for the United States Government: A Study in the Liturgy of Politics and the Politics of Liturgy." In *Liturgy in the Life of the Synagogue: Studies in the History of Jewish Prayer*, ed. Steven Fine and Ruth Langer, 205–224. Grand Rapids, MI: Eisenbrauns, 2005.

On the Prayer for the State of Israel

Golinkin, David. "Who Wrote the Prayer for the State of Israel?" In "Prayers for the Government and the State of Israel." https://web.archive.org/web/20080206065742/http://judaism.about.com/od/conservativegolinkin/a/israel_prayers.htm

On Liturgy for Yom HaShoah

Marx, Dalia Sara. "Memorializing the Shoah." In *May God Remember: Memory and Memorializing in Judaism—Yizkor*, ed. Lawrence A. Hoffman, 39–62. Woodstock, VT: Jewish Lights, 2013.

On Israel in American Liberal Jewish Liturgy

Ellenson, David H. "Envisioning Israel in the Liturgies of North American Liberal Judaism." In Ellenson, *Between Tradition and Culture: The Dialectics of Modern Jewish Religion and Identity*, 153–178. Atlanta: Scholars Press, 1994.

On *Mishkan T'filah* and Its Development

Frishman, Elyse D. "Entering *Mishkan T'filah*." *CCAR Journal*, vol 51:4 (Fall 2004): 57–67.

——, ed. *Mishkan T'filah: A Reform Siddur*, ix–xviii. New York: CCAR Press, 2007.

Hoffman, Lawrence A. "The Prayer Book of the People." *Reform Judaism* vol. 53:3 (Summer 2006): 30–35.

——. "Re-imagining Jewish Worship." *CCAR Journal* vol 49:1 (Winter 2002): 69–87.

Knobel, Peter S. "The Challenge of a Single Prayer Book for the Reform Movement." In *Platforms and Prayer Books: Theological and Liturgical Perspectives on Reform Judaism*, ed. Dana Evan Kaplan, 155–170. Lanham, MD: Rowman & Littlefield, 2002.

Knobel, Peter S., and Daniel S. Schechter. "What Congregants Want in Worship: Perceptions from a CCAR Study." *CCAR Journal* vol 53:1 (Winter 2006): 35–48.

"Recommendations of the Project on 'Lay Involvement in Worship and Liturgical Development.'" Adopted by the [CCAR] Executive Board, March 1998. https://www.ccarnet.org/media/filer_public/2014/07/30/recommendations_of_the_project_on_lay_involvement.pdf.

Stevens, Elliot L. "The Prayer Books, They Are A'Changin'." *Reform Judaism* vol 53:3 (Summer 2006): 36–41.

"Symposium: Preparing a New Siddur." *CCAR Journal* vol 39:3 (Summer 1992), 1–31.

Issues behind *Mishkan T'filah*

POSTMODERNISM

Borowitz, Eugene B., and Jacqueline Mates-Muchin. "The Postmodern Mood in the Synagogue: A Symposium." *CCAR Journal* vol 49:1 (Winter 2002): 113–128.

Margolis, Peter. "Postmodern American Judaism: Origins and Symptoms." *CCAR Journal* vol 48:2 (Spring 2001): 35–50.

FEMINISM AND IMAGES OF GOD

Berman, Donna. "The Feminist Critique of Language," *CCAR Journal* vol 39:3 (Summer 1992): 5–14.

Graham, Edward. "Religious Language for a New Millenium." *CCAR Journal* vol 39:3 (Summer 1992): 15–22.

Spiegel, Fredelle Zaiman. "The Impact of Women's Participation on the Non-Orthodox Synagogue." *CCAR Journal* vol 39:4 (Fall 1992): 37–46.

HEALING AND SPIRITUALITY

Hoffman, Lawrence A. "From Common Cold to Uncommon Healing" *CCAR Journal* vol 41:2 (Spring 1994): 1–30.

T'CHIYAT HAMEITIM: HUMAN METAPHOR OR DIVINE MYSTERY?

Alexander, Daniel S. "Is God Stronger Than Death? *Tehiyyat Hametim* Reconsidered." *CCAR Journal* vol 44:1 (Winter 1997): 47–53.

Levy, Richard N. "Upon Arising: An Affirmation of *Techiyyat Hameitim*." *Journal of Reform Judaism* vol 29:4 (Fall 1982): 12–20.

HEBREW AND TRANSLITERATION

Gamoran, Hillel. "Say Kaddish for Hebrew?" *CCAR Journal* vol 44:2 (Spring 1997): 82–92.

ON THE YOM HASHOAH LITURGY IN *MISHKAN T'FILAH*

Bob, Steven M. "Understanding and Observing Yom HaShoah: A Beginning." *CCAR Journal* vol 46:3 (Summer 1999): 64–73.

Reform Prayer Books Referenced in This Volume

EUROPE

1819 סדר העבודה *Ordnung der öffentlichen Andacht für die Sabbath- und Festtage des ganzen Jahres. Nach den Gebrauche des Neuen-Tempel-Vereins in Hamburg* [Order of Public Devotions for Sabbaths and Festivals throughout the Year, according to the Custom of the New Temple Association in Hamburg]. Edited by S. I. Fränkel and M. I. Bresselau. Hamburg: Self-published, 1819. 2nd ed., 1841.

1841–42 סדר התפילות *Forms of Prayer Used in the West London Synagogue of British Jews*. Edited by David W. Marks. Vol. 1, *Daily and Sabbath* (1841); vol. 2, *Festivals* (1842); vol. 3, *New Year* (1842); vol. 4, *Atonement* (1842); vol. 5, *Various Occasions* (1842). London: J. Wertheimer and Co., 1841–42.

1848 *Gebetbuch der Genossenschaft für Reform in Judenthum* [Prayerbook of the Society for Reform in Judaism]. Vol. 1, *Weekly Prayer and Domestic Devotion*; vol. 2, *Festivals and Holy Days*. Berlin: Self-published, 1848.

סדר תפילה דבר יום ביומו *Israelitisches Gebetbuch für den öffentlichen Gottesdient im ganzen Jahre, mit Einschluss der Sabbathe und saemmtlicher Feier- und Festage. Geordnet und mit einer neuen deutschen Bearbeitung versehen von Dr. Abraham Geiger, Rabbiner der Israeliten-Gemeinde in Breslau.* [Israelite Prayerbook for Public Worship throughout the Entire Year]. Edited by Abraham Geiger. Breslau: Verlag von Julius Hainauer, 1854.

עבודת הלב *Service of the Heart: Weekday, Sabbath, and Festival Services and Prayers for Home and Synagogue.* Edited by John D. Rayner and Chaim Stern. London: Union of Liberal and Progessive Synagogues, 1967.

סדור לב חדש *Siddur Lev Chadash: Services and Prayers for Weekdays and Sabbaths, Festivals and Various Occasions.* Edited by John D. Rayner and Chaim Stern. London: Union of Liberal and Progressive Synagogues, 1995.

NORTH AMERICA

1855 סדר תפילה *The Order of Prayer for Divine Service.* Edited by Leo Merzbacher. Vol. 1, *Daily, Sabbath and Holidays*; vol. 2, *Day of Atonement.* New York: J. Muhlhauser, 1855. 2nd ed., revised by Samuel Adler, New York, 1860; 3rd ed., revised by Samuel Adler, New York: Thalmessinger & Cahn, 1864.

1857 מנהג אמעריקא: תפילות בני ישורון *Minhag America: T'filot B'nei Yeshurun, The Daily Prayers, Part I.* Revised and Compiled by the Committee of the Cleveland Conference [Isaac Mayer Wise, Isidor Kalisch, and Benjamin Rothenheim]. English translation by Isaac M. Wise. German translation by Isidor Kalisch and Benjamin Rothenheim. Cincinnati: Bloch & Co., 1857. 2nd rev. ed., Cincinnati: Bloch & Co., 1872.

עלת תמיד *Gebetbuch für Israelitische Reform-Gemeinden.* Edited by David Einhorn. Baltimore: C.W. Schneidereith, 1858 [a preliminary version, including Sabbath services only, was published in Baltimore, 1856]. English version: *Book of Prayers for Israelitish Congregations*, translated with emendations by Bernard Felsenthal, New York and Baltimore: C.W. Schneidereith, 1872.

1866 תפילות בני ישורון לראש השנה, ליום הכפורים כפי מנהג אמעריקא *The Divine Service of American Israelites for the New Year, for the Day of Atonement.* 2 vols. Edited by Isaac M. Wise. Cincinnati: Bloch & Co., 1866.

1892 תפילות ישראל *Union Prayer Book,* as adopted by the Central Conference of American Rabbis, published by the Ritual Committee. *Part I: The Sabbath, the Three Festivals, and the Daily Prayers.* Chicago, 1892 (withdrawn, 1893).

סדר תפילות ישראל *The Union Prayer-Book for Jewish Worship.* Edited and published by the Central Conference of American Rabbis. *Part II: New Year's Day, Day of Atonement.* Cincinnati, 1894.

סדר תפילות ישראל *The Union Prayer-Book for Jewish Worship.* Edited and published by the Central Conference of American Rabbis. *Part I: Prayers for the Sabbath, the Three Festivals, and the Week Days,* Cincinnati, 1895.

Dr. David Einhorn's עלת תמיד*: Book of Prayers for Jewish Congregations.* New translation [by Emil G. Hirsch] after the German original. Chicago: S. Ettlinger, 1896.

סדר תפילות ישראל *The Union Prayerbook for Jewish Worship.* Rev. ed. Edited and published by the Central Conference of American Rabbis. Part I, Cincinnati, 1918 (corrected, 1919; reset with new copyright date, 1924).

1922 סדר תפילות ישראל *The Union Prayer-Book for Jewish Worship.* Rev. ed. Edited and published by the Central Conference of American Rabbis. Part II, Cincinnati, 1922.

סדר תפילות ישראל *The Union Prayerbook for Jewish Worship.* Newly rev. ed. Edited and published by the Central Conference of American Rabbis. Part I, Cincinnati, 1940.

סדר תפילות ישראל *The Union Prayerbook for Jewish Worship.* Newly rev. ed. Edited and published by the Central Conference of American Rabbis. Part II (first printing, with traditional Aramaic text of *Kol Nidre,* withdrawn; subsequent printings lack the text of *Kol Nidre*; pp. 130–131 reset), Cincinnati, 1945.

שערי תפילה *Gates of Prayer: The New Union Prayerbook: Weekdays, Sabbaths, Festivals; Services and Prayers for Synagogue and Home.* Edited by Chaim Stern. New York: CCAR Press, 1975.

1978 שערי תשובה *Gates of Repentance: The New Union Prayerbook for the Days of Awe.* Edited by Chaim Stern. New York: CCAR Press, 1978 [revised gender-sensitive edition, 1996].

1994 שערי תפילה לשבתות ויום חול *Gates of Prayer for Shabbat and Weekdays: A Gender Sensitive Prayerbook.* Edited by Chaim Stern. New York: CCAR Press, 1994.

2007 משכן תפילה *Mishkan T'filah: A Reform Siddur; Weekdays, Shabbat, Festivals, and Other Occasions of Public Worship.* Edited by Elyse D. Frishman. New York: CCAR Press, 2007.

2015 משכן הנפש *Mishkan HaNefesh: Machzor for the Days of Awe.* Edited by Edwin C. Goldberg, Janet Marder, Sheldon Marder, and Leon Morris. New York: CCAR Press, 2015.

ISRAEL

1992 העבודה שבלב: סידור תפילות לימות החול, לשבתות ולמועדי השנה. התנועה ליהדות מתקדמת בישראל, ירושלים, תשמ"ב Jerusalem: The Movement for Progressive Judaism in Israel, 1982. 2nd rev. ed., 2002.

1999 כוונת הלב: מחזור התפילות לימים הנוראים. התנועה ליהדות מתקדמת בישראל, ירושלים, תשמ"ט Jerusalem: The Movement for Progressive Judaism in Israel, 1989.

AUSTRALIA, NEW ZEALAND, SOUTH AFRICA

2010 משכן תפילה *Mishkan T'filah: World Union Edition; A Progressive Siddur.* Edited by Elyse D. Frishman. New York: CCAR Press, 2010.

NOTES

1. Most notably, by Lawrence A. Hoffman, in *Beyond the Text: A Holistic Approach to Liturgy* (Bloomington: Indiana University Press, 1987), and *The Art of Public Prayer: Not for Clergy Only*, 2nd ed. (Woodstock, VT: Jewish Lights, 1999).
2. I am reminded here of the words—about words—of my teacher, Rabbi Sheldon Blank, which appear in *Mishkan T'filah*, p. 284, and nicely characterize the ideal liturgical word:

   Lend us the wit, O God,
   to speak the lean and simple word;
   give us the strength to speak
   the found word, the meant word;
   grant us the humility to speak
   the friendly word, the answering word.

   And make us sensitive, God,
   sensitive to the sound of the words
   which others speak—
   sensitive to the sounds of their words—
   and to the silences between.

3. See additionally the introductory essay by the editor, Rabbi Elyse D. Frishman, *Mishkan T'filah*, pp. ix–xi. This essay was adapted from Elyse D. Frishman, "Entering *Miskkan T'filah*," *CCAR Journal: A Reform Jewish Quarterly* (Fall 2004): 57–67.
4. See Peter S. Knobel and Daniel S. Schechter, "What Congregants Want in Worship: Perceptions from a CCAR Study," *CCAR Journal: A Reform Jewish Quarterly* 53:1 (Winter 2006): 35–48.
5. See Jakob J. Petuchowski, *Guide to the Prayerbook* (Cincinnati: Hebrew Union College–Jewish Institute of Religion, 1992), 54–55.
6. To avoid confusion, we should point out immediately that there was a *Union Prayer Book* before the standard first publication of 1894–95. This was the "original" *Union Prayer Book*, vol. 1, edited by Rabbi Isaac S. Moses, and published in 1892. It was immediately rejected by Rabbis Kaufmann Kohler and Emil G. Hirsch, the two sons-in-law of the then-deceased Rabbi David Einhorn. In an effort to bring Einhorn's heirs and followers, and their congregations,

to adopt the *UPB*, the CCAR decided in 1893 to withdraw this version and to appoint Kohler as the chair of the Prayerbook Committee, whereby he became the main editor of the as-yet-unpublished vol. 2 (1894) and a new version of vol. 1 (1895). See Lou H. Silberman, "The Union Prayer Book: A Study in Liturgical Development," in *Retrospect and Prospect: Essays in Commemoration of the Seventy-fifth Anniversary of the Founding of the Central Conference of American Rabbis, 1889–1964*, ed. Bertram Wallace Korn (New York: CCAR, 1965), 46–80.

7. This ambiguity of number will be discussed below in the chapter on the weekday *T'filah* petitions; briefly it refers to the fact that the *T'filah* comprised eighteen benedictions in the Land of Israel, but nineteen in Babylonia. The medieval rites and their modern descendants all follow the Babylonian custom.
8. The World Union Edition of *Mishkan T'filah* (2010), which was adapted from the North American original by the Union for Progressive Judaism, Australia, New Zealand, and Asia and the South African Union for Progressive Judaism, does not include any *Musaf* services.
9. In the Land of Israel, twelve blessings were recited; in Babylonia, one of these was split into two, and the Babylonian custom was followed in all of the medieval rites, on which our modern rites are based.
10. Reading from the Torah on Monday and Thursday mornings is already taken for granted in the Mishnah (*M. M'gilah* 4:1). The choice of Monday and Thursday mornings as occasions for reading the Torah is usually explained as deriving from the fact that these were days of public gathering, when the courts were in session (see *T. Taaniyot* 2:4). A homiletical explanation is given in *M'chilta D'Rabbi Yishmael, Vayasa* 1 (ed. Jacob Lauterbach, 1933, vol. 2, pp. 89–90), on Exodus 15:22, "And they went three days in the wilderness and found no water"—and for this reason, the Israelites rebelled against Moses. Figuratively, the Rabbis liken Torah to water and maintain that, in order to prevent any further rebellions, the elders and prophets ordained that Israel should not go more than three days without hearing words of Torah read publicly, such that Mondays and Thursdays were fixed as additional days for Torah reading after Shabbat.
11. The *Tosefta* (3rd century CE) is a collection of early rabbinic traditions, some of the same vintage as those in the Mishnah, some elaborating on those in the Mishnah, but all earlier than the Talmuds. The Talmuds use many of these traditions to discuss the Mishnah.
12. Two traditions are recorded in *B. Shabbat* 127a. The first lists six items and reads as follows:

> Rabbi Judah bar Shila said that Rabbi Asi said that Rabbi Yochanan said: There are six things of which a person enjoys their fruits in this world, while the principal remains for him in the world to come, and these are:
> hospitality to guests;
> visiting the sick;
> devotion in prayer;
> early arrival at the study house;
> one who raises his sons in the study of Torah;
> one who judges others on the side of merit [i.e., giving them the benefit of the doubt].

The second lists four items, and reads as follows:

> We have learned: These are the things that, if a person does them, he enjoys their fruits in this world, while the principal remains for him in the world to come:
> honoring father and mother;
> deeds of lovingkindness;
> making peace between a man and his fellow;
> and the study of Torah is equal to them all.

The last two items in the first list do not appear at all in our liturgical text (in their place, we have "providing for the wedding couple" and "accompanying the dead for burial"). The liturgical text thus either reflects a medieval variant of the Talmudic tradition in *B. Shabbat* 127a or, more likely, a conscious alteration for the liturgical context.

13. The liturgical recitation of Psalm 145, the *Ashrei* psalm, ends with an additional verse, Psalm 115:18, which concludes with this word: *Vaanachnu n'vareich Yah mei-atah v'ad olam, hal'luyah!* ("We will bless You, God, now and always. Hallelujah!"). See below, pp. 31–32.
14. Cantor Bruce Ruben, Ph.D., "Psalm 145: Ashrei Three Times a Day Part 3," in *10 Minutes of Torah: Delving into T'filah*, January 1, 2009, URJ, http://tmt.urj.net/archives/4jewishethics/010109.htm, last accessed May 30, 2017.
15. In the early Greek translation of the Hebrew Bible, called the Septuagint, there is actually an additional Psalm 151 at the end of the book. This additional psalm also appears in the Christian Syriac translation, called the Peshitta, and in the Psalms scroll from Qumran cave 11, 11QPsalms[a], col. xxviii.
16. Ari L. Goldman, "Reconstructionist Jews Turn to the Supernatural," in *New York Times*, Feb. 19, 1989, http://www.nytimes.com/1989/02/19/us/reconstructionist-jews-turn-to-the-supernatural.html, last accessed May 30, 2017.

17. Interestingly, the English version of *Olat Tamid* published in 1896 by Einhorn's son-in-law, Emil G. Hirsch, at Temple Sinai in Chicago, does *not* instruct the congregation to rise for the *Sh'ma*. This is one of several departures from the German original in this version.
18. No blessing is recited after reading from the three *m'gilot* (Song of Songs, Ruth, Ecclesiastes) on the festivals.
19. *GOP* had included, under the rubric of "alternative *Yotzer*," both this Shabbat insertion (*Hakol yoducha*, "All shall thank You," pp. 315–316), as well *El Adon* ("God is Lord of all creation"), a poetic portion of the traditional Shabbat *Yotzeir* benediction that elaborates the praise of God as Creator of the heavenly lights and transitions into a description of the heavenly hosts acclaiming God's sanctity in the *K'dushah* (pp. 316–317, while deleting the final transitional line). *MT* retains this form of *El Adon* in the Shabbat Morning Service II (pp. 314–315) but drops *Hakol yoducha*.
20. Sephardic liturgy tends to follow more closely the prescriptions of the prayer manuals of the Babylonian *geonim* Amram and Saadyah. Saadyah, as noted here, polemicized against the incluson of this phrase, and the extant medieval manuscript copies of *Seder Rav Amram* have incorporated Saadyah's stricture (even though it is, in fact, later than the text of *Seder Rav Amram*).
21. The custom of reciting nineteen, rather than eighteen, blessings in the weekday *T'filah* is Babylonian and is attested only in Babylonian sources (beginning with the Babylonian Talmud, where, in *B. B'rachot* 28b–29a, the need is felt to justify this discrepancy in number; it is attributed to the introduction at Yavneh of an additional, nineteenth, "blessing"—actually a curse—against *minim*, heretics). In the Land of Israel, on the other hand, it remained customary to recite eighteen blessings; this is attested in those fragmentary prayer books from the Cairo Genizah (some as late as the twelfth or thirteenth centuries) that follow the old rite of the Land of Israel. These prayer books also show us, incidentally, that the "nineteenth" Babylonian blessing was *not* the curse against heretics (which already appears in early sources from the Land of Israel); instead, a nineteenth benediction was generated when an Eretz Yisraeli prayer for the restoration of Jerusalem and the Davidic dynasty was split in Babylonia into two prayers, since the Babylonian Rabbis thought that each theme required its own separate blessing. Virtually all of the subsequent medieval rites derive primarily or exclusively from the Babylonian rite, which is why all traditional rites today have nineteen, rather than eighteen, blessings in the weekday *T'filah*.
22. The formulations in the old rite from the Land of Israel, as transmitted in fragmentary prayer books in the Cairo Geniza, do not explicitly sound the

messianic theme here. They simply transition at this point to the concluding benedictory formula (*chatimah*), invoking God as "our Shield and the Shield of our ancestors, our sure Protector in every generation."

23. Wise also was uncomfortable with the traditional theological motif of appealing to *z'chut avot*, the merits of our ancestors, when our own merits in our own eyes are deemed insufficient to warrant God's favor. That stance did not sit well with a modern "can-do" disposition, so Wise replaced the phrase *v'zocheir chasdei avot* ("and remembers the loyal deeds of the ancestors") with *v'zocheir b'rit avot* ("and remembers the *covenant* with the ancestors"). This emendation was not maintained in the *Union Prayer Book* or subsequent CCAR liturgies.
24. Rather different imagery is used in the versions of this benediction from the Land of Israel, as depicted in prayer books from the Cairo Genizah: there God humbles the haughty and judges the arrogant—the accent is on God's retributive justice as the Master of all things.
25. Some variants of this Mishnah text are lacking the words "found in the Torah"; the issue then is simply the outright denial of this belief.
26. Traditional Christianity, however, also looks forward to a resurrection of the dead at the time of the second coming of Christ and the Last Judgment.
27. Rabbi Isaac Mayer Wise for K.K. Bene Jeschurun, Cincinnati, *Minhag America* 1857 (revised 1872), pp. 41; 95, et passim.
28. For more on this topic, see David Ellenson's essay, "The Prayers for Rain . . . ," in his volume of essays *After Emancipation: Jewish Religious Responses to Modernity* (Cincinnati: HUC Press, 2004), 123–136.
29. Cited and translated in W. Gunther Plaut, *The Rise of Reform Judaism* (New York: World Union for Progressive Judaism Ltd., 1963), p. 158. The German original is found in Ludwig Geiger, ed., *Abraham Geiger's Nachgelassene Schriften* (Berlin, 1875), vol. 1, p. 209. This was part of an 1861 article by Geiger entitled, "Nothwendigkeit und Maas einer Reform des jüdischen Gottesdienst: Ein Wort zur Verstandigung" ("The Need for, and Extent of, a Reform of the Jewish Worship Service: A Word of Explanation.")
30. Abraham Geiger, ed., *Israelitisches Gebetbuch für den öffentlichen Gottesdient im ganzen Jahre* (Breslau: Verlag von Julius Hainauer, 1854), pp. 38–39.
31. In this verse, the threefold *kadosh—kadosh—kadosh* signifies an *endless, ongoing* extension of this praise in "surround sound"—that is, the word is flung back and forth among the angelic choirs, such that there is a constant "buzz" of praise utterance. *Adonai Tz'vaot* (sometimes translated as "Lord of hosts") is a divine epithet in biblical literature that refers to God as majestic Ruler surrounded by and commanding a huge retinue of divine beings (the "heavenly

court"). God's *kavod* (sometimes translated as "Glory") usually refers to God's immanent Presence—so, "His Presence fills all the earth" in the new Jewish Publication Society translation.

32. The new Jewish Publication Society translation, in a note to this verse, suggests the emendation *b'rum* for *baruch*. The text then would read, "Then a spirit carried me away, and behind me I heard a great roaring sound *as the Presence of Adonai rose from where it stood.*" The emendation is made likely by similar verbal usage elsewhere in this chapter of Ezekiel. If we are dealing with a textual corruption here (as is likely), it is very old, since *baruch* is reflected in all of the ancient versions.
33. *L'dor vador* does *not* mean "from generation to generation" (that would be *midor lador*); it means "to all generations, eternally."
34. Hebrew learners, please note: *lach* here is not the feminine inflected indirect object (as this form would be characterized in standard Biblical Hebrew), but the masculine inflected indirect object of "Middle," or rabbinic Hebrew, which has been influenced by the forms of Aramaic. The same form also appears in Biblical Hebrew as a pausal (that is, at the end of a major syntactic unit of text).
35. We cannot know for certain whether the Mishnah here is accurately reporting a practice from late Second Temple times or whether the Rabbis are retrojecting their own imaginative reconstruction of how things should have been done. What is clear is that they are consciously drawing a connection between their own post–70 CE liturgical practices and those of the Temple, real or imagined.
36. The Ashkenazic rite uses two different wordings of this prayer: *Sim Shalom* in the morning service, and *Shalom Rav* in the afternoon and evening services. The other medieval rites use *Sim Shalom* for all services. Most Reform prayer books (but not all) are descendants of the Ashkenazic rite in this regard.
37. A midrash on the Priestly Benediction reads, "Great is peace, for all the [priestly] blessings conclude only with peace" (*Sifrei B'midbar* 42).
38. *Oseh hashalom* is the *chatimah* (peroration) for this blessing in the old rite of the Land of Israel, known to us from Genizah fragments. As with the Eretz Yisraeli *chatimah* for the *Avodah* benediction, *she-ot'cha l'vadcha b'yirah naavod*, this was taken into the Ashkenazic liturgy for the festivals and High Holy Days together with liturgical poems (*piyutim*) from the Land of Israel. Nineteenth-century Reformers such as Isaac Mayer Wise, David Einhorn, and Samuel Adler, who substituted these formulas in their prayer books for the standard ones, knew them from the Ashkenazic festival liturgies. As Eric L. Friedland has pointed out (*Were Our Mouths Filled With Song: Studies in Liberal Jewish Liturgy* [Cincinnati: HUC Press, 1997], 230), the *UPB* wording of *Sim*

Shalom goes back to the original (1857) edition of Isaac Mayer Wise's prayer book, *Minhag America* (in the second, 1872 edition, the wording was changed but not necessarily improved!).

39. As with all spontaneous and occasional prayers in Rabbinic Judaism, this one too is given a verbal and rhetorical shape that must be followed: "May it be Your will, O Lord my God and God of my ancestors, that You speedily send a complete recovery from heaven, a healing of both soul and body, to the patient (*name*), son/daughter of (*mother's name*) among the afflicted of Israel" (translation by Rabbi Jonathan Sacks in the *Koren Sacks Siddur* [Jerusalem, 2009]). As we will see below, spontaneous private prayers are supposed to conform to rabbinically mandated rhetorical forms and patterns.
40. "One should not utter words [of private petition] after *Emet V'yatziv* [between the final *Sh'ma* benediction and the *T'filah*], but one may utter words after the *T'filah*, even if the prayer is as long as the Confession [*Vidui*] on Yom Kippur" (*T. B'rachot* 3:6). There is also an opinion in *B. B'rachot* 31a that private prayers could be recited at the end of the petitionary section of the weekday *T'filah*, in the *Shomei-a T'filah* benediction ("Adonai, who hearkens to prayer"), but this is not the preferred practice even in the Talmud.
41. Here, too, what begins as an opportunity for spontaneous, private prayer ends as a requirement to recite a rabbinically formulated prayer text.
42. The text in square brackets appears in the Talmud, but not in the prayer books.
43. The indented text appears in the prayer books, but not in the Talmud; it is a separate petition, the last phrase of which is a psalm verse.
44. The custom of reading the Torah on Shabbat evenings at a late Friday night service is a North American Reform innovation that dates from the early twentieth century and became fairly standard practice by the 1940s. Most men had to work on Saturdays during this era, and the late Friday night service proved to be a successful alternative to a Sunday morning service.
45. Traditional practice follows the old Babylonian custom that reads through the entire Torah in a single year; in the Land of Israel it was read over a period of three and a half to four years, so the weekly readings were much briefer.
46. See Ruth Langer, "From Study of Scripture to a Reenactment of Sinai: The Emergence of the Synagogue Torah Service," *Worship* 72 (1998): 43–67, and "Celebrating the Presence of the Torah: The History and Meaning of Reading Torah," in *My People's Prayer Book: Traditional Prayers, Modern Commentaries*, vol. 4, *Seder K'riat HaTorah (The Torah Service)*, ed. Lawrence A. Hoffman (Woodstock, VT: Jewish Lights, 2000), 19–27.
47. The sole exception is on Yom Kippur, when traditionally the *Musaf*

(additional) and afternoon services do not end with these prayers. The reason is that supplicatory prayer is supposed to continue throughout the day, with no interruption. Therefore, even if a slight break is taken between these services, they are deemed formally not to "end." This tradition has been carried forward in the *Union Prayer Book*, *Gates of Repentance*, and *Mishkan HaNefesh*, where the morning and afternoon services do not conclude with these two prayers.

48. The memorable Reform hymn "All the World Shall Come to Serve Thee" is a translation by Israel Zangwill of a medieval Rosh HaShanah hymn (*piyut*), *V'ye-etayu chol l'ovdecha*, which articulates the same *Malchuyot* theme. That hymn can be found, in both Hebrew and English, in *Gates of Repentance*, pp. 160–161 and 447–449 (at the conclusion of the Rosh HaShanah morning and Yom Kippur afternoon services), and in the Rosh HaShanah volume of *Mishkan HaNefesh*, p. 201 (at the beginning of *Malchuyot*; the Hebrew there is abbreviated).
49. Since the *Musaf* service corresponds to the additional sacrifice offered in the Temple on Shabbat, the festivals, and the High Holy Days, it has been omitted in most (though not all) Reform liturgies, in order to avoid both repetition and the service's sacrificial references. The shofar-blowing ritual described here takes place instead in the morning service (see, for example, *Gates of Repentance*, pp. 139–151, and *Mishkan HaNefesh*, pp. 199–207, 262–269, 278–285; one of the novelties in *Mishkan HaNefesh* is to spread the three sections throughout the service).
50. Only the Ashkenazic rite includes in the daily service the second part of *Aleinu*, beginning with the phrase *Al kein n'kaveh* ("We therefore we hope") and ending with *Bayom hahu*; all other rites end with *Hu Eloheinu ein od* ("He is our God; there is none else"). See Ismar Elbogen, *Jewish Liturgy: A Comprehensive History* (Philadelphia: Jewish Publication Society, 1993), 71–72.
51. See Stefan Reif, *Judaism and Hebrew Prayer: New Perspectives on Jewish Liturgical History* (Cambridge: Cambridge University Press, 1993). Reif, rightly discounting the characteristic medieval "persecution explanation" for virtually all Jewish liturgical change, suggests that *Aleinu* and Mourner's *Kaddish* may have been appended to the end of every service for structural reasons, in order formally to conclude the service with striking themes of messianic expectation and comfort.
52. Beyond the generalized suspicion that "they" in the prayer referred to Christians rather than to pagans, it was repeatedly pointed out by Jewish apostates to Christianity that in gematria (Hebrew numerology), the word *varik* ("and emptiness") in the prayer had the same numerical value (316) as the common medieval Hebrew name for Jesus, *Yeishu*, thus substantively equating the two.

53. A Prussian edict of August 1703 required the elimination of certain words from the prayer, prohibited "spitting and hopping" during its recitation, and demanded that the prayer be recited out loud so that government inspectors could verify compliance with the edict. Similar Prussian edicts were issued in 1716 and 1750. See Elbogen, *Jewish Liturgy*, 71–72; and Lawrence A. Hoffman, ed., *My People's Prayer Book*, vol. 6, *Tachanun and Concluding Prayers* (Woodstock, VT: Jewish Lights, 2002), 46–47.
54. The popular *UPB* version "Let us adore the ever-living God" is included in *MT* as the second option on p. 587 (corresponding to *GOP*, p. 617). The emended Hebrew text that this translates is given in *MT* as the first option on p. 586 (also corresponding to *GOP*, p. 617). The name "Adoration," by the way, was an innovation of Leo Merzbacher, rabbi of Temple Emanuel in New York, who produced that congregation's first Reform prayer book in 1855; this translates *hishtachavayah* (literally "prostration"), the Hebrew name that he also assigned to this prayer. See Eric L. Friedland, "The Historical and Theological Development of the Non-Orthodox Prayerbooks in the United States" (PhD diss., Brandeis University, Waltham, MA, 1967), 25.
55. This is the only two-page spread in *Mishkan T'filah* where the right page gives two entirely different textual options instead of a single text in Hebrew together with a reasonably faithful English translation. Service leaders: note this carefully!
56. The standard melody for *Vaanachnu* by Salomon Sulzer, cantor at the Neue Synagogue in Vienna from 1826 to 1881, was written as a choral setting first published in *Schir Zion* (1840), p. 55.
57. Another instance of standard Reform performance practice influencing our sense of liturgical structure is the singing of *Mi Chamochah*. This text (a verse from the Song at the Sea, Exodus 15:11, followed by Exodus 15:18) is simply a part of the *G'ulah* benediction (*Emet V'yatziv* in the morning; *Emet Ve-emunah* in the evening), not a separate prayer. (See above, p. 56.)
58. In some of the traditional rites, a comparable function is served by reciting scriptural verses of hope and comfort *after* the recitation of Mourner's *Kaddish*. The Ashkenazic rite (only in the afternoon service) gives:

    Have no fear of sudden terror
    or of ruin when it overtakes the wicked.
    Devise your strategy, but it will be thwarted;
    propose your plan, but it will not stand,
    for God is with us.
    When you grow old, I will still be the same.

When your hair turns gray, I will still carry you.
I made you, I will bear you,
I will carry you, and I will rescue you.
(Proverbs 3:25; Isaiah 8:10, 46:4)

The Spanish-Portuguese Sephardic rite (only in the morning service) gives:

Hope in the Lord, be strong and of good courage;
Yea, hope in the Lord.
There is none other holy as the Lord,
for there is none besides Him,
nor Rock like our God.
For who is God except the Lord;
who is the Rock other than our God?
(Psalm 27:14; I Samuel 2:2; 2 Samuel 22:32)

59. For example, Rabbi Adolph Huebsch's prayer book for Congregation Ahawath Chesed, New York (1872; English translation by Rabbi Alexander Kohut, 1889), and Rabbi Isaac S. Moses's prayer books for Congregation Emanu-El, Milwaukee (1884 and 1887). The following brief address to the mourners, from Moses (1887, p. 20), is typical of these books:

> Brothers and sisters, who are mourning for dear lives departed, remember your beloved ones and honor their names in the midst of the congregation of Israel. May the memory of the righteous inspire you to noble deeds and works in their honor. Rise, and praise with me the name of the most High, according to the ancient custom of our fathers.

It is noteworthy that such a text does not appear in any of the major earlier American Reform prayer books: those of Rabbi Leo Merzbacher for Temple Emanuel, New York (1855; revised by Rabbi Samuel Adler, 1860), Rabbi Isaac Mayer Wise for K.K. Bene Jeschurun, Cincinnati (*Minhag America*, 1857; revised 1872), and Rabbi David Einhorn for Har-Sinai Congregation, Baltimore (*Olat Tamid*, 1856–58). What these latter prayer books and all the German Reform prayer books *do* give in the vernacular are the *Yizkor* prayers for Yom Kippur and the festivals. The first German Reform prayer book of an ongoing congregation, that of the Hamburg Tempelverein (1819), includes a Hebrew-language introduction to the Mourner's *Kaddish* (with vernacular translation), which derives from the Spanish-Portuguese Sephardic *Hashkavah* (memorial) prayer, recited on Sabbaths. Rabbi Benjamin Szold's prayer book for Congregation

Ohev Sholom, Baltimore (1864) and its later revision by Marcus Jastrow for Congregation Rodef Sholom in Philadelphia (1885) carry forward this practice.

60. For more information on the poet, see www.merritmalloy.com.
61. An excellent account of German Jewish innovativeness in rites of memorialization (including reciting *Kaddish, Yizkor, yahrzeit*, and lighting a memorial candle) may be found in Ivan G. Marcus, *The Jewish Life Cycle: Rites of Passage from Biblical to Modern Times* (Seattle: University of Washington Press, 2004), 221–244. Marcus convincingly demonstrates the influence of the medieval German Christian surroundings on many of these practices. Many of these customs subsequently spread from medieval Ashkenaz to other Jewish communities around the world. David I. Shyovitz, "'You Have Saved Me from the Judgment of Gehenna': The Origins of the Mourner's Kaddish in Medieval Ashkenaz," *AJS Review* 39, no. 1 (April 2015): 49–73, argues that changing notions of the afterlife in twelfth- and thirteenth-century German Christianity, specifically focusing on the idea of Purgatory and of the efficacy of expiatory rites performed on behalf of the dead to shorten their time of punishment in Purgatory, have influenced the development here of their Jewish counterparts.
62. A special, extended version of the first paragraph of the *Kaddish* traditionally is recited at the graveside at the time of burial. This same text is also recited at a *siyum*, a joyous ceremony that marks the completion of the study of a tractate of the Talmud. Both of these occasions are deemed propitious for intensified prayers that God's kingdom may come speedily: "May the great name of God be exalted and sanctified in the world that, in the future, He will renew. May He revive the dead and raise them to everlasting life, and rebuild the city of Jerusalem, and restore in it the Sanctuary, and uproot all foreign worship from the world, and restore the worship of God to its proper place, and reign in glory during your lifetime and that of all Israel, speedily and soon, and let us say: Amen." The first paragraph of the Hamburg *Kaddish* incorporates some of this language as follows: "May the great name of God be exalted and sanctified, for in the future He will renew the world and revive the dead. May He establish His kingdom speedily in your lifetime and that of all Israel, speedily and soon, and let us say: Amen."
63. See Elbogen, *Jewish Liturgy*, 95.
64. The Hebrew University musicologist Edwin Seroussi has written an interesting study on this topic, *Spanish-Portuguese Synagogue Music in Nineteenth-Century Reform Sources from Hamburg: Ancient Tradition in the Dawn of Modernity* (Jerusalem: Magnes Press, 1996). The earliest Western musical notation of Sephardic liturgical melodies in fact is found in the musical manuscripts of

the Hamburg Reform Tempelverein, as Seroussi points out. Those manuscripts are now housed in the Eduard Birnbaum Collection in the Klau Library at Hebrew Union College–Jewish Institute of Religion in Cincinnati.

65. See Elbogen, *Jewish Liturgy*, 71.

66. This appears in the 1932 *Union Hymnal* as "The Lord of All" and is sometimes translated as "Lord of the universe," with the same spatial-extensive sense, but the rendering is surely incorrect. The word *olam* in Biblical Hebrew has a temporal meaning: "eternal," or "eternity." In later, rabbinic, Hebrew it often has a spatial meaning, "world," "universe," but this commonly is accompanied by the definite article: ***ha****olam*. Since the subject of the poem's first two stanzas is God's eternal existence—"who reigned before any being was created," "and after all ceases to be, You alone will reign in majesty"—the contextual meaning must be temporal.

67. Elbogen, *Jewish Liturgy*, 77.

68. In the traditional liturgy, there is a second, prose formulation of Maimonides's Thirteen Principles found at the conclusion of the daily morning service. Each of the assertions begins with the phrase *Ani maamin be-emunah sh'leimah* ("I believe with perfect faith"). The well-known song *Ani Maamin* that is associated with the faith of many Holocaust victims and survivors is a musical rendition of this wording of the twelfth principle, the belief in the coming of the Messiah.

69. Ron Wolfson, *The Spirituality of Welcoming: How to Transform Your Congregation into a Sacred Community* (Woodstock, VT: Jewish Lights, 2006).

70. Wolfson, *The Spirituality of Welcoming*, 106–107.

71. Karaites (Jews who rejected rabbinic authority) and Samaritans, on the other hand, do not permit any lights to be burning on Shabbat. In the early Islamic period, the Sabbath lamp was a point of contention between rabbinic and non-rabbinic Jews.

72. In rabbinic law, blessings over various activities are always recited *before* the action: the blessing functions in part as the *kavanah*, or articulated intentionality, that defines the action. In the case of kindling the Sabbath light(s), however, the activity is to be performed first, because the blessing acts to acknowledge the sanctity of Shabbat, when an act of kindling is prohibited. This is why people often close their eyes while reciting the blessing, so that upon opening them and beholding the lit Shabbat candles, this blessing also turns out to be "preceding" something.

73. The custom of reciting seven psalms is observed by Ashkenazim (Central and Eastern European Jews). The Sephardic (Mediterranean) custom is to recite

only Psalm 29 before *L'cha Dodi*, followed by Psalms 92 and 93.

74. Elie Kaunfer explores this issue and examines an alternative *L'cha Dodi* poem in his article "The History and Meaning of the 'Other' *Lekha Dodi* Poem(s)," *Hebrew Union College Annual* 79 (2008): 87–105.

75. "The Pious Customs of Abraham Galante," excerpt translated by Lawrence Fine, *Safed Spirituality: Rules of Mystical Piety, The Beginning of Wisdom* (New York: Paulist Press, 1984), 43–44.

76. "The Pious Customs of Abraham Berukhim," excerpt translated by Lawrence Fine, *Safed Spirituality*, 51.

77. The "field of holy apple trees" is a kabbalistic symbol for the *Shechinah*, the last of the ten *s'firot* that represent the dynamic and fluid power of God. *Shechinah* (also called *Malchut*) is deemed to be feminine and to unite on Shabbat with the masculine aspect of the Godhead (the seventh *s'firah*, called *Tiferet*).

78. "The Pious Customs of Isaac Luria," excerpt translated by Lawrence Fine, in *Safed Spirituality*, 74–75.

79. *B. Bava Kama* 32a–b repeats these traditions with the following variants: *Bo-u v'neitzei likrat kalah malk'ta* ("Come, let us go out and welcome the bride, the queen") and *Bo-u v'neitzei likrat Shabbat kalah malk'ta* ("Come, let us go out and welcome Shabbat the bride, the queen").

80. Many commentators on the liturgy have suggested that this custom of standing and facing west to greet the Sabbath bride likely is a remnant of the older practice when the entire ritual was performed outside facing the setting sun, first in an open field, then in the synagogue courtyard.

81. This is why the intermediate benedictions of the weekday *T'filah/Amidah*, which are all petitionary, are omitted on Shabbat; in their place comes a single benediction praising God for the gift of Shabbat and its sanctity (*K'dushat HaYom*, "Sanctification of the Day"). Interestingly, the same pattern is found in a pre-rabbinic weekly liturgy discovered at Qumran, the so-called *Divrei HaM'orot* ("Words [of prayer] having to do with the luminaries"). This text contains a sequence of penitential-type prayers for each day of the week, followed by a hymn of praise recited on Shabbat.

82. *MT*, like earlier North American Reform prayer books, omits the verse about the punishment of the wicked, as appearing too vindictive in its depiction of God.

83. The *Kiddush* ("Sanctification") blessing recited over a cup of wine on these occasions is functionally identical to the one in the *T'filah*. This is indicated by the fact that, although some of the wording differs, the *chatimah* ("seal" or summary at the end) is the same: *Baruch atah Adonai, m'kadeish haShabbat* (or, on

the festivals, *m'kadeish Yisrael v'haz'manim*; or on Rosh HaShanah, *m'kadeish Yisrael v'Yom HaZikaron*).

84. Other examples would be the extended version of the *Yotzeir* benediction before the *Sh'ma* in the traditional (not Reform) Shabbat morning service, which interweaves the theme of Shabbat with that of the benediction itself (creation of light); the extended *P'sukei D'zimrah* section on Shabbat morning with additional psalms and an extended *Birkat HaShir* (the text *Nishmat Kol Chai*) at the conclusion (on which, see below); the full Torah and haftarah readings on Shabbat; the additional, or *Musaf*, service prayed traditionally on Shabbat; and the *Havdalah* service and additions to the *T'filah* at the end of Shabbat.
85. *MT* retains the traditional formulation, *m'chayeih meitim* ("Reviving/giving life to the dead") as an option in parentheses, but gives the euphemistic *m'chayeih hakol* ("Giving life to all") as the preferred version, finessing the question of whether the traditional phrase may be taken literally.
86. Careful readers of the liturgy will notice that the wording of this portion of the *Avot* benediction here varies slightly from the standard version: instead of *gomeil chasadim tovim v'koneih hakol* after the words *El elyon*, this text simply reads: *koneih shamayim vaaretz*. The latter phrase was, in fact, the standard wording at this point of the benediction in the old rite of the Land of Israel (as attested in texts from the Cairo Genizah; the entire phrase in the rite of the Land of Israel, beginning with *El elyon*, derives from Genesis 14:19). As often happens when liturgical poetry from the Land of Israel is incorporated into the medieval rites (particularly the Ashkenazic rite), standard prayer formulas from the rite of the Land of Israel that preceded or followed these poems are incorporated together with them.
87. Although *GOP* (pp. 315–317) gives parts of the traditional Shabbat extension as an "alternative *Yotser*" and *MT* (C, pp. 314–315; Sh, pp. 196–197) retains a portion of this; see note 17 above.
88. In the Ashkenazic rite, the full text of *Yism'chu* appears only in the *Musaf* version of *K'dushat HaYom*; the morning version lacks the first line and begins, *Am m'kadshei shvi'i* ("The people that hallow the seventh day"). In the Sephardic rite (in both its Spanish-Portuguese and Middle Eastern branches), the full text is also found in the morning service.
89. Rabbi Ruth Langer has done an extensive historical and comparative study of the rituals accompanying the removal of the Torah from, and its return to, the ark. She concludes that these rituals symbolically reenact the giving of the Torah at Sinai, the primal act of revelation. In this light, the public reading of the Torah is experienced as a reenactment of its original proclamation. See

Ruth Langer, "Celebrating the Presence of the Torah: The History and Meaning of Reading Torah," in *My People's Prayer Book: Traditional Prayers, Modern Commentaries*, vol. 4, *Seder K'riat HaTorah (The Torah Service)*, ed. Lawrence A. Hoffman (Woodstock, VT: Jewish Lights, 2000), 19–27; and "From Study of Scripture to a Reenactment of Sinai: The Emergence of the Synagogue Torah Service," *Worship* 72, no. 1 (January 1998), 43–66.

90. *MT* generally prefers not to give directions, acknowledging the variation in practice among local Reform congregations, but here the direction to open the ark and to remove the Torah is given before *Ein Kamocha*, rather than later (as in traditional practice).
91. In the gender-sensitive version of this prayer book (1994), the language was changed to *El harachamim* ("compassionate God"). *MT* retains the original wording.
92. It is worth remarking in this context that three other verses from Proverbs figure prominently in the Torah liturgy. When returning the scroll to the ark, we recite Proverbs 4:2 (*Ki lekach tov*, "For I have given you good instruction"), followed by Proverbs 3:18 (*Eitz chayim hi*, "It is a tree of life") and Proverbs 3:17 (*D'racheha darchei no-am*, "Its ways are ways of pleasantness"). In the Book of Proverbs, the last two of these verses (in reverse order!) follow directly upon *Ashrei adam matza chochmah*, "Happy is the one who finds wisdom," and their subject is, as we noted, divine wisdom, which the Rabbis identify with Torah. See below, p. 147.
93. In early rabbinic practice, as attested in the Mishnah (*M'gilah* 4:2), those who were called up to the Torah actually read brief sections of the text (a minimum of three verses); the blessings over the Torah were each recited only once, before the first reading and after the last reading. This was the practice in the Land of Israel, where the weekly readings were briefer and the reading of the Torah was completed over a period of between three and a half and four years. The Babylonian custom of completing the reading of the scroll annually entailed longer weekly Torah portions (the ones that are customary today) and a regular, "professional" reader. In Babylonia, the seven people called up to the Torah on Shabbat were required only to recite the blessings; that is the custom that has persisted until today.
94. See Joseph Heinemann, "Private and Non-Statutory Prayer," chap. 7 in *Prayer in the Talmud: Forms and Patterns*, translated from the Hebrew by Richard S. Sarason (Berlin and New York: Walter de Gruyter, 1977).
95. In the case of a newborn boy, this will take place at the *b'rit milah*.
96. Although in the Ashkenazic pronunciation of Hebrew familiar to many

second-generation American Jews, the two words *Torah* (pronounced TO-raw) and *haftarah* (pronounced haf-TAW-raw) sound similar, they are not etymologically related at all and come from entirely different roots.

97. The earliest literary evidence for this practice might be found in the third Gospel of Christian Scriptures (Luke 4:16ff.), which dates from the last decades of the first century CE. The author relates how Jesus, attending the synagogue in his hometown of Nazareth on the Sabbath, stood up to read and was given the scroll of Isaiah, from which he selected verses pertinent to his messianic calling. The evidence is partly suspect because of its obvious ideological shaping and its failure to mention any reading from the Torah ("the Law").

98. Suggestive evidence for this practice is found in midrashic texts from the Land of Israel dating to the fourth to sixth centuries CE, where such verses routinely conclude literary homilies.

99. *The Torah: A Modern Commentary*, edited by W. Gunther Plaut (New York: Union of American Hebrew Congregations, 1981). Rabbi Plaut also published a separate volume, *The Hafatah Commentary* (New York: Union of American Hebrew Congregations, 1996), which includes further traditional haftarah readings not found in the original volume (or its revised edition). By contrast, *The Torah: A Women's Commentary*, edited by Tamara Cohn Exkenazi and Andrea L. Weiss (New York: URJ Press, 2008), does not include haftarot.

100. This unusual placement may be due to the fact that some of these prayers—for bar/bat mitzvah, weddings, and the prayer for the new month (Rosh Chodesh)—are occasional and thus are not recited every Shabbat. But the prayers for the congregation, the country, and the State of Israel are (in most communities) recited every week.

101. Jonathan D. Sarna has written a seminal article on this topic: "Jewish Prayers for the United States Government: A Study in the Liturgy of Politics and the Politics of Liturgy," in *Liturgy in the Life of the Synagogue: Studies in the History of Jewish Prayer*, ed. Steven Fine and Ruth Langer (Grand Rapids, MI: Eisenbrauns, 2005), 205–224.

102. See David Golinkin, "Who Wrote the Prayer for the State of Israel?" in "Prayers for the Government and the State of Israel," at http://judaism.about.com/od/conservativegolinkin/a/israel_prayers.htm.

103. See, for example, Philip Birnbaum, *Hasiddur Hashalem: Daily Prayer Book* (New York: Hebrew Publishing Company, 1949), pp. 731–734 (for many decades, the standard prayer book used in most North American modern Orthodox congregations), and its most recent successor, Jonathan Sacks, *The Koren Sacks Siddur* (Jerusalem: Koren Publishers, 2009), 1010–1011.

104. The prophet Elijah often appears to rabbis in the Babylonian Talmud, as here, to give them wise counsel and advice.

105. In the Ashkenazic rite, this last paragraph (beginning with the words *Y'chad'sheihu HaKadosh Baruch Hu*) is chanted according to the special melody of the month—a melody associated with the holiday that falls during that month (when there is one); so this text is sung to the tune of *Maoz Tzur*, for Chanukah, in Kislev; *Adir Hu*, for Pesach, in Nisan; *Akdamut*, for Shavuot, in Sivan; *Eili Tzion*, for Tishah B'Av, in Av; and so on. (The latter two are less well known to Reform Jews. *Akdamut* is an Aramaic hymn from medieval Germany traditionally sung before the reading of the Ten Commandments on Shavuot; *Eili Tzion* is the best known of the dirges that are chanted on the Ninth of Av, the traditional anniversary of the destruction of the Temples.) Traditionally, *Birkat HaChodesh* is not recited on the Shabbat preceding Rosh Chodesh Tishrei, because that is Rosh HaShanah, and the new year trumps the new month.

106. The word *minchah* means "an offering, gift, or tribute"; in ancient Israelite worship, it referred specifically to a food or grain offering. During the period of the Second Temple, this was made during the afternoon or late afternoon; hence the rabbinic association of the word for this offering with the *time* for the offering. The Rabbis purposely used Temple cultic terminology to refer to the prayers of the synagogue, which were deemed to replace the sacrifices after the Temple's destruction. By contrast, the words *shacharit* ("dawn") and *arvit* ("twilight, evening"), used of the morning and evening prayers, refer directly to the time of day. These words, too, have cultic associations, since these were the times when the daily animal sacrifices (*tamid shel shachar* and *tamid shel bein haarbaim*; regular offerings at dawn and dusk) were offered in the Temple.

107. Some manuscripts of this passage do not include the reference to three times a day, enjoining only a daily recitation of this psalm. The "three times a day" variant apparently reflects either a local or a later custom.

108. It is this practice of reading from the Torah on Shabbat afternoons, together with the traditional custom of coming together in the late afternoon to recite both the *Minchah* and *Maariv* services in sequence, that has generated the recent Reform practice of holding *Havdalah* bar/bat mitzvah ceremonies, combining the afternoon Torah reading with the evening service that includes the *Havdalah* blessings. This recent practice may be another reason why *MT* makes no distinction between the form of the Shabbat morning and Shabbat afternoon Torah reading liturgies—for an afternoon bar or bat mitzvah, one might want to use the more elaborate ritual.

109. Interestingly, the Torah readings listed in the Mishnah (*M'gilah* 3:5) for

Pesach and Shavuot are *not* the mythic narratives that we read today, but excerpts from the festival calendars in Leviticus 23 and Deuteronomy 16. Possibly this reflects the custom in the Land of Israel of reading briefer sections from the Torah on Shabbat and the festivals. The Torah readings familiar to us are first recorded in *T. M'gilah* 3:5 (for Shavuot, as an alternative custom) and in *B. M'gilah* 31a (for Pesach, also as an alternative custom).

110. The association of *Kohelet* with Sukkot is later than that of the other two scrolls with their respective festivals. It is first attested in *Machzor Vitry*, which represents the liturgical customs of twelfth-century Ashkenaz (Franco-Germany), particularly those of Rashi's disciples.

111. The Babylonian rabbinic cycle of Torah readings was annual, but in the Land of Israel the reading of the Torah took place over a period of three and a half to four years. So in the Land of Israel and in places (like one of the synagogues in Fostat, old Cairo) that followed its liturgical customs, Simchat Torah would take place only once every three and a half to four years.

112. Geonic legal-liturgical works like *Seder Rav Amram* and *Siddur Rav Saadyah* do not know this custom. *Seder Rav Amram* indicates that the annual cycle of reading the Torah is concluded on the second day of Sh'mini Atzeret (not called Simchat Torah there), but does not know the custom of beginning the reading again on the same day nor the special festivities that go with that. See below, pp. 165–68 regarding the two-day observances of festivals in the Diaspora (*yom tov sheini shel galuyot*).

113. By contrast, the Islamic calendar is fully lunar—that is why the major, month-long observance of Ramadan travels around the solar calendar, never at the same solar time each year. The Gregorian calendar in use in Western countries is a solar calendar—that is why the holidays of the Jewish year can fall out on it with as much as a month's variance over a period of several years. A 364-day schematic solar calendar was used by the Jewish sectarians at Qumran during the late Second Temple period. It is attested in the calendrical scrolls found there. This calendar is also known from the Enochic Astronomical Book (I Enoch 72–82) and the Book of Jubilees, both texts from the late Second Temple period. See the article "Calendars," in John J. Collins and Daniel C. Harlow, *The Eerdmans Dictionary of Early Judaism* (Grand Rapids, MI: Eerdmans, 2010), 457–460.

114. The names of the Hebrew months in use today—Tishrei, Cheshvan, Kislev, and so on—are actually Babylonian. The old Hebrew/Canaanite names are found in the older sections of the biblical narrative—Aviv, Bul, Ziv, Eitanim (only these four are mentioned by name). Before the Babylonian exile, the

Hebrew year began in the spring (cf. Exodus 12:1, "This month [Aviv, during which Pesach falls] shall mark for you the beginning of the months; it shall be the first of the months of the year for you"). The Babylonian year began in the fall—this custom is preserved in the post-exilic and rabbinic calendars. In the rabbinic calendar, Rosh HaShanah, the beginning of the year, is the first day of Tishrei; while in the biblical calendar, this day, referred to as the day of loud blasts (*yom t'ruah; zichron t'ruah*) falls on the first day of the *seventh* month, seven months after Aviv.

115. For a fuller account, see the article "Calendar," in the *Encyclopaedia Judaica* (Jerusalem: Keter, 1971), 5:43ff.
116. The vernal equinox is the point at which days and nights are the same length while the days are getting longer.
117. The autumnal equinox is the point at which days and nights are the same length while the days are getting shorter.
118. But the situation envisaged here, during Temple times, is quite specific. See the discussion on this entire issue by Charles L. Arian and Clifford E. Librach, "The 'Second Day' of Rosh Hashanah: History, Law, and Practice," *Journal of Reform Judaism* [*CCAR Journal*] 32 no. 3 (Summer 1985): 7–83.
119. The earliest German Reform congregational prayer books (from the Hamburg Tempelverein, 1819; rev. 1841) retained the second-day festival observance.
120. Although it is increasingly common for Reform Jews and Reform congregations to observe the second seder during Pesach.
121. For a full account of this issue, see Arthur Spier, The *Comprehensive Hebrew Calendar*, 3rd rev. ed. (New York: Philip Feldheim, 1986), 12.
122. See the remarks of Rabbis Solomon B. Freehof, *Current Reform Responsa* (Cincinnati: Hebrew Union College Press, 1969), 42–43; A. Stanley Dreyfus, in the Table of Scriptural Readings for *Gates of Prayer* (1975) (= *Gates of Understanding*, 1:271; *Gates of the House*, 283); Walter Jacob, *Contemporary American Reform Responsa* (New York: CCAR, 1987), 276; and Mark Washofsky, *Jewish Living: A Guide to Contemporary Reform Practice* (New York: UAHC Press, 2001), 109. Rabbi Chaim Stern, *On the Doorposts of Your House* (New York: CCAR Press, 1994), 364; 2nd ed. (2010), 309, reproduces verbatim the note in *Gates of Understanding* and *Gates of the House*.
123. Rabbi Levy had prepared preliminary work on the festival services for the Siddur Editorial Committee, and Rabbi Frishman served as the general editor of the siddur. Danny Siegel is a well-known poet, author, and lecturer, who has taught much about *tzedakah* and other Jewish values.
124. Sephardim recite here *Yism'chu* (also found in the morning and additional

[*Musaf*] services); *Mishkan T'filah* gives this as a left-page alternative to *V'shamru*, as we have noted above (p. 124).

125. There are also special verses inserted at this point on Rosh HaShanah (Psalm 81:4–5, about blowing the shofar on the new moon) and Yom Kippur (Leviticus 16:30, about how the people will be purified from sin will be on this day). These texts appear in the *machzor*, the High Holy Day prayer book (see *Mishkan HaNefesh*, vol. 1, p. 15, and vol. 2, p. 66; although, as in *GOP*, these verses are not used in their traditional evening location before the transition to the *T'filah*).
126. There is even a partial parallel to this petition in the festival prayer manuscripts from Qumran that have been preserved in fragmentary form.
127. The Ashkenazic rite does not have an insertion for dew in the *G'vurot* benediction during the dry season. *MT*'s use of this derives from the Sephardic rite, by way of the Israeli prayer books, which universally include it.
128. The poem *B'tal'lei Orah* comes from the Sephardic rite and appears in *GOP* in Hebrew and English, p. 495. The version here is adapted from Ronald Aigen, ed., *Renew Our Days: A Book of Jewish Prayer and Meditation* (Montreal: Congregation Dorshei Emet, 1996), 502–503.
129. The poem *Z'chor Av* is in the Ashkenazic rite. The version here is adapted from Aigen, *Renew Our Days*, 527ff.
130. The exception to this rule is the (brief) Shabbat afternoon Torah reading—but here, too, the consideration is that people would not be working on Shabbat and that the day should be spent in prayer and study, as well as in eating and resting. The same consideration holds true for the afternoon Torah readings on Yom Kippur and Tishah B'Av, of course without the eating and resting!
131. Recall that in the Jewish calendar, the new day begins not at midnight but at sunset, based on the imagery of the Creation story at the beginning of the Torah: *Vay'hi erev vay'hi voker, yom echad*, "There was evening and there was morning: one day" (Genesis 1:5, etc.).
132. According to Leviticus 23:15, the counting is to begin *mimochorat haShabbat miyom haviachem et omer hat'nufah*, "on the day after the Sabbath, from the day on which you bring the sheaf of elevation offering." Early rabbinic literature (*M. M'nachot* 10:3; *B. M'nachot* 65a–b) testifies to divergent understandings of this directive during the late Second Commonwealth period: Does "on the day after the Sabbath" mean the day after the first day of Pesach, i.e., the festival day on which there is to be a cessation—*shabbat*—from work, or does it mean the day after, literally, the actual Sabbath day that comes after the first day of Pesach? The Rabbis ruled according to the first interpretation, such that Shavuot always falls on the sixth day of Sivan. Others (including the later Karaites) advocated

the second interpretation, such that Shavuot would always fall on the first day of the week, a Sunday, seven weeks later.

133. See further the article "Omer," in *Encyclopaedia Judaica*, 12:1382–1389.

134. In a fully traditional service, *piyutim* (liturgical poems, hymns) that deal with themes of the specific festival, will be inserted into the benedictions that surround the *Sh'ma*. These poems have been eliminated even in many Modern Orthodox prayer books and services, because they are often perceived as arcane and linguistically difficult.

135. The interpretation appears in *M'chilta D'Rabbi Yishmael, Bachodesh*, 4, and *Sifrei Devarim* 343. Both of these are early midrashic anthologies dating roughly from the third century CE, the former on the Book of Exodus, the latter on Deuteronomy.

136. *Midrash Vayikra Rabbah* 10:14, on Leviticus.

137. The *Birchot HaShachar* texts also are identical with those in the daily morning service; that is why, on Shabbat and the festivals, a traditional siddur will direct you to the weekday morning service for the beginning of the liturgy. The unique texts for Shabbat and the festivals begin with *P'sukei D'zimrah*, where there are considerably more psalms recited on Shabbat than on weekdays. Specifically, the Shabbat (and festival) liturgy in the Ashkenazic rite adds Psalms 19, 34, 90, 91, 135, 136, 33, 92, and 93 before *Ashrei* (which is mostly Psalm 145). The Shabbat and festival liturgy *deletes* the weekday Psalm 100 before these additions.

138. None of this appears in the first two editions of the *UPB*.

139. The portion of the Spanish-Portuguese prayer for dew that appears in *GOP* on pp. 493–495 is retained in *MT*, in English only, as a left-page reading for one of the spreads of the *K'dushat HaYom* benediction, p. 483. The left-side portion of the two previous spreads are a reading by Rabbi Chaim Stern about the Sinai event (p. 491), adapted from the extended *Avodah* service on Yom Kippur afternoon in *Gates of Repentance* (p. 418); and verses from Exodus (23:14–16) about pilgrimage to Jerusalem on the festivals, together with a poem by Yitzhak Yasinowitz about going up to Jerusalem (p. 479).

140. This is why we also contemplate the shadows of our fingers over our hands after reciting the *Havdalah* blessing over the lights of fire and why, having covered our eyes after lighting the Shabbat candles, we then uncover them to behold the light of the flames that had been lit before receiving upon ourselves the Shabbat prohibitions against work and kindling a flame.

141. The use of the Greek transcription, *Hosanna*, in Christian scripture (Matthew 21:9; Mark 11:9–10) and subsequent Christian liturgy, misconstrues the

meaning of the original Hebrew, which is a cry for help rather than an exclamation of praise.

142. The recitation of *Hallel* on the festivals and Chanukah is an early rabbinic custom, already attested in *T. Sukkah* 3:7. The recitation on Rosh Chodesh was a local Babylonian custom, noted as such in the Babylonian Talmud, *Taanit* 28b. During the intermediate and last days of Pesach and on Rosh Chodesh, a shortened form of *Hallel* is recited, omitting the first eleven verses of both Psalms 115 and 116.
143. In Sephardic communities, it is also recited during the Pesach eve service in the synagogue before the seder.
144. This latter theme is elaborated particularly in the Sukkot prayers for rain.
145. This form is sometimes called "Half *Hallel*" and is not to be confused with the short form of the *Hallel* found in *Mishkan T'filah* on C, pp. 558–559; W/F, pp. 294–295, which consists only of Psalms 117 and 118. It appears instead in *MT* as the fuller form of *Hallel*, C, pp. 560–569; W/F, pp. 296–305. The actual "full" *Hallel* does not appear in *MT* at all. In this regard, *MT* follows the precedent of *Gates of Prayer*, which gives the same two options for *Hallel*.
146. This differentiation is quite old; it appears in early rabbinic literature (*T. Sukkah* 3:2).
147. For an excellent presentation and analysis of the literary and inscriptional evidence from the Hellenistic, Greco-Roman, and Byzantine periods, see Lee I. Levine, *The Ancient Synagogue: The First Thousand Years*, 2nd ed. (New Haven, CT: Yale University Press, 2005).
148. Literally "The Choicest of Songs," "The Best Song"—the Hebrew idiom is a superlative.
149. The Greek name of the book translates the Hebrew somewhat overly literally as "The Gatherer," a title or position, while the Hebrew *Kohelet* is supposed to be the speaker's proper name. Since early tradition assigns the book's authorship to King Solomon, *Kohelet* came to be understood as an epithet rather than a name.
150. These midrashic associations become the basis for many medieval poems recited particularly on the first day of Pesach that connect Song of Songs to the story of Israel's redemption.
151. These explanations for the reading of Song of Songs on Pesach and Ruth on Shavuot may be found in *Machzor Vitry*, 380, and *Sefer Hamanhig*, Laws of Sukkot, 57.
152. It is attested in *Machzor Vitry*, 380; *Siddur Rashi*, 222; and *Sefer Hamanhig*, Laws of Sukkot, 57. The first two of these works date from the early twelfth

century (they were written or compiled by Rashi's students). The latter work, by Nathan ben Abraham of Lunel (Provence), was written in Toledo around 1205.

153. The somewhat strained homiletical reason given in the three works listed in the preceding note is that the reference to "seven or even eight" in Ecclesiastes 11:2, "Distribute portions to seven or even to eight, for you cannot know what misfortune may occur on earth," signifies the seven days of Sukkot and the eighth day, Sh'mini Atzeret, the days of the autumn harvest, when one must separate and distribute in a timely fashion the priest's due and tithes from the harvested produce, rather than delaying, in order to enjoy God's festival blessing.

154. It also uses a separate mode for Esther and another mode for Lamentations, for a total of six modes for chanting Scripture in the synagogue (Torah, haftarah, High Holy Day Torah, festival scrolls, Esther, Lamentations).

155. The biblical verse does not end where its liturgical citation ends; instead it continues: "Yet God does not remit all punishment, but visits the iniquity of the parents upon children and children's children, upon the third and the fourth generation." Indeed, the last word of the liturgical citation, *v'nakeih*, translated in the liturgy as "and granting pardon" (more accurately, "remitting" or "wiping the slate clean"), in the biblical text is actually the first word of the next clause, where it serves as an emphatic: "God will *not* grant pardon, remit all punishment"! Here is a famous instance of rabbinic textual interpretation that turns the meaning of the biblical text on its head when it does not comport with the Rabbis' own conception of God and the need for divine forgiveness.

156. In this context, it is worth noting that the final *parashah* of the Torah, *V'zot Hab'rachah*, is not part of the weekly cycle of Shabbat Torah readings. It is read only on Simchat Torah, when it is immediately followed by the beginning of *B'reishit*. The full *parashah* of *B'reishit* is then read on the Shabbat following Simchat Torah. It is as if concluding the reading of the Torah takes place on another plane entirely and is not allowed to happen without immediately beginning the cycle again.

157. Erev Yom Kippur (Yom Kippur eve), when all of the Torah scrolls are removed from the ark to bear witness, as it were, to the public nullification of vows effected by the *Kol Nidrei* formula, is not, strictly speaking, an exception to this rule. The scrolls are being used in a legal ceremony that precedes the evening prayer. (That is why, traditionally, *Kol Nidrei* is recited, three times, before the sun has fully set and the holy day has begun.)

158. The two earlier editions of the *UPB*, vol. 1 (1895 and 1918), do not include a

separate Torah service for Simchat Torah (Sh'mini Atzeret) or any provision for *hakafot*.

159. This is why a traditional congregation must own at least three scrolls, since there are occasions during the year when three different sections of the Torah are read one after the other. These occur on Simchat Torah, when separate scrolls are used to read the end of the Torah (*V'zot Hab'rachah*) and its recommencement (*B'reishit*), as well as the pertinent paragraph from Numbers 29 about the sacrificial offerings for the festival day. Three scrolls are also used when Rosh Chodesh, the new month (which has its own special reading from Numbers 29), falls on the Shabbat during Chanukah (Rosh Chodesh Tevet), or when it falls on Shabbat Shekalim (Rosh Chodesh Adar) or Shabbat HaChodesh (Rosh Chodesh Nisan)—all of these are days on which two scrolls otherwise would be used, reading the regular weekly Torah portion and a special portion for the occasion.

160. For an excellent account of the development of these memorial customs in the Rhineland, see Ivan G. Marcus, *The Jewish Life Cycle*, 224–241.

161. *Gan Eden*, the Garden of Eden, is the traditional Jewish image for paradise, the heavenly afterlife, just as *Geihinom*, Gehenna, is the traditional image for the place of punishment or purgation. (*Gei ben Hinom*, the Valley of Ben Hinnom, outside of Jerusalem, in II Chronicles 28:3, 33:6 and Jeremiah 7:31, 19:2–6, is where sacrifices were made to foreign deities, including child sacrifice, "passing one's children through the flames"; it thus came to represent a place of fiery divine punishment after death.)

162. As we have noted several times above, this is one of the instances of wordings from the old rite of the Land of Israel that are preserved only on the festivals and High Holy Days in the Ashkenazic rite, because they have been incorporated together with Byzantine liturgical poetry (*piyutim*) from the Land of Israel. Another example is *sheot'cha l'vadcha b'yirah naavod* ("whom alone we serve in reverence"), the *chatimah* for the *Avodah* benediction from the Land of Israel. When nineteenth-century Reformers elected to use these phrases in their liturgies (as being more universalistic than the traditional ones), they took them from the Ashkenazic holiday liturgies, not knowing that the phrases had originated in the Land of Israel.

163. When the twenty-seventh of Nisan falls on a Friday, the observance is advanced one day to Thursday the twenty-sixth, so as not to interfere with Shabbat preparations. Similarly, when the twenty-seventh falls on a Sunday (the calendar is structured such that it can never fall on Shabbat), its observance is

delayed one day to Monday the twenty-eighth, so that the observance will not begin directly at the end of Shabbat.

164. For this attribution, see the Wikipedia entry "Ani Ma'amin," https://en.wikipedia.org/wiki/Ani_Ma'amin, accessed on February 1, 2017.

165. See, for example, the Wikipedia entry "Zog nit keyn mol," https://en.wikipedia.org/wiki/Zog_nit_keyn_mol, accessed on February 1, 2017.

166. Noteworthy in the context of an increased interest in the musical traditions of Jewish communities around the world is a Sephardic version of *Ein K'Eloheinu* that intersperses Hebrew text with its Ladino translation (C, p. 631; Sh, p. 327; W/F, p. 367). Musical notation can be found in the second volume of the *Shabbat Anthology* (New York: Transcontinental Music Publications, 2004), 106–109.